KIDS DON'T WANT TO FAIL

KIDS DON'T WANT TO FAIL

Oppositional Culture and the Black-White Achievement Gap

ANGEL L. HARRIS

HARVARD UNIVERSITY PRESS
Cambridge, Massachusetts
London, England
2011

Library of Congress Cataloging-in-Publication Data
Harris, Angel L., 1975–
Kids don't want to fail : oppositional culture and the Black-White achievement gap / Angel L. Harris.
p. cm.
Includes bibliographical references and index.
ISBN 978-0-674-05772-2 (alk. paper)
1. African American students. 2. Academic achievement—United States. 3. Educational equalization—United States. 4. Minorities—Education—United States. I. Title.
LC2717.H37 2011
371.829'96073—dc22   2011002394

To Okirah and Victoria Caitlyn Harris

CONTENTS

PREFACE

Since completing the Ph.D. program in Public Policy and Sociology at the University of Michigan in 2005, I have had countless discussions with many black people about the racial achievement gap. I am always struck by how the notion that black children resist education consistently emerges as the primary explanation for why they perform poorly academically. Among these discussions, there are three instances that stand out and led me to the conclusion that this book needed to be written.

In a recent trip to Mississippi, I talked to Mrs. Jones, a veteran middle school teacher, about her experiences in the classroom. I asked her why she thought black students performed worse than whites, to which she replied, "These kids just want to sit there and do nothing. They look at you like you are crazy. They just want to pass notes to each other all day long." Her frustration was genuine, and I did not doubt her observations. I was humbled at the thought that her experiences and perceptions of black youth were similar to those that I have heard countless times from other educators. I have even witnessed this belief among educators at the college level. An example of this is my experience with Dr. Smith. Dr. Smith received his Ph.D. from a prestigious institution and now works at a teaching college in the South that caters predominantly to black students. He is absolutely convinced that black students have an oppositional culture toward schooling. I sat in on several of his classes, in which he chastised the students for not being prepared for class. These "lectures" devolved into diatribes about how too many of the students at the university were preoccupied with their physical appearance and "hooking-up" with one another, avoided taking challenging classes, and had a general apathy toward schooling. Such tirades were seamlessly incorporated into his lectures, and the students seemed unsurprised. Dr. Smith's go-to quote is: "These kids today don't want anything out of life." Dr. Smith's story reminds me of the numerous educators that I have encountered throughout the United States who interpret poor academic performance as oppositionality.

The previous two examples might be written off as blacks from a previous generation expressing their displeasure with what they perceive to be a lack of ambition in today's generation of blacks. However, perhaps the most unexpected place where I have heard this belief echoed was during a discussion with Q, a close friend who is really more like a brother to me. Q is not an educator or a scholar by any means. He is a black male who has fathered eight children and has served a six-year prison sentence for dealing drugs. During a recent phone conversation, Q asked me what I was working on, to which I replied, "A book." This answer must have seemed odd, as Q thought that my job as a professor was simply to teach students. Needless to say, the notion that I was on leave for a full year with pay seemed like a fantasy tale to Q, as his conception of my occupation did not include the all-important research component. Curious, Q asked me what the book was about, to which I replied, "Kids and schools." Unsatisfied with my response, Q pressed further, asking, "What about kids and schools?" to which I replied, "Why blacks do not perform as well as whites." Q's response reinforced my desire to write this book: "Because them Niggas don't want to. That's why." The fact that this narrative about black oppositionality to schooling had reached Q reminded me of how persuasive and pervasive a theory it is.

Given his history as a drug dealer, if I were to place Q along a distribution of his peers, he would represent those in the left tail of that distribution. That is, only a small proportion of all black youth become drug dealers (left tail), and only a small proportion go on to pursue postgraduate education (right tail); the large majority occupy the middle of this distribution. However, the Qs of the world receive a disproportionate share of attention, and their experiences define how the entire distribution of blacks is perceived. Similarly, what is missing from Dr. Smith's narrative is any acknowledgment of the fact that his students are in college—a costly investment in education beyond compulsory schooling, which alone makes the resistance model inapplicable to these students—and are attending a nonselective institution with a mission of historically serving minority students with limited academic preparation. And like many teachers with whom I have spoken, Mrs. Jones failed to consider whether she was observing a general phenomenon among youth rather than a "black" approach to schooling, as her classes were comprised almost exclusively of low-income black students.

I believe that we must break the race monolith and understand that although some black youth resist schooling, the overwhelming majority of them do not enjoy academic failure, and a select few decide to become overachievers (college and postcollege graduates). Furthermore, each of these groups has a white counterpart, as some whites serve time in prison, some pursue postgraduate education, and the overwhelming majority sit somewhere in between. Only once this is realized will we be able to move the discourse on racial disparities in education in this country forward in a fruitful manner. My hope is that this book moves us in that direction.

KIDS DON'T WANT TO FAIL

1

INTRODUCTION TO OPPOSITIONAL CULTURE

By age 17, the average black student is four years behind the average white student; black twelfth graders score lower than white eighth graders in reading, math, history, and geography (Thernstrom and Thernstrom 2003).[1] This racial achievement gap should be considered a national crisis and recognized as one of the biggest social problems facing the United States during this century. Interestingly, however, when blacks and whites have the same twelfth-grade test scores, blacks are more likely than whites to complete college (Jencks and Phillips 1998). Furthermore, even after young people enter the workforce, the black-white gap in basic premarket skills remains a factor in the inequality in earnings between blacks and whites. Although racial disparities in wages persist after accounting for the racial achievement gap, the difference is smaller between blacks and whites with similar test scores than among those with different scores (Farkas and Vicknair 1996; Neal and Johnson 1996; O'Neill 1990).[2] This is important, considering that relative to whites, blacks have roughly half the percentage of college graduates and three-fourths as much in earnings (U.S. Census 2009). Jencks and Phillips (1998) posit a viewpoint shared by many scholars that reducing the test score gap is necessary and sufficient for substantially reducing racial inequality in educational attainment and earnings, which could in turn help decrease racial disparities in crime, health, and family structure.

The purpose of this book is to provide an in-depth examination of a popular explanation for the racial achievement gap: the idea that black students develop attitudes that are oppositional toward schooling (Ogbu 1978). This cultural deficit model, which I refer to as the "oppositional culture theory" (or the resistance model), has received widespread attention among both academics and teachers. While many academics might believe that the basic tenets of this theory have been discredited, the perspective lives on, perhaps nowhere more actively than among our nation's teachers. In a study of the perceptions among both secondary mathematics teachers and their school or district supervisors and university faculty of factors that contribute to the achievement gap, Bol and Berry (2005) use both qualitative and quantitative data to show that teachers are more likely to attribute the achievement gap to students' characteristics (and resistant culture). In contrast, supervisors and university faculty are more likely to attribute the gap to differences in the exposure or access to quality curriculum and instruction. Bol and Berry's study illustrates the difference between school teachers' and academicians' beliefs regarding the black student cultural deficiency narrative. As I discuss later in this chapter, many teachers, who are on the front lines in the battle against the achievement gap, observe what appears to be an oppositional culture among minority youth. In addition, strong support for the theory still exists in some quarters of the academy. The work of scholars who promote the theory (which I discuss later in this chapter) has been influential in both the social science community and among the general public. In short, the theory remains a powerful narrative for explaining persistent patterns of inequality.[3]

In the past two decades, the theory has moved from the academy into the mainstream press. In the *Atlanta Journal-Constitution*, for example, Thomas Sowell (1994) wrote, "The most painful of the new developments has been the growth of an attitude in ghetto schools across the country that trying to learn is 'acting white.'" Similarly, Brent Staples (1996) of the *New York Times* wrote, "Some education experts demean the gifted programs as elitist and unfair. Even rival students get into the act, harassing the achievers for 'acting white.'" Bob Herbert (1995) of the *New York Times* provides a more scathing description: "Some African Americans, unable to extricate themselves from the quicksand of self-defeat, have adopted the incredibly stupid tactic of harassing fellow blacks who have the temerity to take their studies seriously. According to the poisonous logic of the harassers, any attempt at acquiring knowledge is a form of 'acting white.'" This sentiment was also expressed by President Barak Obama in his speech during the 2004 Democratic National Convention, in which he stated, "Go into any inner city neighborhood, and folks will tell you that government alone can't teach our kids to learn; they know that parents have to teach, that children can't achieve unless we raise their expectations and turn off the television sets and eradicate the slander that says a black youth with a book is acting white" (Organizing for America 2004). These excerpts illustrate the pervasiveness of the belief that blacks have an antagonistic relationship toward schooling which they express through antischooling behavior.

Another indicator of the theory's popularity is the strong sales of books propagating this belief (Cosby and Poussaint 2007; McWhorter 2000; Steele 1990). The theory that blacks resist schooling has been embraced by educators and the general public and is practically regarded as common sense. Although many studies fail to find support for this theory, Farkas, Lleras and Maczuga (2002:154) conclude that "it is premature to reject oppositional culture as one of the possible mechanisms influencing lower school performance among ethnic minorit[ies]." Regardless of whether the debate regarding the theory's merit is still ongoing among scholars, the case seems to be closed for many teachers around the country, who are convinced that a culture of resistance is prevalent among black youth. In fact, Lucas (2008) presents findings that suggest the general belief that blacks prefer failure to upward mobility is held by many teachers. Specifically, using data from the General Social Survey, a major source of nationally representative trend data on attitudes since the mid-1970s, Lucas (2008:32) shows that roughly one-third of teachers believe that blacks' long-standing socioeconomic disadvantage relative to whites persists because blacks "just don't have the motivation or willpower to pull themselves up out of poverty." That is, the narrative of oppositional culture among blacks is so prevalent that it extends beyond the domain of schooling even for many teachers.

This book represents my attempt to move the discourse toward a more fruitful direction. My aim in this study is to determine whether the oppositional culture theory is a plausible explanation of the black-white achievement gap. My lack of satisfaction with previous quantitative assessments of the resistance model, which have ignored substantial aspects of a rich framework, and my countless discussions with teachers, principals, and other school administrators who remain frustrated with students who seem not to care about school, have motivated me to write this book. Although explaining the achievement gap is beyond the scope of this study, below I provide background on the achievement gap—the problem the resistance model is intended to explain. I then briefly discuss some common justifications used to explain the gap. This discussion is not intended to be exhaustive, but rather to provide some context to how the resistance model is situated within the larger sociological literature. Next, I summarize studies that suggest that the oppositional cultural narrative is popular among the most important agents in children's educational experience: teachers. I follow this with a description of the oppositional culture theory and discuss why further research is necessary before the framework can be accepted or dismissed. I conclude this chapter with an outline of the theoretical model that will serve as a guide for the rest of this book.

Racial Disparities in Academic Outcomes

The racial achievement gap is arguably the most well-known problem facing schools within the United States. Black and white youth are excelling at drastically different rates in schools. Nationally representative datasets show that the racial achievement gap is rather large by adolescence. For example, in a study using the National Longitudinal Study of Adolescent Health, Fryer and Torelli (2010) find that the mean grade point average (GPA) for black students is 12 percent lower than their white counterparts during grades 7 through 12. In an analysis based on the National Education Longitudinal Study, Harris and Robinson (2007) find that black students trail whites in GPA by 10 percent during middle school. They also show that blacks score 26 percent lower than whites in grade 12 on a composite measure of grades in reading, math, science, and social studies. The black disadvantage in schooling extends to later educational attainment. For example, among adults aged twenty-five and older, twice as many blacks (16 percent) dropped out of high school than whites (8 percent), and only 19 percent of black adults hold at least a bachelor's degree compared to 33 percent of their white counterparts (U.S. Census 2009).

While the racial disparities in grades and educational attainment are disconcerting, it is the gap in standardized test scores that concerns policy makers. Although standardized tests are intended to provide *an* assessment of students' academic proficiency, testing has become *the* defining motif of school reform initiatives, leading some to suggest that the preoccupation with standardized testing is actually the tail wagging the dog (McNeil 2000; Meier 2000; Sacks 1999). For example, twenty-six states (encompassing two-thirds of the nearly 17 million youth in high school) require high school exit exams (Center on Education Policy 2009), and standardized tests serve as the primary mechanism of stratification for colleges (SAT/ACT), graduate programs (GRE), and professional schools (MCAT/LSAT); good grades are not enough to graduate from high school or to gain admission to top-flight colleges, graduate programs, and professional schools. Since policy makers seem to focus entirely on test scores, any discussion of racial achievement gaps must document the trends in standardized test scores. Therefore, despite the limitations of testing, I focus much of this discussion on the achievement gap in test scores.

The Racial Achievement Gap in Test Scores[4]

The academic achievement gap between whites and blacks has narrowed over the past thirty years, with black children's test scores gaining both absolutely and relative to whites (Ferguson 2001; Hedges and Nowell 1998; Jencks and Phillips 1998). However, the convergence in black-white test scores that occurred from the early 1970s to approximately 1990 has been slow (Grissmer, Flanagan, and Williamson 1998; Hedges and Nowell 1999). For example, the rate of change in the gap observed during the last four decades of the twentieth century in the National Assessment of Educational Progress (NAEP)—created by Congress in 1969 to regularly test nationally representative samples of students in grades 4, 8, and 12 (or sometimes ages 9, 13, and 17)—suggests that achieving gap convergence would take thirty years in reading and about seventy-five years in math (Hedges and Nowell 1999). Analysis of non-NAEP surveys during the same time period yields even more startling projections. Using five national datasets to estimate twelfth graders' achievement across four decades, Hedges and Nowell (1999) conclude that the linear rate of decline from 1965 to 1992 suggests gap convergence would take approximately six decades in reading and slightly over a century in math.

If these projections were not disconcerting enough, more recent analysis of achievement trends in the 1990s indicates that the modest convergence in reading and math gaps that were observed in the 1970s and 1980s has either ceased (Smith 2000) or reversed (Grissmer et al. 1998). I provide evidence of this in Figure 1.1, which shows SAT reading and math scores for white and black youth from 1996 through 2008. The data are for seniors who took the SAT any time during their high school years through March of their senior year. If a student took the test more than once, the most recent score is used. The graph shows that the achievement gap has remained constant in both reading and math since the mid-1990s. Racial inequality exists even among high achievers. Hedges and Nowell (1998:167) note that "blacks are hugely underrepresented in the upper tails of the achievement distributions, and this underrepresentation does not seem to be decreasing."

In addition to its long-standing persistence, the achievement gap is pervasive across subject areas. Figure 1.2 shows the percent of white and black twelfth graders with scores that place them at the basic proficiency level. Whereas two-thirds of white students are achieving at a level considered "basic proficient" on all but U.S. history, less than one-third of blacks are

Figure 1.1:   SAT Reading and Math Scores since the Mid-1990s for White and
Black Youth

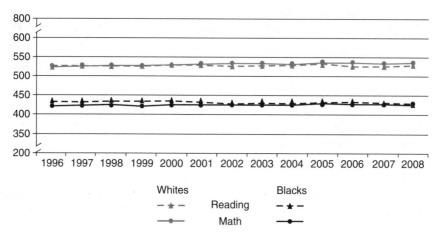

Source: College Entrance Examination Board, *National Report on College-Bound Seniors,* years
1995–1996 through 2007–2008.

Figure 1.2:   Percent of Students at or above Basic Proficiency Level, Grade 12

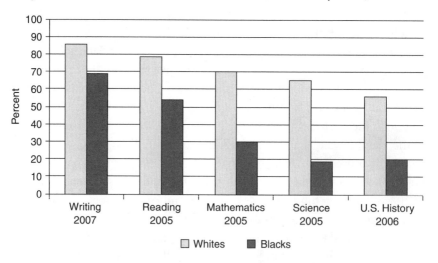

Source: National Assessment of Educational Progress (NAEP) Data Tools.

"basic proficient" in math, science, and U.S. history, and barely over half are "basic proficient" in reading. Thus, not only do educators and policy makers have to consider strategies for accelerating gap convergence, but they must also provide a solution that considers a wide range of school subjects.

Despite the usefulness of standardized tests as a barometer of the differences in the quality of schooling received by black and white youth, it is important to note that standardized tests are not without limitations. The aura of objectivity projected onto standardized tests has led to the presumption that the persistence of racial disparities in test scores is evidence of blacks' resistance to schooling. However, it would be a mistake to use standardized tests as an outcome to assess oppositional culture. Black youth can still display an oppositional culture even if they have average scores similar to whites, just as an achievement gap can still exist without the presence of a pervasive oppositional culture. While a thorough critique of the testing and accountability movement that increasingly characterizes schooling in the United States is beyond the scope of this study, highlighting the limitations of testing is relevant to a discussion of oppositional culture theory, as there is often a tendency to invoke culture to explain persistent patterns of inequality in test scores.

The achievement gap as measured by test scores may now lead to even greater racial disparity on many life-chance outcomes because of anti–affirmative action initiatives and litigation. Elite colleges and professional schools are relying more heavily on test scores despite the fact that standardized tests, and the Scholastic Aptitude Test (SAT) in particular, are weaker predictors of college performance for blacks than for whites (Mattern et al. 2008; Vars and Bowen 1998).[5] Proposition 209 in California and Initiative 200 in the state of Washington banned the use of race in student admissions to attain diversity in public colleges. *Hopwood v. Texas* (78 F.3d 932 5th Cir. 1996) has also led to the same ban in both public and private institutions throughout Texas, Louisiana, and Mississippi. Since affirmative action programs tend to be concentrated among the most selective four-year institutions (Kane 1998), fewer blacks may gain admission to flagship universities, as has been the case in California, Texas, and the state of Washington since affirmative action was repealed (Brown and Hirschman 2006; Harris and Tienda 2010; Swain 2001). Given that graduates from elite universities receive greater returns from education than those from nonelite institutions (Espenshade and Radford 2009), blacks' underrepresentation in these types of schools can be expected to exacerbate racial inequality. With the advent of the school voucher movement and the push to end affirmative action programs over the past decade, the issue of race-based and ethnicity-based test score gaps has garnered increased attention from policy makers and the general public. Specifically, there is increasing interest in identifying the factors that contribute to the black-white achievement gap.

Common Explanations of the Achievement Gap

Researchers have proposed numerous theories to explain the black-white achievement gap. Perhaps the most controversial of these theories is the notion that achievement differences are substantially genetic in origin. The works of Arthur Jensen (1969), and more recently Herrnstein and Murray's (1994) publication of *The Bell Curve*, have been central in advancing the hypothesis that blacks are genetically inferior. However, there is a lack of convincing empirical evidence to support this claim (for a review, see Dickens 2005; Fischer et al. 1996; Nisbett 1998). While the genetic argument can be critiqued on the basis of the evidence presented by its proponents (for example, most of the evidence that undergirds the arguments in *The Bell Curve* are based on minuscule R^2 reported in the book's fourth appendix), it is more intuitive (and less technical) to present evidence that counters the genetic deficiency thesis.

Studies show that test scores are strongly conditioned by social class, particularly among young children. In a study of racial differences in intelligence tests among children in preschool, Brooks-Gunn, Klebanov, and Duncan (1996) found that 52 percent of the black disadvantage in IQ scores can be attributed to family and neighborhood economic characteristics, and that there is no substantial black-white difference when quality of the home learning environment is taken into account. Although the study was conducted using data from the Infant Health and Development Program, a study on low birth-weight children in eight sites across the United States, the findings are consistent with studies that use nationally representative samples. For example, using data from the Early Childhood Longitudinal Study-Kindergarten (ECLS-K), Fryer and Levitt (2006) show that after accounting for social class, black children actually enter school with an advantage in reading achievement relative to whites and that social class accounts for 85 percent of the black-white gap in math. They show that blacks lose ground relative to whites as they matriculate through the first three years of schooling. Furthermore, over the past forty years, blacks have gained on their white counterparts on standardized tests, both on achievement-based tests and intelligence tests (Dickens and Flynn 2006). Using data from nine standardization samples for four major IQ tests, Dickens and Flynn (2006) show that the black-white gap in IQ declined from 4 to 7 points between 1972 and 2002, and these reductions were fairly uniform across the entire range of cognitive ability. These findings suggest that either the genetic deficiency thesis is flawed or that blacks have experienced a genetic boost over the past forty years that has eluded whites.[6]

Perhaps the most common factor implicated in the origin and persistence of the black-white achievement gap is socioeconomic. Specifically, researchers have pointed to economic disadvantages that typically characterize the communities many black children inhabit. Sampson, Morenoff, and Earis (1999:636) note that since economic resources and social-structural differentiation in the United States are "very much a spatial affair . . . ecological differentiation is fundamental to a full understanding of what communities supply for children." The out-migration of middle-class residents from urban areas has resulted in the uneven distribution of racial groups across spatial units within large geographic areas (that is, segregation) (Massey and Denton 1993). Furthermore, structural transformations of the U.S. economy in areas in which ethnic minorities tend to live has led to concentrated poverty within these segregated contexts. Wilson (1987, 1996) and Massey and Denton (1993) note that disadvantaged communities lack the resources to adequately sustain neighborhood institutions and public services and are characterized by persistent joblessness, all of which contribute to making high-poverty areas breeding places for crime, violence, substance abuse, and sexual promiscuity. These conditions inhibit the development of educational skills, thereby depressing school achievement, which in turn discourages teachers. Wilson (1987:57) argues that "a vicious cycle is perpetuated through family, through the community, and through the schools." In contrast, neighborhoods where most adults have steady employment foster behaviors and attitudes conducive to success in both school and work (Wilson 1987).[7]

Schools have not been free of criticism with regard to the racial achievement gap. Social reproduction theorists argue that schools maintain existing patterns of inequality because they are structured to reproduce the current social order. This line of reasoning is often attributed to Bowles and Gintis (1976) and Bourdieu and Passeron (1977), who argue that schools reflect and reproduce social class inequality; schools socialize children to occupy the segments in society from which they originate. Whereas blacks and other disadvantaged minority groups attend schools that "emphasize behavioral control and rule following . . . schools in well-to-do suburbs employ relatively open systems that favor greater student participation, less direct supervision, more electives and in general a value system stressing internalized standards of control" (Bowles and Gintis 1976:132). Thus, given the repressive and coercive authority structure in predominantly minority schools, along with constrained advancement opportunities that mirror inferior job situations, minority youth are not trained to feel and appear prepared to occupy jobs beyond the low-wage sector. Tracking is a major mechanism through which social class distinctions are perpetuated (Bowles and Gintis 1976; Lucas 1999).[8]

Proponents of the oppositional culture thesis will quickly note that socioeconomic differences generally account for roughly a third of the achievement gap among adolescents (Ogbu 2003). To underscore the point that oppositional culture is endemic within blacks' culture rather than being a class-based phenomenon, Ogbu (2003) conducted his final study in the affluent school district of Shaker Heights, Ohio. The lack of robust structural (or situational) explanations has given rise to a cultural narrative that suggests that black underachievement is a product of blacks' own attitudes and beliefs, of their own presumed tendency to undervalue education.[9]

The Popularity of Oppositional Culture Theory

In addition to the popularity of oppositional culture within the academy and the mainstream press, several studies show that teachers perceive a pervasive oppositional culture among black students. For example, using data from the National Council of the Teachers of Mathematics (NCTM), Bol and Berry (2005) find that teachers (grades 6–12) are more likely to attribute the achievement gap to student characteristics such as differences in motivational levels, work ethic, and family support—factors that serve as mechanisms through which oppositional culture is expressed—than to causes stemming from curriculum and instruction or school characteristics. Bol and Berry's qualitative findings show that "teachers seemed to view socioeconomic status and a culture opposed to achievement as connected. This is exemplified in the responses that depict poor families as not valuing academic achievement or making education a priority" (2005:38).

Analysis of two large nationally representative datasets—the ECLS-K and the National Education Longitudinal Study (NELS)—shows that teachers perceive black students as having a greater oppositional disposition toward schooling (for example, being disruptive or argumentative) and lower pro-schooling disposition (for example, effort, attentiveness, eagerness to learn) than white students (Downey and Pribesh 2004). The notion that teachers perceive lower academic orientation—students' cognitive/psychological and behavioral stance toward education—for black youth relative to their white counterparts cannot simply be attributed to children's school performance. McKown and Weinstein (2008) find that teacher expectations favor white and Asian students over black and Latino/a students with comparable academic records, particularly in highly diverse classrooms and classrooms with high student perceptions of teacher bias.

The view among teachers that black youth do not value schooling seems to exist from the outset of the schooling process. Downey and Pribesh (2004) show that teachers attribute a greater antischooling disposition and lower favorable academic orientation to black students relative to whites even as early as kindergarten. Ronald Ferguson (2003:479) notes that teachers perceive the greatest black-white difference in general academic orientation in the first three years of schooling. His conclusion was based on his construction of an "effort" scale using results from the *Prospects* survey, a congressionally mandated study of educational growth using a national sample of teachers. The scale consisted of items that asked teachers to rate specific students on the extent to which they (1) care about doing well, (2) get along with teachers, and (3) work hard at school. Ferguson found that teachers rated black children lower than whites on all three items as early as the first grade. Diamond, Randolph, and Spillane (2004) find a similar pattern using ethnographic data from five urban elementary schools. They find that teachers hold more deficit-oriented beliefs about children in predominantly black and low-income schools than they do about children in schools with a majority of white or Chinese students, or who come from middle-income families. Furthermore, they conclude that when students' deficits were emphasized, teachers believed students' lack of motivation was a major factor that undermined their own abilities to teach effectively. This phenomenon continues into middle and high school: Downey and Pribesh's (2004) analysis of the NELS shows that teachers of adolescents persist in attributing to blacks a culture oppositional toward schooling. Another line of research that highlights teachers' belief in a black culture oppositional to schooling involves studies that show school personnel place greater emphasis on black children's behavior. Ethnographic work by Ann Ferguson (2000), Morris (2005), and Lopez (2003) reveals that school personnel regard black males as recalcitrant and oppositional; moreover, such personnel constantly regulate black male students' dress, behavior, and speech. These scholars show how children are often oblivious to the reasons behind the stricter regulations they encounter. Their participant observations also reveal that school personnel (often unintentionally) do not enforce standards of behavior uniformly across racial and ethnic groups; positive behaviors by minority youth tend to go unnoticed (and therefore unrewarded), while their negative behaviors are often noticed, which is not the case for their white counterparts.

Although most studies in this line of research focus on males, who receive the bulk of the differential treatment, Morris (2007) finds that black girls are not immune; negative stereotypes about "blackness" also follow them into the classroom. His ethnographic study of a predominantly black and Latina middle school shows that school personnel were disproportionally concerned with how black girls enacted femininity. He notes, "[Black] girls did not experience the same forms of classroom discipline and teacher-student interaction as White girls, Latina girls, Latino boys, or Black boys . . . The stereotypes and resulting treatment pertaining to Black girls were unique to them" (2007:510). Morris notes that the assertiveness subtly encouraged for white and middle-class children (Lareau 2003) was interpreted as abrasive and aggressive when enacted by black girls. Thus, in school settings black girls often appear inadequately feminine and in need of femininity reform towards more acceptable and traditional aspects of female deference such as passivity and silence.

Studies suggest that black youth do not have to misbehave in order to be considered oppositional by teachers. Tyler, Boykin, and Walton (2006) conducted a study of how teachers perceive classroom motivation and achievement based on students' culture-based classroom behaviors. They had elementary school teachers rate students' motivation and achievement after reading scenarios of hypothetical students who behaviorally manifested a European (or mainstream) cultural ethos (competition, individualism) or Afrocultural ethos (communalism, verve). Teachers rated students displaying competitive and individualistic classroom behaviors higher on motivation and achievement than those displaying communal behaviors or who approached schooling with verve. Neal et al. (2003) reach similar conclusions using teacher assessments of students' achievement, level of aggression, and need for special education services, based on a review of videotape of carefully paired white and black youth engaging in similar day-to-day behaviors in middle school. They found that teachers assign worse ratings on all three outcomes to both black and white students who enact so-called black physical movements (that is, body mechanics commonly associated with African Americans) than to the black/white pair that enacted "standard" styles of walk and behavior movements. These studies show that the value teachers assign to academic success is not independent of cultural considerations, as disadvantaged minority groups are perceived as outsiders to the academic setting (Delpit 1995). Fordham (1988, 1996) notes that the black community's collective ethos conflicts with the individualistic ethos sanctioned within the school context, which means that black children have the added burden of unlearning or modifying their culturally sanctioned interactional and behavioral styles once they enter school.

The use of cultural explanations for racial inequality is not new. The attribution of racial differences in achievement to culture is part of a larger debate that originated in the 1960s about whether persistent patterns of racial inequality across nearly every life-chance outcome was due to culture rather than to societal conditions. Disadvantaged groups are posited to have a "culture of poverty," a thesis that can be traced to anthropologist Oscar Lewis (1961, 1968). Based on ethnographic studies of Latin American poverty, Lewis argued that prolonged exposure to factors that characterize disadvantaged communities such as unemployment, low income, lack of home ownership, and chronic shortage of basic necessities (for example, food and health care) promotes behavioral patterns that compromise upward socioeconomic mobility. Specifically, these conditions give rise to feelings of marginality and helplessness and contribute to a lack of impulse control or ability to defer gratification and plan for the future. Lewis argued that although this culture emerges in response to constrained opportunities, it becomes entrenched and self-sustaining within these communities and serves as a primary factor in the maintenance of disadvantage. Once the values and attitudes that comprise this culture of poverty are absorbed, people "are not psychologically geared to take full advantage of changing conditions or increased opportunities which may occur in their life-time" (Lewis 1968:188).

The cultural thesis gained notoriety in the political arena with the release of *The Negro Family: A Case for National Action* (1965), a report by sociologist and then Assistant Secretary of Labor Daniel Moynihan commissioned by President Lyndon B. Johnson. Moynihan presented a sharply pointed argument that government economic and social welfare programs, both existing and prospective ones, should be systematically designed to encourage the stability of the Negro family, which he claimed was unstable and thus a central feature of "the tangle of pathology" of life in the ghetto. He warned that the absence of employment opportunities in black communities was leading to the disintegration of the black family and that a major consequence of this disintegration was poor academic achievement and educational attainment. Thus, the large proportion of nontraditional families found in black communities has been used to explain almost all forms of racial inequality, including academic outcomes, as black children have been much more likely to reside in single-parent homes than whites over the past fifty years (Sandefur et al. 2001).

Although the cultural explanations advanced by Lewis and Moynihan suggest that cultural behavioral patterns are strategies for coping with feelings of hopelessness and despair that arise from depressed socioeconomic conditions, the structural (societal) component occupies a subordinate status to the cultural aspect of their thesis. Both Lewis and Moynihan view racial inequality as maintained by an autonomous culture of poverty among blacks. In fact, their work fueled the cultural side of the structure versus culture debate within the scientific community, the political arena, and popular culture that began in the 1960s and continues into the twenty-first century. Most readers will recognize this debate along the conservative-liberal continuum. At one extreme, proponents of the conservative perspective argue that blacks have to be culturally rehabilitated before they can take advantage of the opportunities for advancement in society (Banfield 1970; Wax 2009). At the liberal end of the spectrum, new generations of blacks and other disadvantaged groups are viewed as sharing cultural behavioral patterns with their predecessors because they experience similar economic conditions and constraints to upward social mobility (Massey and Denton 1993; Wilson 1987, 1996). However, norms, aspirations, and patterns of behavior are not seen as intractable and undergo change or "rise and fall with changes in situations" (Gans 1968:211). Thus, what appears to be a self-perpetuating cultural defect is actually a structurally created and sustained adaptation to concentrated disadvantage.

Despite being only one of a number of frameworks to guide research on stratification and education over the past half century, the cultural deficit thesis remains prominent. Conservatives in particular continue to use it to explain the persistence of racial differences in achievement and on many other life-chance outcomes such as family structure, unemployment, and crime. Cultural explanations are consistent with a major premise upon which the ideology of the American Dream rests; America is the land of limitless opportunity in which individual effort and hard work determine who succeeds. Getting ahead is ostensibly based on individual merit. Furthermore, addressing structural conditions such as poverty, residential segregation, and other forms of socioeconomic disadvantage seems impractical. Thus, the residual achievement gap net of structural factors—despite the difficulty associated with adequately measuring structural forces—provides compelling evidence for the plausibility of cultural explanations. The research literature makes the gap appear intractable, which creates fertile ground for theories suggesting its origin lies in the culture of minorities and their own refusal to succeed. The popularity of the resistance model among teachers and the general public alone is enough to warrant further research on this framework. In the next section I discuss a variation of the cultural deficit model that has gained popularity within the research literature on education and the general public: Ogbu's oppositional culture theory.

The Oppositional Culture Theory

The oppositional culture theory (more formerly known as the *cultural-ecological theory*), was developed by Nigerian-American cultural anthropologist John U. Ogbu (1938–2003), who was interested in exploring differences in academic outcomes between minority and nonminority groups in the United States and other societies. The theory, which has been refined to explain achievement variation between different minority groups, relies on two components to explain racial/group differences in achievement: 1) societal and school forces and 2) community and individual-level forces. These components coincide with the *ecological* (environmental) and *cultural* portions of the cultural-ecological framework, respectively. The first factor captures the unfair treatment members of minority groups typically face within a given society. Ogbu (1978) notes that minority groups are systematically denied access to educational opportunities equal to those received by the dominant group. They also experience barriers to success in future employment and earnings due to racial/ethnic discrimination and structural inequalities, which Ogbu refers to as the *job ceiling*. Thus, minorities are precluded from competing for the most desirable roles in society on the basis of individual training and abilities. Even after a society abandons formal mechanisms responsible for the unequal treatment of minority groups, vestiges of past discriminatory policies in the labor market and education remain in effect.

Basically, children's academic investment is seen as driven by the prevailing system of social mobility, which is an important backdrop for the resistance model. The system of social mobility refers to the arrangements within any society by which people gain (or lose) resources that allow them to move up the socioeconomic ladder. These resources are not always financial; they can also include social status or other forms of nonmonetary capital. The system typically contains two components: one is the mechanism by which people acquire tools that can be exchanged for resources, and the other is the structure that serves as the market that assigns value to these tools and distributes rewards accordingly. One's ability to ascend the economic hierarchy relies on 1) the acquisition of tools/skills and 2) how these tools are received by the market. In a properly functioning system of social mobility, opportunities for the acquisition of both skills and rewards are structured such that they are equally available to all who wish to pursue them, and everyone is rewarded equally for the same set of skills. When the system fails to provide equal opportunities or the relationship between skills and rewards is less than optimal, and when these inefficiencies affect people with a particular set of characteristics, then the system suffers from structural discrimination. Within the United States, education is the primary mechanism for upward (socioeconomic) mobility, and the labor market is the institution that provides rewards commensurate with the skills acquired within the educational domain.

Among minority groups, differential access to opportunities triggers responses attached to community identity, a phenomenon that corresponds to the second component of the oppositional culture theory. Ogbu (1978) notes that the motivation for maximizing school achievement results from the belief that more education leads to better jobs, higher wages, higher social status, and more self-esteem. When members of minority groups encounter barriers within the opportunity structure, they develop the perception that they receive lower rewards for education than the dominant group. Regardless of the accuracy of these perceptions, they give rise to community and individual-level forces characterized by an oppositional culture that includes resisting educational goals. Ogbu (1994) describes a *cultural inversion* that takes place whereby some minority groups define certain behaviors, in this case achievement, as inappropriate for them because these behaviors are the domain of their oppressors. This repudiation is marked by truancy, lack of serious effort, dismissive attitudes toward school, delinquency, and even early withdrawal from school altogether.

The effects of societal and community forces are not posited to be the same for all minority groups. Their effects are especially acute for members of subordinate minority groups—groups who have historically been specific targets of exclusionary policies. These groups occupy a subordinate status in a rigid stratification system—a societal structure in which people are arranged hierarchically according to their social class and in which access to resources is not based entirely on *acquired* social class. Ogbu refers to these groups as *caste-like minorities*. Ogbu (1978) published a comparative assessment of differences in school achievement between minority groups in six countries (Britain, India, Israel, Japan, New Zealand, and the United States) and found that subordinate minorities exist in each context.

Together, the societal *(ecological)* and community *(cultural)* level forces provide a general understanding of how societal forces influence individual-level behaviors to produce achievement differences between dominant and minority groups across numerous contexts. However, while all minority groups experience and perceive barriers to upward mobility, not all groups respond similarly. Ogbu refined his framework to include a minority classification scheme useful for understanding the variability between different minority groups.

Group Classification

Within the oppositional culture framework developed by Ogbu, minority groups are placed into three distinct classifications: autonomous minorities, voluntary minorities, and involuntary minorities. Autonomous minorities are groups that may be small in number and/or different in race, ethnicity, religion, or language from the dominant group. Voluntary or immigrant minorities are groups who *willingly* move to a host country, typically in search of better opportunities in employment or greater political or religious freedom. In contrast, involuntary minorities are groups who have been historically enslaved, colonized, or conquered and who thereby interpret the incorporation of their group into their host country as forced by the dominant group.

Since the framework is used to understand racial differences in achievement within the United States, race is often used as a proxy for group classification. Examples of autonomous minorities include Amish, Jews, and Mormons, and examples of voluntary minorities include Asian Americans and West-Indian Americans. Examples of involuntary minorities include African Americans, Hawaiians, and Native Americans. However, the fact that African Americans are involuntary minorities and immigrant blacks (for example, Caribbean) appear to be voluntary minorities illustrates that not all blacks have the same minority status. Group classification does not necessarily correspond with race. Nevertheless, researchers typically use Asian Americans, blacks, and whites to represent voluntary, involuntary, and dominant groups, respectively.

A group's place within the classification scheme is not always obvious. Although most Hispanic groups within the United States are either immigrants or descendants of immigrants, Ogbu claims that Mexican Americans—who comprise nearly two-thirds of the Hispanics living in the United States (U.S. Census Bureau 2000)—are involuntary minorities. He argues that they feel alienated from American society because they have bitter memories of their incorporation into the United States via American imperialistic expansion in the 1840s. However, roughly fifty thousand Mexican nationals remained within the newly acquired U.S. territory, a small fraction of the more than forty-five million people of Mexican ancestry currently in the United States; most Mexican Americans are immigrants or descendants of immigrants who arrived after the Mexican revolution of 1910 (see Jaffe, Cullen, and Boswell 1980). Since nearly all Hispanic children in American schools derive from voluntary immigration, Ogbu's classification of this group as an involuntary minority is highly implausible (Thernstrom and Thernstrom 2003).

The same applies for black immigrants, particularly those from Africa, who account for nearly half of black immigrants to the United States over the past two decades (Kent 2007). For example, the creation of independent nation-states in much of sub-Saharan Africa after the end of European colonial rule in the 1960s was accompanied by political and economic turmoil. Africans faced extreme poverty, widespread unemployment, political instability, and deteriorating infrastructures as African economies struggled, prices for Africa's major exports dropped, and the costs of imported manufacturing goods increased. Additionally, many national governments were ineffective, rife with corruption, and plagued by civil violence and strife. After the passage of the Refugee Act of March 17, 1980, which ended the acceptance of only refugees from communist countries the United States opposed during the Cold War, the flow of Africans to the United States accelerated. Much of this immigration was from the horn of Africa (especially Somalia, Ethiopia, and Eritrea), where civil and international conflicts displaced thousands of people (for further discussion, see Kent 2007).

Similarly, Cuba and Haiti have been major sources of refugees in the United States as residents fled repressive communist or dictatorial regimes. Thus, given the wide variation in "push" factors—educational and employment opportunities, reunification of relatives, and individual safety—it is unclear whether black immigration is voluntary or involuntary. Immigration for any of these reasons could be classified as voluntary or involuntary, though the lack of economic opportunities in many of the countries from which blacks immigrate make the involuntary minority classification more plausible for them than the voluntary minority classification.

Group Classification and Schooling Responses

The minority classification scheme is intended to provide an understanding of why ethnic minority groups differ on schooling behaviors, and subsequently, school achievement. Autonomous minorities, despite the fact that they experience some discrimination, are not dominated or oppressed and have levels of school achievement similar to the dominant group (Ogbu 1990). Therefore, this group is not discussed within the oppositional culture literature.

Members of voluntary minority groups are posited to view education as the primary mechanism through which they can realize the opportunities that originally led them to immigrate. Therefore, they fail to adopt counterproductive schooling behaviors/attitudes and often overcome experiences of discrimination and difficulties in school to do well academically. Their distinction from the dominant group—in culture, language, and social or collective identity—is characterized by *primary cultural differences*, differences that existed prior to their immigration and acquisition of minority status. These groups understand that their cultural ideals are distinct, and they view learning aspects of the dominant group's mainstream culture as necessary for success. Thus, they attribute the barriers they initially experience to cultural differences and interpret them as temporary obstacles to overcome. In addition, with little history of being targeted for oppression by the dominant group, they trust both it and its institutions, and believe that this dominant group will support their quest for upward mobility.

Involuntary minorities are posited to hold caste-like minority status, which means that they experience greater and more persistent forms of discrimination. They perceive themselves as direct targets of the barriers to success with regard to future employment and earnings. As such, they become disillusioned about the future and begin to doubt the value of schooling. They undergo a *cultural inversion* whereby they develop a culture oppositional to the dominant group (Ogbu 1994). They hold *secondary cultural differences*—differences that emerge after two groups have been in continuous contact, particularly when the contact involves one group's domination over another. Whereas cultural differences from the dominant group for voluntary immigrant minorities are based on *content* (for example, differences driven by lack of familiarity stemming from cross-country migration), for involuntary minorities they are based on *style* (for example, differences perceived to be driven by preferences). Therefore, they see these differences as markers of group identity to be maintained.

In sum, the oppositional culture theory claims *some* minorities adopt counterproductive schooling behaviors because of the knowledge or belief that the system of social mobility has been rooted in educational and occupational discrimination based on group membership. Ogbu's group classifications are intended to identify *which* minority groups are likely to adopt counterproductive schooling behaviors and to explain why minority groups differ in their responses to societal barriers. Thus, the major premise of the oppositional culture theory is that the prevailing system of social mobility greatly determines achievement motivation and behavior largely through students' beliefs about the opportunity structure. Ogbu views the lower academic performance of involuntary minorities as an adaptation to the barriers they encounter. He therefore attributes the lower academic performance of blacks to their disinvestment in schooling, which is the result of their belief that the system of social mobility is rooted in educational and occupational discrimination against them.

Ogbu (1978:196) describes the dilemma that results from lower value being placed on blacks' educational credentials: "On the one hand, they were asked to compete with whites in acquiring academic skills, and presumably in preparing themselves for similar roles in adult life; on the other . . . when they succeeded in achieving qualifications similar to those of whites, they were denied equal rewards in terms of occupations, wages, and the like." In one sense, the notion that blacks put forth less effort and commitment for schoolwork appears quite rational. The theory implicitly assumes, however, that the only way to counter this trend and to ameliorate the achievement gap is to change the culture of black youth.

Although there is no shortage of research on the oppositional culture theory, previous studies that both support and challenge the theory provide an incomplete assessment of the framework. Below I describe the limitations of these studies and discuss the need for further research.

The Need for Further Research on Oppositional Cultural Theory
The notion that blacks resist schooling is not without empirical support; however, the studies most often cited as providing support for the resistance model fail to establish definitive evidence for the theory. For example, in a survey conducted among high school seniors in eight public high schools in the Los Angeles area, Roslyn Mickelson (1990) showed that blacks held less positive attitudes about education as a mechanism for upward mobility than did whites, which she attributed to the material realities blacks experience that "challenge the rhetoric of the American Dream" (1990:59). She found that the attitudes about school on which blacks were less favorable than whites—perceptions of school derived from personal experiences or the experiences of significant others—were consequential for academic achievement, which might explain why blacks have lower academic outcomes than whites. However, Mickelson's study was not based on a random sample, which introduces the possibility of selection bias, and the measures used to gauge schooling attitudes among blacks were relatively unclear—issues I address further in Chapter 4. Despite these limitations, Mickelson's study is one of the most widely cited articles within the literature on the oppositional culture theory. Furthermore, Mickelson's findings have been reinforced by some ethnographic studies that find support for the notion that blacks perceive fewer returns to education in the labor market than whites (Fordham and Ogbu 1986; Ogbu 2003). Thus, this finding deserves serious consideration.

There is also some evidence consistent with the hypothesis that black youth resist educational goals because they equate academic success with "acting white" (Fordham and Ogbu 1986; Fryer and Torelli 2010; Ogbu 2003). The locus classicus for the burden of "acting white" variant of the oppositional culture theory is the study conducted by Fordham and Ogbu (1986). Using ethnographic data from eight students in a high school in Washington, D.C., Fordham and Ogbu conclude that the fear of being accused of "acting white" causes a social and psychological situation that diminishes black students' academic efforts and compromises their achievements. However, based on the evidence presented by Fordham and Ogbu, there are several factors that call into question the appropriateness of the term "acting white" and their support for the existence of the phenomenon—that fear of "acting white" is responsible for achievement gaps. First, the study was conducted only among black students. Analysis conducted on one group cannot explain differences between groups. It is impossible to

determine whether Fordham and Ogbu documented a general phenomenon that occurs during adolescence among youth from all ethnicities, as
documented by previous studies (Coleman 1961; Steinberg 1996) or one
that is limited to just black youth.

Second, no youth in their study made reference to "acting white." Instead,
the term "brainiac" appeared in some of the student narratives. Interestingly,
when "brainiac" was used by the students, the term was not used in reference to race. The term "fear of acting white" seems to be used by the researchers to describe the phenomenon of nerd disdain that they document.
The colloquial "acting white" is an apt term for a concept within a theory
that attributes a group's disadvantage to their adoption (and maintenance)
of an identity that is in opposition to an advantaged counterpart. Given the
importance of this concept to the theory, it is surprising that none of the
narratives from the eight students upon which the study was based ever
made reference to "acting white."

Third, whereas some students reported that they could perform better in
school, it is never established whether the students were overestimating
their own abilities based on previous success at lower levels of schooling.
Although some students might claim that they can perform much better
than they show, it is important to establish whether their lower academic
performance is indeed a choice, particularly since a major premise of the
theory is that students *purposefully* avoid attaining good grades. The study
(and indeed the theory) suffers from the omission of students' skill sets:
Fordham and Ogbu never establish whether the behaviors they observed
were a result of students' becoming discouraged with their inability to perform well in school. Instead, they speculate in the case of one student that
her loss of enthusiasm occurred because she finally submitted to peer pres-
sures not to act white, despite the fact that the loss of enthusiasm occurred
after the student was placed in an all-academic section, of which she stated,
"You know, everyone in there was smart, so it wasn't recognized—they recognized everybody as being a smart section (sic), instead of an individual"
(1986:190).

Finally, Fordham and Ogbu (1986:195) provide some evidence that contradicts the notion that high achieving black students are negatively sanctioned for their high achievement. They describe how a student named
Norris maintained high achievement despite negative peer pressure: "At
the elementary and junior high schools, where his peers thought that he got
good grades without studying, they attributed his academic success to his

'natural talent' or special gift. Therefore they did not view him as a pervert brainiac" (1986:195). This quotation suggests that blacks are not against high achievement. I address this issue in Chapter 5.

A third source of evidence for the oppositional culture theory is the ethnographic study conducted by Ogbu (2003) in the school district of Shaker Heights, located in an affluent suburb of Cleveland, Ohio. The purpose of the study was to determine why black students in one of the best districts in the nation, serving an upper-middle-class, highly educated community (with over 60 percent of the residents over twenty-five years old holding at least a bachelor's degree), still performed far below their white counterparts. Interestingly, Ogbu concluded that he found support for the notion that black underachievement resulted from the black community's resistance to education—despite the fact that the study came about at the behest of black parents. A group of concerned members in the black community had contacted Ogbu to conduct the study, which was jointly funded by the community and school district. Furthermore, Ogbu undermined his own evidence by noting that some of the black students who expressed countereducational attitudes were not free from self-doubt about their ability to succeed. This is consistent with Ronald Ferguson's analysis (2001) of Shaker Heights, which shows that the factors that predict black-white GPA differences implicate skills much more than effort, an issue I address further in Chapter 7.

A fourth highly cited study that can be used to promote the "acting white" hypothesis was conducted by Roland Fryer and Paul Torelli (2010). In a study using the National Longitudinal Study of Adolescent Health, which contains data on a nationally representative sample of more than ninety thousand junior high and high school students, Fryer and Torelli find some support for the notion that the "acting white" phenomenon has a significant effect on black student achievement in public schools with high interracial contact among high-achieving students. However, they note that the phenomenon is nonexistent in predominantly black schools—or in schools in which blacks comprise over 20 percent of the student body—and in private schools. Additionally, the relationship between academic achievement and popularity for black students is positive for those with a GPA lower than 3.5; the extent of the support Fryer and Torelli find for the "acting white" hypothesis is the negative relationship between academic achievement and popularity for black students with a GPA of 3.5 or greater who attend schools in which blacks comprise less than 20 percent of the student body. This would apply to roughly one-tenth of the black student population if we were to disregard the finding related to school racial composition (blacks with a GPA of 1.25 standard deviations above the mean). Given that most black youth do not attend schools in which they comprise less than 20 percent of the student body, it appears that the "acting white" hypothesis applies to an estimated 5 percent of the black student population. Furthermore, Fryer and Torelli's findings produce no support for the sabotage model proposed by McWhorter (2000), which posits that blacks seek to compromise the achievement of their peers. I confront the "acting white" hypothesis in greater detail in Chapter 5.

Studies that challenge the oppositional culture theory also suffer from numerous limitations. Previous quantitative studies test only certain aspects of the theory (Ainsworth-Darnell and Downey 1998; Cook and Ludwig 1997, 1998; Harris 2006, 2008; Harris and Robinson 2007). For example, Ainsworth-Darnell and Downey (1998) and Cook and Ludwig (1997, 1998) systematically compared African Americans and whites across resistance measures but were unable to provide a more exhaustive test due to the relatively few indicators of school resistance across waves within the NELS. This data limitation forced them to employ a cross-sectional design. Although I have attempted to build on these studies (Harris 2006, 2008; Harris and Robinson 2007), my previous studies also fail to consider various components of the theory and therefore provide limited snapshots of the framework. Additionally, these studies do not address the reasons why proponents of the resistance model continue to find evidence supportive of the framework that non-proponent have not been able to duplicate.

Previous qualitative studies that challenge the theory have provided rich narratives from students with regard to oppositional culture (Akom 2003; Carter 2005; Horvat and Lewis 2003; O'Connor 1997; Tyson 2002; Tyson, Darity, and Castellino 2005), but they too suffer from several limitations. Many of these studies give a disproportionate amount of attention to whether blacks receive greater negative sanctions from their peers for high achievement than whites (in other words, the "acting white" hypothesis), and are typically conducted in only a few schools. The limitations of these studies have much to do with the intent of their authors, since each sought to address very specific aims; nevertheless, questions can always be raised about whether their findings can be generalized beyond the few purposeful cases they examined.

In sum, the popularity of the resistance model among many educators and the lack of consensus within the scientific community regarding the framework's viability suggest that further research is necessary before the theory can be either accepted or rejected. Although the resistance model is an incredibly rich theory with many components, many people think about the theory as a literal reflection of its name (that blacks have an oppositional culture). Also, the theory is often reduced to the "acting white" hypothesis, which is the component of the framework that receives most attention. However, many of framework's components have not received attention from researchers. It is this void in the literature that I seek to address in this book.

Purpose and Guiding Framework for This Book

The resistance model has received much attention among teachers and other school personnel, as well as from the mainstream press. It has also generated a great deal of research within the scholarly community (Ainsworth-Darnell and Downey 1998; Akom 2003; Carter 2005; Cook and Ludwig 1997; Downey and Ainsworth-Darnell 2002; Farkas, Lleras, and Maczuga 2002; Fordham and Ogbu 1986; Harris 2006, 2008; Harris and Robinson 2007; Horvat and Lewis 2003; Mickelson 1990; O'Connor 1997; Ogbu 2003; Tyson 2002; Tyson, Darity, and Castellino 2005). However, for various reasons it is difficult for these authors to provide a systematic assessment of the theory that accounts for many of its nuances. I am particularly frustrated with quantitative studies—my own included—because they fail to capture a substantial portion of the story. This stems either from challenges such as data limitations and other methodological obstacles or from the fact that the structural norms of publishing in scientific journals generally require researchers to write narrowly focused studies.

This book represents my attempt to provide educators and the social scientific community with an examination of the resistance model that considers most aspects of the framework. Rather than providing the narrow snapshots of the proverbial elephant, my aim is to conduct an analysis that rivals the richness and depth often provided by my qualitative colleagues yet is able to assess the prevalence of the patterns identified by the data. In order to adequately capture the theory's multidimensionality, I draw on a rich collection of measures by using data that follow students over time from six datasets. Because my goal is to determine if an oppositional culture exists among blacks relative to whites, Latino/as are excluded from this study.[10]

I provide the outline for the chapters that follow in a conceptual framework in Figure 1.3. Arrows represent the relationships between the concepts written within the boxes. For example, the arrow from group status to achievement signifies that racial differences exist in academic achievement. Thus, the dashed arrow represents the achievement gap. The path denoted by *a* signifies that race determines one's experiences with opportunities within the United States. I focus on this link in Chapter 2, in which I discuss the relationship between race and opportunities as it pertains to the resistance model. I discuss whether some basis exists for blacks to believe in racial barriers and to be skeptical about education as a means to circumvent these barriers. In order for the resistance model to be viable, black Americans must perceive barriers to upward mobility. Therefore, I review the empirical evidence for the existence of barriers that are posited to compromise academic investment among black Americans.

My examination of the framework begins in Chapter 3 with an assessment of the implications that parents' experiences with the opportunity structure have for youth perceptions of opportunity and academic achievement (denoted by paths *b* and *c*, respectively). In this chapter, I examine the intergenerational transmission of beliefs about the opportunity structure. While there is an extensive literature on the implication of racial socialization for youths' academic outcomes in the field of psychology, this subject has not received much attention within the context of the resistance model.

Figure 1.3:   Chapter Outlines and Guiding Conceptual Framework

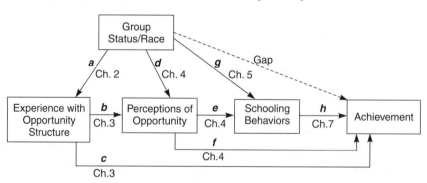

Note: Ch = chapter. This is a conceptual model and not a path diagram for analysis. Chapter 6 is purposefully omitted.

As such, it is not clear how the barriers based on race that parents perceive for themselves or for their children are associated with youths' perceptions of education as a mechanism for upward mobility; empirical evidence for this aspect of the framework is missing from the resistance model literature.

In Chapter 4, I examine whether differences exist in perceptions of opportunity between black and white youth (path *d*) and the implications that these perceptions have for academic investment (paths *e* and *f*). While this aspect of the resistance model has been assessed previously (in particular, Mickelson 1990), the findings from Chapter 4 provide further clarity on the attitude-achievement paradox raised by Mickelson (1990)—that blacks underachieve despite expressing favorable attitudes toward education.

I then turn my attention to path *g* in Chapter 5 by comparing black and white youth on over thirty indicators that capture academic investment. The outcomes of academic investment are varied and include youths' beliefs about the importance of education, affective attitudes toward education, and schooling behaviors based on both traditional survey items and time diaries. Thus, Chapter 5 contains the bulk of the analysis that explores whether racial differences exist in general academic orientation. Although this type of analysis has been conducted by others (Ainsworth-Darnell and Downey 1998; Cook and Ludwig 1997), Chapter 5 extends this line of inquiry by employing three sources of data not previously used to assess the resistance model, one of which is based on a nationally representative sample of young people in England. Assessing the resistance model in the United Kingdom fills an important void in the literature; although the theory was intended to provide a cross-cultural framework for understanding how marginalized groups orient themselves toward education, the cross-cultural dimension of the framework has received little attention. Therefore, Chapter 5 provides a test of the theory based on a richer collection of measures than found in previous studies, including time diaries, and contains the first quantitative assessment of the framework within a non-U.S. context.

In Chapter 6, I shift the focus from the resistance model to examine the effectiveness of a strategy for academic success derived from the resistance model. Specifically, I explore whether black students' achievement would improve if they were to adopt a "raceless" identity or distance themselves from "black culture." While the notion that blacks can increase their achievement by distancing themselves from the black community is not part of the resistance model, it is an idea motivated by the resistance model proposed by Signithia Fordham, a former student and collaborator of John Ogbu.

I return to the framework in Chapter 7 by carefully assessing the link between schooling behaviors and academic achievement (path h). It is in this chapter that I suggest a substantial modification to the resistance model. Specifically, I document the extent to which the resistance model suffers from omitted variable bias by not accounting for academic skills at early levels of schooling. This has implications for understanding whether oppositional culture is responsible for poor academic achievement or whether oppositional culture results from poor academic preparation. If the latter scenario is the case, then oppositional culture cannot be the cause of the racial achievement gaps observed among adolescents. If blacks do behave in ways inconsistent with school success, the latter scenario would suggest that it is not because they purposefully resist schooling, but because they do not receive academic skills critical for academic success prior to adolescence. This would shift the spotlight to alternative factors, perhaps such as living in isolated neighborhoods where the effective academic habits that lead to success are less present. There is no study that formally examines whether black students display oppositionality to schooling at the elementary school level, despite the existence of an achievement gap at this stage of development. In fact, the ethnographic work of Karolyn Tyson (2002, 2003) lends support for the latter scenario.

I continue to suggest new grounds for exploration in Chapter 8 by further examining the notion that marginalized groups resist schooling. In order to test the generality of this marginalization hypothesis, I conduct a class-based analysis using a sample from both the United Kingdom and the United States. Although Ogbu's work rests squarely on explaining racial differences in schooling, I discuss the possibility that the theory's underlying assumption might be supported more by a class-based rather than a race-based analysis. This discussion is important because it is possible that proponents of the theory attribute a class-based phenomenon to black youth. Since it is difficult to cognitively control for social class, some educators might incorrectly (and inadvertently) attribute a culture of resistance to schooling to black students.

Finally in Chapter 9, I provide a discussion of the theoretical and practical implications of the findings from this book. The findings from this study do not allow me to present a solution to black-white achievement disparities; rather, this book is intended to provide a careful and rigorous quantitative assessment of one theory of the racial achievement gap. Although explaining the achievement gap is beyond the scope of this study, in Chapter 9, I propose avenues that can help educators and policy makers refocus and refine their understandings of the racial differences in academic outcomes between black and white youth.

Figure 1.3 thus represents a conceptual representation of the oppositional culture theory rather than a diagram intended for path analysis. Given the richness of the theory, I opt to assess the framework in chapters along a "path-by-path" basis. This organization allows me to break down and unpack the thesis into its main components, an approach that can serve to clarify many issues. Each component of the diagram is critical to the oppositional culture theory. The pivotal point here is that if any of these "causal" links does not hold, then the oppositional culture theory cannot be true; each of the links is necessary to sustain the theory. Or to put it another way, each empirical chapter on its own (between Chapters 3 and 7) has the potential to invalidate the oppositional culture theory. I report on the viability of the theory at the conclusion of each chapter, and throughout the book I revisit the diagram to reorient the reader toward the aspect of the framework being addressed or to revise the framework to be more consistent with the evidence that emerges from the chapters.

At the simplest level, the task for teachers is to teach students the skills called for by the age- or grade-appropriate curriculum. Ideally, teachers should hope that the K-12 education system will help students to develop open minds; this outlook will enable students to weigh evidence carefully and to assess the quality of others' arguments and thereby prepare them to construct arguments of their own. If students have set opinions and have concluded that they will not be swayed, regardless of the evidence presented to them, then we have all failed. Similarly, as educators, we too must practice these principles. If evidence runs counter to what we believe, we must remain open to the possibility that we have misinterpreted our observations. If not, the discourse does not move and intellectual progress is compromised. We must always remain willing to change our position if called for by new evidence. There will be readers for whom the findings from this study contravene their expectations. My hope is that at a minimum these readers do not disregard the findings but instead engage in dialogue about the evidence presented here. As educators, we owe this to our students. Given the projections I discuss above for the convergence of the achievement gap, the stakes are too high not to do so.

2

DISCRIMINATION AND BARRIERS:
BASIS FOR BLACK CYNICISM
TOWARD SCHOOLING

A major premise of the oppositional culture theory is that blacks disinvest from academic goals because they do not believe that education will enable them to overcome barriers to upward socioeconomic mobility. The black American experience is deeply rooted in socioeconomic disadvantage and in a history of being targets of government-sanctioned discriminatory treatment, dating back to the era of slavery (pre-1865) through the era of Jim Crow, which mandated *de jure* racial segregation in public spaces (1876–1965). State-mandated discrimination officially ended in 1964 with the Civil Rights Act; this legislation was followed by the passage of the Voting Rights Act of 1965. But the persistence of racial inequality, as seen in many socio-economic indicators—education in particular—after the repeal of state-mandated discrimination, has fueled the black cultural deficit narrative. According to the oppositional culture theory, the vestiges of past discriminatory practices lead blacks to go beyond academic disinvestment to outright resistance to schooling.

The issue of whether black youth perceive these barriers is the subject of Chapters 3 and 4. In this chapter, I discuss whether a basis exists for blacks to remain cynical about education as a mechanism for upward mobility. I begin by reviewing previous research on racial inequality within the labor market. Although pervasive discrimination across various domains contributes to a societal structure in which some groups occupy a caste-like minority status, the resistance model posits that it is unfair treatment in the labor market that undermines black youths' investment in school. Therefore, I review studies that suggest blacks continue to experience labor market discrimination as well as studies that challenge those findings. Making a case for whether or not discrimination exists lies beyond the purview of this book—what is key here to the oppositional culture theory is that blacks attribute disparate treatment to discrimination. It is important to establish whether a basis exists for blacks to remain skeptical about their chances for advancement within the opportunity structure, because the oppositional culture theory posits that the black experience occurs within an unfair system of social mobility. A major premise of the theory is that barriers to upward mobility are persistent enough to create caste-like minorities whose unfair experiences with the labor market lead them to disinvest from education. Thus racial barriers are an integral component of the resistance model.

I then discuss how beliefs in the existence of barriers have shifted over time within the United States and whether blacks believe that they still experience barriers to upward mobility. In this discussion, I highlight the beliefs of both whites and blacks. Whereas the discussion of whether whites believe that blacks experience barriers is important for understanding the increased popularity of the narrative of black cultural deficiency, the discussion of belief in barriers among blacks is necessary to determine whether the oppositional culture theory remains viable. The resistance model rests on the assumption that blacks believe in barriers. In the final section of this chapter, I place blacks' belief both in barriers and in the importance of education in historical context. Although a culture of resistance to schooling is attributed to blacks, the oppositional culture theory is silent on when this culture emerged.

Racial Differences in Labor Market Experiences
Disparities in Promotions

Previous research suggests that there is a legitimate basis for blacks' perceptions of an unfair opportunity structure (Baldi and McBrier 1997; Elliott and Smith 2004; Smith 2005). For example, using data from the National Organizational Study—interviews conducted with the employers of respondents from the National Opinion Research Center's General Social Survey—Baldi and McBrier (1997) find that relative to whites, black workers with comparable education, experience, and training, and in similar types of firms, are only half as likely to receive a promotion. In a study on differential access to workplace power, Elliott and Smith (2004) find that racial inequality in promotion increases at higher levels of power. Specifically, using data from the Multi-City Survey of Urban Inequality (MCSUI)—a multistage stratified area-probability sample of respondents in Atlanta, Boston, Detroit, and Los Angeles—they find that both black males and females are less likely to receive promotions at the higher end of the occupational hierarchy than white males. These differences exist even if the comparisons are made among individuals with similar years of education, total work experience, prior job-specific experience, and employer tenure. In the case of black women, this form of inequality appears to be a result of direct discrimination, since familial obligations that might lead females to opt out of consideration for higher-level positions were taken into account. Thus, studies on racial differences in promotion suggest that these disparities cannot be attributed to differences in human capital or type of firm.

Smith (2005) shows that racial differences also exist in the processes that determine promotions in the labor force. He finds that before receiving a promotion, relative to white men, black men must work longer periods of time after leaving school, and black women must have more prior job-specific experience and log more time on the job—*ceteris paribus*.[1] Furthermore, previous research provides some evidence that blacks' human capital credentials receive more intense scrutiny than whites' credentials when blacks and whites are in contention for promotions (Baldi and McBrier 1997), particularly when vying for managerial (Wilson, Sakura-Lemessy, and West 1999) and supervisory positions (Smith 2001).[2]

Blacks are also disadvantaged when it comes to experiencing job layoffs. Wilson and McBrier's (2005) analysis based on the Panel Study of Income Dynamics (PSID), an ongoing survey of a nationally representative sample of Americans collected since 1968, shows that the percentage of layoffs for blacks is nearly twice that for whites (31 percent and 16 percent, respectively). The greater layoff rates for blacks exist in both the private and public sector. They also find that blacks are more vulnerable to being laid off than whites; increases in tenure with employer, college and postcollege education, and union membership are associated with decreases in the layoff likelihood for whites but not for blacks. Thus, blacks face a route to downward occupational movement that is structured less by traditional stratification-based causal factors, and they experience this mobility faster than whites (Wilson and Roscigno 2010). Along the same line, reentrance into the labor market comes with additional costs for blacks, as shown by Tomaskovic-Devey, Thomas, and Johnson (2005), who find that blacks experience longer periods of job search than white job seekers with similar levels of human capital (for example, education and cognitive skill). This suggests that blacks on average accumulate general labor market experience at slower rates across their careers than do white workers.

Disparities in Wages

In addition to racial differences in upward mobility within the workforce, another factor that might contribute to blacks' perceptions of discrimination is racial differences in wages. Studies based on the National Longitudinal Survey of Youth (NLSY)—which contains panel data on the school-to-work transition and labor market experiences of a nationally representative sample of over twelve thousand men and women that spans four decades—show that while no black-white wage gap exists at entry to the labor force, a racial wage gap develops as experience accumulates primarily because blacks reap smaller gains from job mobility (Oettinger 1996; Tomaskovic-Devey, Thomas, and Johnson 2005). The black wage disadvantage persists net of education, experience, hours worked, occupation, authority, region, and city size (Smith 1997). Furthermore, Smith (1997) finds that although this income gap declined over the last quarter of the twentieth century, blacks in supervisory positions earned roughly 80 percent of the income earned by whites near the end of the century. However, the black-white wage gap remained constant among workers in nonsupervisory positions.

Many of these patterns also exist among women. Despite the wage gains black women made between 1940 and 1980, they continue to earn less than their white counterparts (Anderson and Shapiro 1996). Furthermore, Anderson and Shapiro (1996) show that black women are less likely to hold high-wage occupations than their white counterparts, even if they have the same levels of education, work experience, tenure, and type of occupation. They must also have higher levels of education, work experience, and tenure relative to their white counterparts to access high-wage occupations.

The cost of "blackness" is estimated in a study conducted by Goldsmith, Hamilton, and Darity (2006), who examine whether skin tone is a determinant of wages. They find that whereas the wages for light-skinned blacks are similar to whites, wages substantially decline as skin tone darkens, with medium- and dark-skinned blacks earning substantially less (by at least 10 percent) than whites. These findings hold even if the comparison is made between people with similar occupations, levels of education, retrospective high school performance level, labor market experience, health status, and self-esteem. They also account for respondents' socioeconomic background and neighborhood quality, as well as for employment-specific factors such as union status, full-time work status, firm size, having a supervisory role, and degree of contact with customers. Since skin shade is separate from culture and unrelated to intelligence among blacks (Hill 2002), these differences cannot be attributed to cultural or genetic factors.[3]

Figure 2.1 relates the annual income of white and black Americans over the age of twenty-five to educational attainment for 2008 using the Current Population Survey. Both whites and blacks experience increased earnings with each additional level of schooling. The increases in the slopes are virtually identical, indicating that the returns from education are about the same for each race. However, whites earn somewhat more than blacks at each level of schooling. Furthermore, the black-white pay differential widens slightly as the level of education increases. Thus, given the racial pay differentials, it appears that a basis exists for blacks to perceive that there are certain barriers within the labor market that education may not help them overcome.

Along with Figure 2.1, the aforementioned studies show that blacks experience an increase in earnings with greater levels of schooling. Nevertheless, according to the resistance model, there are two forms of inequality with regard to wages that undermine blacks' investment in schooling. First, the

Figure 2.1:   Mean Annual Income by Educational Attainment for People Ages 25 and Over, 2008.

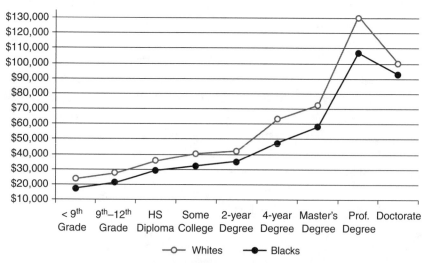

Source: Data are from the U.S. Census Bureau, Current Population Survey, 2008 Annual Social and Economic Supplement.

inequality can take the form of a main race effect—racial differences in mean wages at each level of education. Second, unfair treatment can take the form of racial difference in returns on education—the rate of increase in earnings for each additional year or level of education. Even if blacks receive the same increase in earnings for each additional level of education as whites, blacks' lower wages compared to whites with similar levels of schooling is posited to compromise their academic investment. The same should hold true with regards to promotions. That is, a slower rate of ascent in the occupational hierarchy or holding a lower occupational rank, despite similar levels of education compared to whites, should contribute to blacks' school disinvestment, because these forms of inequality tap into the job ceiling aspect of the oppositional culture theory.

The aforementioned studies suggest that blacks have some basis for perceiving that they are treated differently from whites in the labor market along both the *race effect* and the *rate of increase* standard of inequality in both promotions and wages.[4]

The Skills versus Discrimination Debate

A major critique raised against this line of research that applies to many of the aforementioned studies is that they do not adequately account for productivity characteristics, and many of them lack measures of skill. Some scholars have suggested that the racial wage gap stems from blacks' deficiencies in human capital—skills in particular—or the labor market characteristics of blacks rather than discrimination. Using the NLSY, Neal and Johnson (1996) show that about two-thirds of the wage disadvantage for black men and all the difference for black women age twenty-six to twenty-nine can be attributed to their lower scores on the Armed Forces Qualification Test (AFQT) administered when they were aged sixteen to eighteen. Similar conclusions were reached by O'Neill (1990) and Johnson and Neal (1998), though the latter researchers found that less of the racial wage gap is explained when annual earnings rather than hourly wages are used as the outcome. This line of research prompted Nobel Laureate–winning economist James Heckman (1998:101) to claim that labor market discrimination is "no longer a first-order quantitative problem in American society." In fact Carneiro, Heckman, and Masterov (2005) conclude that social policy for dealing with racial inequality should not focus on discrimination in the labor market because addressing early skill deficits for blacks holds much greater promise than heightened legal activism in the workplace. They make this recommendation despite their finding that adjusting wage gaps by both years of completed schooling and the age when the test was taken widens the wage gaps reported by Neal and Johnson (1996) for all groups, particularly for black males.

Although some scholars suggest that discrimination in the labor market has abated, based on equations that show racial wage gaps are greatly reduced (or eliminated) when blacks and whites are matched on premarket skills, the studies upon which these conclusions are based rely on the AFQT as the measure of skills. Studies that rely on the AFQT do not include people with zero wages, which could apply to a greater proportion of blacks excluded from the labor market due to discrimination. Also, when the AFQT is adjusted for the school grade completed and the respondent's age at the time the test was taken, the AFQT's impact on wages all but disappears (Rodgers and Spriggs 2002). Furthermore, Rodgers and Spriggs (1996) show that AFQT scores are racially biased—they do not measure the same set of skills (or job skills) across racial groups. If the AFQT measures skills acquired as a result of school quality, motivation, and family background, then these factors should contribute similarly to AFQT scores across racial groups, even if the mean scores on these factors vary by race. Rodgers and Spriggs (1996) show that this is not the case; these factors predict higher scores for whites than blacks. Additionally, the skills measured by the AFQT lack job specificity.

Studies that use alternative measures of cognitive skill do not support the argument that the racial wage gap is due to racial differences in cognitive skills. For example, Mason (2000) shows that premarket (that is, cognitive) skills as measured in the PSID account for less than one-third of the racial wage gap. Similarly, Tomaskovic-Devey, Thomas, and Johnson's (2005) analysis of the NLSY shows that the black wage disadvantage relative to whites increases over the career trajectory even after controlling for level (and quality measured as cognitive skills) of education. These findings run opposite to theories of statistical discrimination, which predict that the wage gap should be largest at the point of initial hire, when uncertainty among employers regarding employees' abilities is highest, and that as employers get to know workers, they will reward them more for their actual characteristics than for their assumed attributes. Although Tomaskovic-Devey, Thomas, and Johnson's (2005) findings suggest that racial differences in earnings develop as a result of labor market forces, the fact that racial wage inequality increases over the career trajectory can also be interpreted as evidence of lower productivity among black workers, discovered only after the point of hire. Coleman's (2003) study provides further clarity on this issue by examining the role of job-specific skills for the racial wage gap. He uses employers' evaluations of workers' skills based on actual on-the-job ability ratings relative to other workers contained in the MCSUI Employer Survey and finds that blacks earn 19 percent less than whites, nearly half (42 percent) of which could be attributed to blacks' lower levels of human capital (that is, education, job tenure, and age). However, when white and black men have the same competitive performance rating from their employers, in addition to similar levels of human capital, racial wage differences actually increase slightly. Thus, human capital and employers' job-specific skill ratings—a more relevant form of skill evaluation than tests purported to measure cognitive aptitude—explain less than half of the black male wage disadvantage. Coleman's data included every major business sector except farming and mining.

Within this line of research, the major issue of concern is whether the racial wage gap can be attributed to blacks' lower skills relative to whites or to labor market discrimination. Theoretically, blacks and whites with similar levels of educational attainment and job-relevant experience should receive similar wages. If under this scenario blacks receive lower earnings than whites, the difference should be accounted for by racial differences in skills. Previous studies differ on the extent to which the skills argument explains these gaps. Proponents of the discrimination argument claim that the racial wage gap net of skills is real and reflects labor market discrimination. Proponents of the skills explanation claim that the AFQT is an adequate measure of skills and that any remaining wage gap after accounting for skills reflects the fact that the measure of skills is imperfect, because discrimination in the labor market has abated. The case can always be made that any residual wage gap between blacks and whites after all major characteristics (for example, level of education, experience, hours worked, occupation, level of authority, skills) are taken into account results because the measure of skill being employed is inadequate. The side that one takes in this debate depends on the confidence one has in the quality of the measure of skill being used in a particular study. In order to gain greater purchase on whether blacks have a legitimate basis for believing in racial barriers, I turn to a discussion on audit studies, which test for evidence of labor market discrimination in a manner that does not rely on workers' skill levels.

Direct Evidence of Discrimination

Studies that attempt to explain racial wage differences by accounting for premarket skills provide only an indirect assessment of labor market discrimination. There is a long line of studies that *directly* test for (and find) discrimination in the labor market. Much of this evidence comes in the form of audit studies, which match job applicants on every category (for example, on the basis of résumés or credentials) other than the factor on which the discrimination is being tested (for example, sex or race). In studies that use actual job applicants, the auditors are thoroughly trained throughout the course of the study to act in identical ways, given nearly identical résumés, and sent on interviews for the same jobs.

A recent study that used this approach was conducted by Bertrand and Mullainathan (2004), who randomly sorted résumés into two groups: those with very white sounding names (for example, Emily Walsh or Greg Baker) and to those with very African American sounding names (for example, Lakisha Washington or Jamal Jones). To examine whether credentials affect the racial gap in callbacks from employers, Bertrand and Mullainathan experimentally varied the quality of the résumés sent in response to a given ad; higher-quality applicants were assigned slightly more labor market experience, fewer gaps in employment history, some certification degree, foreign language skills, or were awarded some honors. After sending nearly 5,000 résumés to over 1,300 employment ads in the sales, administrative support, and clerical and customer services job categories, Bertrand and Mullainathan found large racial differences in callback rates. Applicants with white names had a callback rate of one for every ten résumés, compared to one in fifteen for résumés belonging to applicants with black names. In fact, the effect of having a white-sounding name was similar to that of having an additional eight years of work experience. Furthermore, they found that the racial gap in callbacks widened with an increase in résumé quality, which contradicts the notion that improved credentials alleviate employers' fear that black applicants are deficient in some unobservable skills. Black résumés were not treated more preferentially by federal contractors, who are generally more constrained by affirmative action laws, nor by larger employers or employers who explicitly state that they are "Equal Opportunity Employers."

Perhaps the most disconcerting evidence of barriers experienced by blacks emerges from the results of an audit study conducted by Devah Pager (2007). In one of the best-known audit studies in sociology, Pager compared the job prospects in the low-wage labor market of black and white men who were recently released from jail. She found that the likelihood of receiving an interview for blacks *without* a criminal record was the same as whites *with* a criminal record. She also found that the benefits of making personal contact with employers moderated the negative effects of having a criminal record for whites but not for blacks; contact with employers increased the callback rate for whites with a criminal record by more than 350 percent, compared to 50 percent for blacks with a criminal record.

Although audit studies provide powerful evidence of the persistence of racial barriers experienced by blacks, they are not without limitations. Most of the critiques against audit studies come from Heckman and Siegelman (1993) and Heckman (1998), who argue that audit studies employing individuals (auditors) from different racial groups matched on various characteristics — as is commonly done in studies on housing discrimination — produce biased estimates of discrimination. Heckman and Siegelman (1993) note that audit studies assume that the distributions of unobserved characteristics considered important by the job or housing agent are identical among the white and nonwhite worker or home seeker. Despite the training that auditors undergo to ensure that their behaviors follow common protocols, there are some behavioral cues (both verbal and nonverbal) that auditors cannot control.

Zhao, Ondrich, and Yinger (2006), who find evidence of discrimination in the housing market, minimized this type of bias by accounting for actual auditor characteristics not employed in previous audit studies that may influence the way an auditor is treated. However, Heckman (1998) notes that the training process sometimes instructs auditors on the problem of discrimination in the United States, which might lead auditors to find or perceive discrimination where none might exist or be perceived during the course of normal interaction. Furthermore, Heckman and Siegelman (1993) argue that problems exist in effectively matching auditors (or résumés) and in the methods by which firms are selected. Although some audit studies do not employ auditors, such as that conducted by Bertrand and Mullainathan (2004), who randomly sorted résumés to test for discrimination in the labor market, these concerns about auditor selection present threats to the overall validity of audit studies.

Perceptions of Racial Barriers within the United States

The large racial disparities in key social and economic domains discussed above and in Chapter 1 — and the findings from the aforementioned studies — can easily be interpreted as evidence of unequal opportunity for upward mobility between racial groups. However, some prominent scholars have declared that discrimination is no longer a major obstacle for blacks within the United States. For example, as mentioned earlier, James Heckman (1998) argues that labor market discrimination is no longer a problem in American society. Eminent sociologist Orlando Patterson (1997) and Stephan and Abigail Thernstrom (1997) make the same claim with regard to the housing market. They argue that white prejudice and discrimination are no longer important causes of housing segregation. Patterson (1997:17) goes further in writing that "being Afro-American is no longer a significant obstacle to participation in the public life of the nation." This position is important because it is the continued persistence of the black-white achievement gap in conjunction with a belief in declining racial barriers that makes the oppositional culture thesis compelling. If one accepts the notion that blacks no longer experience racial barriers, then it seems logical to attribute the persistence of inequality to a cultural deficit that includes purposeful resistance to schooling.

In addition to the aforementioned critiques raised against audit studies, as well as studies that provide evidence for racial discrimination in the labor market, some studies on racial attitudes within the United States have contributed to the notion that racial barriers no longer account for racial inequality. These studies typically show that attitudes about race appear to be shifting in a positive direction. In one of the most comprehensive studies on racial attitudes in the United States, Schuman et al. (1997) find that fewer whites readily endorse statements that blacks are less intelligent than whites and fewer object to increasing levels of interracial mixing in neighborhoods and to interracial marriage (see Krysan 2008 for an updated version of Schuman et al. 1997). For example, whereas in 1977 nearly 30 percent of whites believed that racial inequality in jobs, income, and housing existed because blacks have less inborn ability to learn, less than 10 percent held this belief by 2000. The percentage of whites who support an open housing law that prohibits homeowners from refusing to sell to someone because of their race or color increased from slightly over 30 percent in 1974 to 69 percent in 2006. Similarly, 75 percent of whites approved of interracial marriage in 2007 compared to less than 10 percent in 1960. These trends suggest that an overwhelming majority of whites—the dominant group that has historically oppressed blacks—no longer hold views that can be considered racist. Given that an increasing proportion of whites hold favorable racial attitudes, it is reasonable to conclude that blacks do not encounter obstacles to upward mobility.

The belief that barriers do not account for racial inequality is also becoming increasingly popular, particularly among whites. Schuman et al. (1997) show that over the final quarter of the twentieth century, there was an increasing trend in the percentage of whites who believed that racial inequality in jobs, income, and housing existed because blacks lacked motivation or will power to pull themselves out of poverty. Whereas roughly one-third of whites held this belief in 1977, 51 percent held this belief by 2000 and again in 2006 (Krysan 2008). The belief among whites that discrimination is responsible for racial inequality declined slightly over the same period, from roughly 40 percent during 1977 to 30 percent in 2006. There has also been a steady decline among whites in attributing racial inequalities to a lack of educational opportunities for blacks, from 66 percent in 1977 to 44 percent by 2006 (Krysan 2008; Schuman et al. 1997).

The narrative that blacks are responsible for their socioeconomic disadvantage appears to extend to employers, a trend that might present more challenges for blacks in the labor market. Pager and Karafin (2009) conducted in-depth interviews with fifty-five hiring managers for entry-level positions in the retail, restaurant, and service industry to explore employers' group-level attributions concerning black applicants and workers. They also examined the connection between employers' direct observations of black workers and their general perceptions about the black workforce. They found that only 15 percent of employers attributed the employment problems of black men to structural issues such as poverty, lack of education, disadvantaged neighborhood contexts, and prejudice and discrimination. The most common explanations (about three-fourths of respondents) focused on the individual shortcomings of black men themselves. Employers consistently mentioned factors such as lack of work ethic, poor self-presentation, or a threatening or criminal demeanor. Although fewer than half of the employers interviewed reported observations of their own applicants or employees consistent with their mostly negative perceptions about blacks, Pager and Karafin (2009) found that most employers maintain their original attitudes about blacks in general.

In addition to the decline in the proportion of whites who attribute racial inequality to barriers experienced by blacks, recent Gallup Polls show that an overwhelming majority of whites believe that blacks do not experience barriers. In 2008, most whites believed that blacks had an equal opportunity to receive a good education (80 percent). Similarly, in 2007 most whites believed that blacks do not receive unfair treatment at work (84 percent), neighborhood shops (87 percent), stores downtown or in the shopping mall

(83 percent), in restaurants, bars, theaters or other entertainment places (87 percent), or in dealing with the police (60 percent). In sum, despite the large racial disparities that exist on major indicators of socioeconomic well-being, whites' racial attitudes appear to be improving, fewer whites attribute racial inequality to the existence of barriers, and an overwhelming majority of whites believe that blacks no longer experience racial barriers. These patterns make it easy to understand why the black cultural deficiency narrative has gained in popularity within the United States; if the dominant group believes that racism is on the decline and racial barriers are no longer a major obstacle to blacks' advancement opportunities, then the cultural deficiency narrative becomes a more plausible explanation for persistent racial inequality on socioeconomic outcomes.

Do Black Americans Believe in Barriers?

Whereas a decline in beliefs about barriers among white Americans contributes to the viability of the oppositional culture theory, the theory rests on the assumption that a belief in barriers is prevalent among blacks. In Figure 2.2, I highlight results from a recent *Washington Post–ABC News* poll based on a nationally representative sample within the United States. The top panel shows that 74 percent of Americans regard racism as a problem (72 percent and 85 percent of whites and blacks, respectively), with blacks being twice as likely as whites to believe that racism is a big problem (44 percent compared to 22 percent). Furthermore, 74 percent of whites believe blacks have either achieved (37 percent) or will soon (37 percent) achieve racial equality. In contrast, over 40 percent of black Americans believe that racial equality will not be achieved in their lifetime or will never be achieved. The final outcome in the top panel shows that almost three-fourths of blacks report having experienced racial discrimination, which is actually up from 64 percent in 2003, with nearly half (48 percent) reporting that these experiences occur either occasionally or often (not displayed).

The bottom panel of Figure 2.2 suggests that substantial racial differences exist in beliefs about the extent to which blacks experience unequal treatment because of race. The first three outcomes show that over 80 percent of whites believe that blacks who live in their communities receive fair treatment in the housing market, job market, and when visiting local businesses such as stores, restaurants, or banks. In contrast, less than half of blacks believe this to be the case, with slightly more than one-third perceiving fair treatment in the labor market. The next outcome shows that 60 percent of

Figure 2.2: Beliefs about Racism within the United States

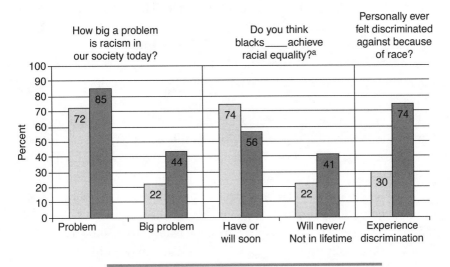

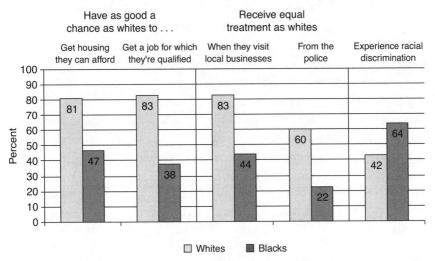

Source: *Washington Post-ABC News* (cell and landline) telephone poll based on a random sample of 1,079 Americans, January 13–16, 2009.

 [a] Three percent of blacks and four percent of whites had no opinion.

whites and only 22 percent of blacks believe that blacks who live in their communities receive fair treatment from police. The percentages for both groups suggest that a substantial proportion of both white and black Americans do not believe that blacks receive fair treatment from the police. Finally, 22 percent more blacks than whites believe that blacks in their community experience racial discrimination (64 percent compared to 42 percent).

While fewer whites believe that blacks are adversely affected by racial barriers, a substantial proportion of blacks still believe that racial barriers continue to persist. Why does such racial discrepancy exist regarding the belief in racial barriers against blacks? Lucas (2008) provides some clarity on this question in a discussion of experiential realities and public contestation. He notes that "different, well-meaning scholars and citizens may live in the same epoch characterized by the same reality concerning discrimination, yet have vastly different experiences of that reality and thus draw diametrically opposed conclusions about the time in which they live" (2008:24). Lucas shows that although the last quarter of the twentieth century saw a decline in the proportion of realtors and police officers who attribute racial inequality to blacks' lack of motivation or will power to pull themselves out of poverty, blacks still have a high likelihood of interacting with individuals from each of these occupations who hold this belief. Specifically, whereas the proportion of realtors and police officers who held this belief in 2000 stood at roughly 55 percent and 42 percent, respectively, the probability of a black person encountering a pair of realtors or police officers of which at least one believes that blacks lack will power is approximately 77 percent and 62 percent, respectively. More relevant for black youth, Lucas shows that given the fact that one-third of teachers believe in the argument that blacks lack motivation and will power, blacks are virtually assured of having at least one teacher in grades 1 through 12 who hold this belief (over 97 percent chance).

Why do Blacks and Whites differ in Beliefs about Racial Barriers

Lucas (2008) argues that in research on discriminatory treatment, the experiences of targeted groups should be of central interest. His analysis shows that whites' attitudes toward blacks and racial issues do not adequately account for the day-to-day experiences of blacks. Despite the fact that prejudicial attitudes have declined, Lucas's systematic analysis of data obtained from a nationally representative probability sample indicates that the likelihood that blacks will encounter prejudiced authorities remains rather high. Lucas explains this seeming paradox in the following manner:

> Observe first that these [prejudicial] attitudes are held by whites, some of whom occupy positions of mundane power . . . Then note that the organization of social, economic, and political life often necessitates repeated interaction with a string of such authorities, as in the case of education, or requires one to do business with those one cannot select, as in the case of Realtors (i.e., the Realtor for the other party to the transaction) or police. Taken together, these features lead to the conclusion that blacks in school, the economy, and in the criminal justice system navigate a minefield of white authorities who doubt their abilities and question their motivation. (2008:35–36)

Lucas notes that blacks' descriptions of their encounters with prejudiced authorities are often disbelieved because many listeners—particularly whites—are aware that the proportion of people who hold prejudicial beliefs is declining. He argues that this triggers the cycle of many blacks doubting the integrity and commitment to justice of their (often white) disbelievers and of many whites doubting the integrity and even sanity of individuals whose description of events invokes racism or discrimination. Lucas (2008:50) claims that we are in an interstitial moment in history that he terms "the era of contested prejudice," which is characterized by "the asymmetry of experience . . . [which] erects a difficult-to-scale wall of misunderstanding between communities." He argues that the appropriate response to charges of discrimination should be cautious consideration rather than outright dismissal or uncritical acceptance.

The work of Eduardo Bonilla-Silva also provides a better understanding of the disparate beliefs blacks and whites hold regarding racial barriers. In *Racism without Racists*, Bonilla-Silva (2006) argues that racist expressions are no longer articulated in terms of black biological inferiority, but rather are expressed in more subtle, institutional, and apparently nonracial forms. One of the primary mechanisms through which whites maintain their disbelief in barriers (and thus maintain their privilege) is by the narrative of colorblindness, as many whites claim that they "don't see any color, but people" (Bonilla-Silva 2006:1).

Bonilla-Silva (2006) discusses how whites receive material gains by adhering to a colorblind ideology, as this ideology does not disturb the current racial hierarchy within the United States. He argues that the narrative of colorblindness mutes discussions about how minorities and whites are steered into separate neighborhoods or how fewer rental and sale units are shown to minorities. Instead, residential segregation is attributed to blacks' desire to live around other blacks rather than to whites' desire (or to the actual practices whites employ) to live separately from blacks. Similarly, factors that contribute to racial disparities within the labor market, such as the advertising of desirable jobs in mostly white networks and ethnic newspapers, are not discussed. Whites explain their success (and the failure of blacks) in individual terms (merit and hard work versus lack of work ethic), rather than attributing it to historically evolving institutional arrangements that unfold in a manner consistent with the interests of the dominant group. Therefore, the narrative of colorblindness does not allow for discussions of how whites benefit from racial barriers, leads to a lack of concern for how racial barriers affect blacks, and allows whites to believe that they are blameless, particularly when they deny being a part of historical wrongdoings and beneficiaries of persistent patterns of inequality. Bonilla-Silva's interview data suggests that racial inequality is stripped of any racial underpinnings and attributed to naturally occurring market dynamics or happenstance and/or blacks' cultural deficiency.

Bonilla-Silva (2006) argues that unlike whites, most blacks have not adopted the colorblind rhetoric. Thus, whites and blacks understand and discuss race differently. Bonilla-Silva notes that many whites have developed an elaborate system to discuss race (or rhetorical moves), which includes both outright avoidance or deflection of discussions about race and incoherence. In contrast, he notes that a majority of blacks readily discuss race, see racism as an everyday phenomenon, and understand the role of white privilege in society. The differences between the ways in which whites and blacks understand and discuss race contribute to the lack of trust and empathy between these groups discussed above. Many whites interviewed by Bonilla-Silva attributed the problems with race within the United States to blacks' continued use of the so-called race card. Furthermore, Bonilla-Silva's findings reveal that not all whites subscribe to the colorblind narrative. In particular, whites who live interracial lives—have black friends or romantic partners—are color conscious. He argues that it is usually whites with working-class backgrounds who are color conscious rather than well-educated, middle-class whites because they understand oppression through their class status, and therefore tend to have more empathy for minority oppression.[5]

Although whites' attitudes about race and racial inequality might appear unrelated to blacks' perceptions of unequal opportunity, the colorblind narrative goes a long way in creating a context in which cultural deficiency narratives can thrive. Below I discuss when the culture of resistance to schooling (or the oppositional culture narrative) attributed to blacks might have begun.

Origin of Oppositional Attitudes toward Education among Blacks

The belief in barriers among blacks does not necessarily mean that blacks will have an antagonistic relationship toward education. Nevertheless, the oppositional culture theory posits that belief in barriers to upward mobility and skepticism that education will effectively enable one to circumvent such barriers because of one's race leads to a culture of resistance to schooling. This resistance takes the form of negative attitudes toward schooling. However, neither the oppositional culture framework nor its supporters adequately address the question of when this attitude developed among black Americans. If resistance to schooling is a response to barriers that render education inconsequential for upward socioeconomic mobility, then oppositional culture among blacks should be lower now than in previous generations. Although blacks have an overwhelming number of reasons to be cynical about education as a mechanism for upward mobility, there is a long line of work by historians that suggests blacks had a reverence toward education during periods in U.S. history in which racial barriers were blatant and overwhelming, such as the eras of slavery (pre-1865), reconstruction (1865–1877), and Jim Crow (1876–1965).

In a discussion of blacks' educational experiences in the South during 1860–1935, James Anderson (1988) describes a ferocious importance ascribed to schooling by black Americans. He discusses how the desire for schooling among blacks was so strong at the turn of the twentieth century that white planters used their power and influence in local and state governments to restrict public school availability to black children. In the few cases where public schools were available to blacks, their parents were willing to accept the loss of child labor—a crucial component to the agricultural economy to which most southern blacks during the reconstruction era were limited—and additional income in order to send their children to school. The central theme that emerges from Anderson's work is that from the time slavery ended through the first half of the twentieth century, most black Americans were persistent in fashioning a system of formal education within a context that denied them complete citizenship, the right to vote, and the freedom to control their labor power (many were trapped in the agricultural economy by statutes and social customs).

Anderson (1988) documents the extraordinary efforts made by blacks to obtain an education, a trend that actually began prior to northern benevolence and the Emancipation Proclamation. The pervasiveness of blacks' desire for schooling was documented in 1866 by John Alvord, the then national superintendent of schools for the Freedmen's Bureau, in the following manner: "Throughout the entire South an effort is being made by the colored people to educate themselves . . . they are determined to be self-taught; and everywhere some elementary text-book, or the fragment of one, may be seen in the hands of negroes (quoted in Anderson 1988:6). Anderson (1988) describes how, in response to the cost-cutting measure of closing black schools taken by the Freedmen's Bureau in 1866, black leaders petitioned for added taxes to be levied upon their community to replenish the bureau's school fund. In addition, he notes how in response to a thirty-foot long petition signed (marked "x" for those who lacked literacy) by ten thousand negro parents, Alvord wrote that "[ex-slaves were] ignorant themselves, but begging that their children might be educated, promising that from beneath their present burdens, and out of their extreme poverty, they would pay for it" (quoted in Anderson 1988:10). Anderson (1988) provides seemingly endless testimonies from former slaves about the punishments they endured for pursuing literacy, including being beaten to forget what they had learned, and the efforts they made to establish schools for blacks.

A similar picture emerges from historian Heather Williams's study, *Self-Taught: African American Education in Slavery and Freedom* (2005). Williams documents the struggles of slaves and black freedmen to obtain literacy and initiate an educational movement during slavery, through the Civil War, and during the first decade of freedom. She notes that during this period, southern states had laws that prohibited the teaching of slaves to read (numeracy, however, was considered important for some slaves in tasks such as weighing cotton or erecting buildings), a prohibition that was extended to include "colored" freedmen. Some laws even prohibited "mental instruction" (that is, memorization), the gathering of five or more slaves outside their plantation, the transporting of written material by blacks across state lines, and the meeting of freedmen in any location that could serve as a place of learning. Punishment for slaves and freedmen who violated these laws included imprisonment with hard labor for life or lashes (for example, no more than twenty in South Carolina, up to thirty-nine in North Carolina and Mississippi). However, the wrath of slave owners was more severe, as numerous slaves reported being beaten with plaited cowhide, having fingers severed, witnessing the hanging of other slaves caught reading or teaching others to read, and fearing the hyperbolic threats made by slave masters (for example, being skinned alive or receiving five hundred lashes). Nevertheless, Williams documents what can be described as a cat-and-mouse game in which slaves and freedmen constantly devised creative and subversive means to acquire literacy. Williams (2005:12) writes that "accounts of such efforts make it evident that even in slavery, with its violence, insults, and punishing labor, many African Americans yearned to become literate." Williams's study highlights how blacks' strategies to obtain literacy evolved over time to adjust for the ever-changing obstacles they encountered.

Pulitzer Prize–winning historian Leon Litwack (1998) also documents the risks and initiative blacks took to pursue education during the age of Jim Crow. He provides many accounts of violence directed toward blacks (such as harassments, beatings, schoolhouse burnings, and murders), as blacks carrying books elicited the same reaction as blacks bearing arms, and documents the many measures blacks took to pursue education (such as hiding books in market baskets, establishing clandestine schools, and relocating to communities that allowed blacks to receive an education). Several of the narratives Litwack provides describe how the desire for schooling was even stronger for blacks than whites. For example, a black preacher in 1865 observed that "the ignorant whites had every chance to learn, but didn't, we had every chance to remain ignorant, and many of us learned in spite of them" (Litwack 1988:53).

Litwack (1988) does mention that not all blacks shared a passion for learning. He notes that many blacks did not pursue an education because of the lack of employment options once schooling was completed, the inability of parents to dispense with the labor of their school-aged children, and parents' fear of their children being killed. However, he notes that this sentiment was not so much a rejection of education as an adaptation to social and economic realities. By the same token, Litwack (1988:54) further notes that many blacks understood the socioeconomic benefits of obtaining an education: "After emancipation, employers, landlords, and store keepers, among others, seized every opportunity to exploit black illiteracy for personal gain. The value of 'book-larnin' was at no time more dramatically impressed on blacks than at 'settling up' time and when it came to signing a labor contract . . . [reading, writing, numeracy] were deemed increasingly essential if blacks were to carve out for themselves a larger degree of independence in the workplace, if they were to cast off the remaining vestiges of slavery that made them economically dependent on whites." Furthermore, Litwack (1988) notes that within the black community, education was a mark of accomplishment, and those who rejected schooling later expressed deep regret.

Interestingly, during this era of government-legislated racial discrimination—the epitome of barriers to upward mobility—historical evidence suggests that blacks attributed more value to schooling than many whites. Anderson (1988) documents how officials from the Freedmen's Bureau were alarmed by lower-class whites' general apathy toward schooling. In 1869 Louisiana's superintendent wrote that unlike the ex-slaves, "the whites [took] little or no interest in educational matters, even for their own race" (Anderson 1988:26). The history of the Freedmen's Bureau is replete with comparisons of the attitudes toward schooling for ex-slaves and lower-class whites. In 1866, Alvord noted: "We make no invidious comparisons of the ignorant freedman, and the ignorant Anglo-Saxon of the South. We only say the former has most creditably won his present position; and he has done it by good conduct, and rapid improvement under that instruction we are now reporting" (quoted in Anderson 1988:26). Anderson does note that the Freedmen's Bureau's description of poor whites as indifferent toward education probably reflects the fact that it was difficult for poor whites to have a different conception of education and society because they were too closely tied to the planters' interests and ideology.

The historical record suggests that if a pervasive culture of resistance to education exists among black Americans, then this culture must have emerged after the era of Jim Crow. On the one hand, it seems counterintuitive to suggest that blacks would resist educational goals because of their belief in the limitations of education *after* rather than before the civil rights movement. No one would question that the effectiveness of education for blacks became greater after 1965. On the other hand, the persistence of racial disparities on numerous socioeconomic indicators after the civil rights movement could have led to the emergence of a cynicism toward schooling among blacks; if there is ever a time when education leads to convergence in the disparities along numerous socioeconomic indicators, surely it should be now. Regardless of when the hypothesized black culture of resistance to schooling emerged, the black cultural deficiency narrative remains a popular part of the mainstream discourse on the racial achievement gap.

Chapter Summary

Although substantial racial progress has been made within the United States, studies show that blacks continue to have some basis to be cynical about education as a mechanism for upward socioeconomic mobility. In the labor market, blacks receive lower wages, are less likely to receive a promotion, are more likely to experience job layoffs, experience longer periods of job search, and must have more prior job experience before receiving a promotion. These disadvantages exist even when blacks and whites have comparable levels of education, experience, cognitive skill levels, and are employed by similar types of firms. Blacks also experience fewer callbacks for job interviews simply based on having names commonly associated with blacks, and employers respond to blacks *without* a criminal record in the same manner as they do to whites *with* a criminal record. Many of these differences increase as blacks move up the socioeconomic ladder; racial inequality in promotion increases at higher levels of power and the racial wage gap widens as occupational status increases. In contrast to most white Americans, who believe that blacks face few racial barriers to upward mobility and attribute blacks' socioeconomic disadvantages to their own lack of motivation to succeed, the majority of blacks perceive barriers to upward mobility. Regardless of whether one accepts the empirical evidence for the existence of racial barriers within the United States, blacks' greater belief in these barriers contributes to the viability of the oppositional culture thesis.

The oppositional culture theory posits that the persistence of racial barriers and blacks' belief in these barriers compromise blacks' commitment to schooling. However, if blacks resist schooling, it is unclear precisely when they began regarding the idea of schooling as worthy of disdain. The position that blacks *always* possessed a cultural resistance to schooling is altogether indefensible, as the historical record denies this view. Virtually every account by historians or contemporary observers stresses that most blacks took unbelievably high risks to obtain literacy skills during slavery and emerged from slavery strongly believing in the importance of schooling. Nevertheless, the narrative of blacks' general cultural deficiency, which gained popularity in the 1960s with Lewis's (1961, 1968) writings about the "culture of poverty" and Moynihan's (1965) description of the "tangle of pathology" within the black community, has gained traction within education.

James Coleman (1966:73–74) writes that "the sources of inequality of educational opportunity appear to lie first in the home itself and the cultural influences immediately surrounding the home; then they lie in the school's ineffectiveness to free achievement from the impact of the home." Conversely, a doyen of the lost cause, historian Philip Bruce (1889), was so taken by the urgency with which black parents encouraged their children to attend school after the Civil War that he attempted to turn it into a marker of inferiority: "The Negro attaches an almost superstitious value to such instruction; he exults in the idea as if it were that of a fetish; it calls up a vague conception to his mind that is pregnant with manifold but ill-defined benefits" (1889:7–8). In the following chapters, I examine which of these statements—Coleman's or Bruce's—is more consistent with the evidence.

3

ORIGINS OF YOUTH PERCEPTIONS OF
OPPORTUNITY AND ACADEMIC INVESTMENT

According to the oppositional culture theory, blacks have developed a cultural norm of underachievement in response to inequitable educational opportunities and discriminatory social and employment policies within the United States. Black Americans have historically experienced barriers toward advancement not just in education, but in other realms such as the labor and housing markets. While these experiences were particularly acute prior to the civil rights movement, racial disparities continue to have an impact on numerous life outcomes, which I discussed in Chapter 2. Some scholars claim that because of these barriers, the larger black community has an antagonistic relationship toward education that stems from their negative perceptions about the opportunity structure (Fordham and Ogbu 1986; Ogbu 1978, 2003; Steinberg, Dornbusch, and Brown 1992).

Although it seems plausible that unequal experiences with the opportunity structure might lead black youth to disengage from the academic domain, this disengagement cannot stem from direct experiences within the opportunity structure. Adolescent youth have limited firsthand experiences in the labor market; they have not had the opportunity to exchange their educational credentials for compensation or rewards within the labor market. Thus, although children may develop perceptions about the opportunity structure for members of their group, these perceptions are based not on their own experiences, but on the experiences of other members of their group who have had sufficient exposure to the unfair opportunity structure.

Youths' perceptions of opportunity and the source of these perceptions are an entry point into the resistance model. I highlight this below in Figure 3.1. Path *a* represents the notion that experiences with the opportunity structure are determined by one's group status, which in turn affects how children perceive the opportunity structure—represented by path *b*—and academic outcomes—represented by path *c*. Therefore, a group's experience with the opportunity structure will indirectly determine the academic investment youth make based on their perceptions about opportunities available to members of their group. Whereas support for path *a*—that blacks experience various aspects of the opportunity structure differently from whites—is well documented, it is unclear the extent to which children base their perceptions of opportunities for upward mobility on the experiences of other members of their group. Thus, before turning my attention in the next chapter to youths' own perceptions about the opportunity structure, I first focus on paths *b* and *c*.

Although normative expectations of achievement can be transmitted through a number of social contexts, youths' perceptions about the opportunity structure are likely to stem from the messages they receive from older family members. Whereas peers can exert influence on achievement, they are likely to be equally inexperienced with the labor market. Similarly, the portrayal of discrimination and inequality on television and through other forms of media probably do not lead to the state of visceral anguish that might occur when one's own skills and academic credentials (or those for members of one's family and friends) have been undervalued in the labor market. Children are likely to learn about the opportunity structure by listening to their parents, aunts, uncles, and adult family friends describe their experiences in the labor market. However, since parents are a vital medium through which beliefs, values, and expectations regarding achievement are transferred to adolescents (Kao 1995), the unfair challenges faced by black parents are likely to have more deleterious consequences on black youths' academic orientation than the experiences of friends and other family

Figure 3.1:   Chapter in Focus: Experiences in Society and Youths' Academic Ethos

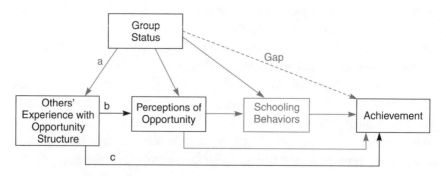

members. I begin, then, with a discussion of the intergenerational transmission of beliefs about the opportunity structure, considering the role of parents as socializing agents.

Parents, Race, and Messages about the Opportunity Structure

Given that blacks and whites differ in their experiences within the work force, it is reasonable to expect that the values and norms parents impart to their children—particularly around race—will differ by race. As major conduits for black children's knowledge about the opportunity structure, parental experiences with an opportunity structure that underrewards blacks' educational accomplishments relative to whites should compromise black children's motivation to achieve academically (Fordham and Ogbu 1986; Mickelson 1990; Ogbu 1978, 2003). According to Ogbu (1978) and Fordham and Ogbu (1986), parental experiences with discrimination limit children's confidence in the system of social mobility, thereby instilling negative attitudes towards future opportunities and diminished appreciation for education. As Mickelson (1990:59) notes, "Young blacks are not bewitched by the rhetoric of equal opportunity through education; they hear another side of the story at the dinner table."

Parents try to inculcate in their children the skills that they themselves need to function effectively in society (Kohn and Schooler 1983). Black parents' experiences in the labor market make this practice particularly salient in black households. The process of emphasizing strategies to cope with racial discrimination in mainstream society is known as racial socialization (Constantine and Blackmon 2002; Demo and Hughes 1990; Hughes and Johnson 2001; Lesane-Brown et al. 2005). Taylor et al. (1990:994) note that racial socialization is a salient aspect of socialization for black parents as they attempt to "prepare their children for the realities of being black in America." Specifically, black parents must educate their children about black culture and lifestyles while simultaneously teaching them how to negotiate interactions in the larger white society.

Racial socialization can consist of black parents either instilling a sense of racial or ethnic pride (Bowman and Howard 1985; Cross, Parham, and Helms 1991) or out-group mistrust—cautions and warnings about whites (Hughes and Chen 1997). Hughes and Chen (1997) find that parents' perceptions of racial bias in the workplace affects the frequency with which they speak to their children about discrimination and communicate messages regarding racial mistrust. Also, parents who experience discrimination are more likely than others to anticipate that their children will also experience discrimination and to provide their children with coping mechanisms (Coard et al. 2004; Hughes 2003; Hughes and Chen 1997). Black parents' cautions and warnings about whites are not isolated to their perceptions of institutional-level discrimination at work. Hughes (2003) finds that experiences of community-based discrimination predict whether black parents incorporate preparing their children for bias into their parenting repertoire. Similarly, Stevenson et al. (2002) find that adolescents who report having a family member who has experienced discrimination receive higher levels of cultural socialization than those whose family members do not report experiencing discrimination. The process of racial socialization leads black children to perceive themselves as members of a black community (Coard et al. 2004), which some posit yields an antagonistic view about education as a mechanism for upward mobility (Fordham 1996; Ogbu 1978).

Since racial socialization is the process of transmitting beliefs and attitudes regarding race and ethnicity from parents to children, black youth are often exposed to messages of group disadvantage. Ogbu (1978) argued that overemphasizing racial barriers and discrimination undermines children's sense of self-worth and promotes distrust and anger towards mainstream institutions. Conversely, numerous studies show that race socialization is beneficial for youths' racial identity and academic outcomes. For example, Bowman and Howard's (1985) seminal study showed that black children who are socialized to be aware of racial barriers generally attain significantly higher grades than those not given these messages. It appears that race socialization instills a positive racial identity, which studies consistently show is associated with better academic outcomes (Edwards and Polite 1992; Sanders 1997; Sellers, Chavous, and Cooke 1998; Wong, Eccles, and Sameroff 2003), and better prepare youth to deal with prejudice, stigmatization, and discrimination (Bowman and Howard 1985; McCreary, Slavin, and Berry 1996; Oyserman et al. 2003; Thomas and Speight 1999). In contrast to previous studies that have examined the importance of race socialization for academic outcomes, in this chapter I focus specifically on parents' beliefs about discrimination they have experienced and the discrimination that they anticipate for their children as determinants both of youths' academic achievement as well as of their perceptions regarding schooling as a mechanism for upward mobility. I also consider whether parents' beliefs about the importance of schooling is a determining factor in youths' perceptions about the importance of school.

In order to examine the intergenerational transmission of beliefs about opportunities for upward mobility, I analyzed survey data from the Maryland Adolescence Development In Context Study (MADICS). The MADICS contains a unique collection of measures on 1,407 black and white families (66 percent and 34 percent, respectively) from a county on the eastern seaboard of the United States. The MADICS provides a good opportunity to examine the intergenerational transmission of beliefs about opportunities for two reasons. First, in addition to containing data on children throughout adolescence (from middle school through high school), the MADICS also contains data collected from youths' parents. Second, the MADICS contains a wealth of survey items regarding perceptions about the opportunity structure, chances for upward socioeconomic mobility, and academic orientation from both parents and peers usually not found in national datasets.[1] Numerous datasets contain basic indicators of academic orientation unrelated to race (for example, educational aspirations), but the MADICS is particularly rich in indicators that measure racialized perceptions of barriers to upward mobility at various stages of adolescence.

I begin my assessment in Figure 3.2, which displays findings for black-white racial comparisons on survey questions intended to measure parental perceptions of racial barriers, including their subjective experiences with discrimination, and their beliefs concerning the potential barriers their children may experience due to race.[2] I display two pairs of estimates for each question—one that shows the average score for both groups and another that shows the averages once several background factors are taken into account. That is, the second pair represents the average scores for both groups if they had similar family income, parental education, and family structure (for instance, a single- or a two-parent household) and can be interpreted as the scores for blacks and whites similarly situated with regards to social class. The figure shows that black parents report experiencing more racial discrimination over the life course than white parents. Parents' expectation that their child will experience discrimination is also greater among blacks than whites. The second pair of estimates shows that these patterns are the same even if the comparison is made among blacks and whites with similar socioeconomic backgrounds.

The bottom panel of Figure 3.2 shows group comparisons on the odds of parents responding "yes" to the question of whether they think it has been harder for them to get ahead in life because of their race and whether they expect the same for their child. The bold line along the y-axis highlights 1.0, which is intended to provide a basis by which to compare the estimates for black parents to those of white parents. Thus, an estimate of 1.0 would indicate that blacks are just as likely as whites to affirm the question. The first pair of estimates shows that black parents are over three times more likely than their white counterparts to view their race as a liability for advancement in life. They are nearly twice as likely to believe race will make it

Figure 3.2:   Parents' Perceptions of Discrimination toward Self and Child (means)

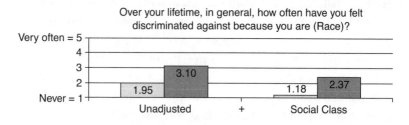

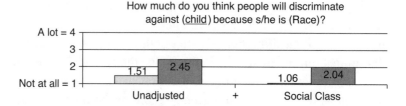

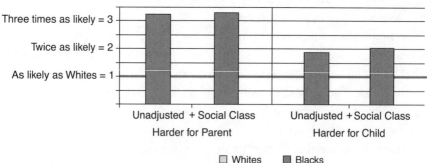

Note: Comparisons on the right-hand side account for family income, parental education, family structure, and youths' sex and can be interpreted as the scores for blacks and whites similarly situated with regard to social class. All racial differences are statistically significant (*p* < .01).

challenging for their children to advance in life. These patterns remain nearly identical when socioeconomic background is taken into account.

The finding in Figure 3.2 that black parents report experiencing more discrimination over their lifetimes than their white counterparts might be an underestimate of the actual racial difference of this phenomenon. There may be a wider racial gap in the experience of discriminatory treatment than the data indicate due to underreporting by blacks and overreporting by whites. Consistent with the current study, Coleman, Darity, and Sharpe (2008) found that black male and female workers are far more likely than whites to report experiencing racial discrimination at work, even when a host of human capital and labor market factors are controlled. However, when they compared reports of wage discrimination against independent measures of wage discrimination, they found black respondents significantly underreported their exposure and white respondents significantly overreported their exposure to discrimination. Their analysis produced statistical evidence of wage discrimination—racial wage gap net of human capital and labor market factors—for 87 percent of black workers (both male and female) who reported having experienced discrimination on the job in the Multi-City Survey of Urban Inequality (MCSUI). In contrast, their results displayed no statistical evidence of wage discrimination for the overwhelming majority of white females (97 percent) and males (89 percent) who reported having been exposed to racial discrimination. Their findings extend to reports of discrimination in raises and promotions, which led them to conclude that reports of job discrimination or discrimination in wages and promotions are generally coupled with a real wage penalty for blacks, but not for whites.

It is important to note that parents' experiences of discrimination and perceptions of barriers are not synonymous with their beliefs about the importance of education. It may seem logical that black parents would attribute less value to education as a mechanism for upward mobility than white parents. However, even the anticipation that their child will experience barriers within the labor market does not necessarily mean that parents will attribute little value to education. It also seems logical that black parents would promote a positive academic orientation in order to increase their children's chances of overcoming the barriers to upward mobility they themselves experienced. I show this in Figure 3.3, which displays black-white comparisons on indicators that gauge how important parents believe education is for their children. Despite reporting a greater belief in barriers, the educational aspirations black parents have for their children are not lower than those of their white counterparts. Figure 3.3 suggests that black parents actually hold higher educational aspirations for their children and believe more strongly than whites that success in school is essential for their child's success in life.[3]

The greater importance attributed to education for black parents despite their greater perceptions of discrimination might reflect an overcompensation effect. In anticipating greater obstacles for their children, black parents may offer more encouragement for school achievement than do white parents—the reverse of the oppositionality hypothesis. In fact, given compa-

Figure 3.3:   Parents' Perceptions of the Importance of Education (means)

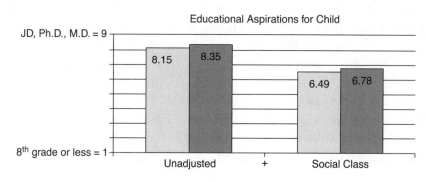

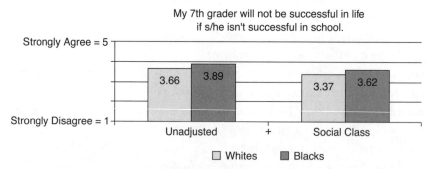

□ Whites   ■ Blacks

Note: Educational aspirations and expectations are coded as 1 = eighth grade or less, 2 = grades 9–11, 3 = high school graduate, 4 = post–high school vocational training, 5 = some college, 6 = graduate from a two-year college, 7 = four-year college graduate, 8 = master's degree, and 9 = J. D., M.D., or Ph.D. The comparisons on the right-hand side account for family income, parental education, family structure, and youths' sex. All racial differences are statistically significant ($p < .05$).

rable family backgrounds based upon ordinary measures of social class (without even taking into account wealth), blacks display higher levels of educational attainment than whites. Mason (1997) found that black students are 6 percent to 7 percent more likely than white students to graduate from high school if the comparison is made among students with similar socioeconomic backgrounds. Mason (2007) also shows that both black men and women obtain more years of education than their white counterparts when raised in similar family environments. Mason's work suggests that black students translate a given set of family status characteristics into more years of educational attainment than otherwise similarly situated white students, which is consistent with an overcompensation effect attributable to parental and family characteristics.

Since some readers might find the results in Figure 3.3 paradoxical, I provide additional evidence to determine whether these patterns are robust. Specifically, in Figure 3.4 I present findings for parents' educational aspirations and expectations using two additional datasets: the National Education Longitudinal Study of 1988 (NELS) and the Education Longitudinal Study of 2002 (ELS). The NELS is a nationally representative study of nearly twenty-five thousand U.S. students who were in the eighth grade during the first wave of data collection in 1988 and were followed through 2000.

Figure 3.4: Parents' Educational Aspirations and Expectations for Child

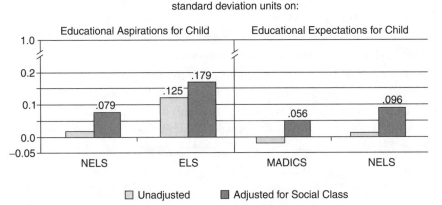

Ratio of black parents relative to white parents in standard deviation units on:

☐ Unadjusted   ■ Adjusted for Social Class

Note: Social class accounts for family income, parental education, family structure and youth's sex. Significant estimates are labeled above the bar ($p < .01$ for significant estimates based on the NELS and ELS, and $< .05$ for the significant estimate based on the MADICS).

The ELS follows a nationally representative cohort of students from the time they entered grade 10 in 2002 through the end of high school.[4] Because the comparison is being made across datasets, I report the standardized coefficient for black parents' educational aspirations and expectations relative to whites.[5]

The findings show that black parents hold higher educational aspirations for their children than their white counterparts in both datasets and suggest that the findings in Figure 3.3 should not be considered as an artifact of the MADICS data. While black parents may have high educational aspirations for their children, their greater anticipation of barriers for their children relative to white parents might lead them to *expect* that their child will attain less education than they would like. Therefore, rather than simply focusing on the amount of education parents *want* their children to attain, I also report parents' response to how much education they *believe* their children will attain on the right-hand side of Figure 3.4 using both the MADICS and the NELS. The standardized estimates for both datasets show that the level of education parents expect their children to attain is higher among black parents net of socioeconomic status (SES). The estimates in the MADICS are actually smaller than those based on national data. These findings suggest that despite believing their children will experience discrimination and that race serves as an encumbrance for their children, black parents still expect their children to attain more education than their white counterparts. Further evidence of this pattern can be found in a national poll commissioned by the National Center for Public Policy and Higher Education, which showed that black parents place higher value on obtaining an education as a means for advancement than whites (Public Agenda 2000).

The findings that black parents have higher educational aspirations for their children and attribute more importance to schooling than their white counterparts are consistent with both quantitative and qualitative studies. Cook and Ludwig's (1997) analysis of the NELS shows that on average, black parents are at least as involved in their children's educations as white parents. Their results show that relative to white parents, black parents are more likely to telephone their child's teacher (65 percent to 58 percent) and attend a school meeting (65 percent to 56 percent), and there are no racial differences in parents' attendance of school events (63 percent) or in helping their children with homework (54 percent). However, when Cook and Ludwig controlled for family socioeconomic status, the racial differences increased on all outcomes in favor of black parents. MacLeod's (2009) ethnographic study of low-income youth yields a similar pattern. He found that the "Hallway Hangers" (white youth) expressed limited belief in the openness of the opportunity structure due in part to the lack of upward mobility achieved by their parents, who were "hesitant to encourage hefty ambitions in their children." McLeod reports, "As the Hallway Hangers tell it, there is little stimulus from home to raise their aspirations" (2009:58). In contrast, the parents of the "Brothers" (black youth) expected them "to perform up to a certain standard at school, both in terms of academic achievement and discipline" (2009:59). MacLeod's narratives suggest that black parents project their frustrated and unfulfilled educational and occupational ambitions onto their children by cultivating in them high hopes for the future.

Do Parents' Beliefs about the Opportunity Structure Have Implications for Youths?

Parental responses considered in isolation are not enough to determine whether parents' experiences and beliefs are consequential. The question of whether black parents contribute to an antiacademic ethos is further complicated by findings that appear paradoxical and seemingly contravene expectations. What should be made of the findings displayed in Figures 3.3 and 3.4 suggesting that black parents are just as reverent toward education as (if not more than) white parents? Additionally, should black parents' negative experiences and perceptions about opportunities suggested by the findings displayed in Figure 3.2 be disregarded?

Prior to addressing these questions, it is important to note that despite the seemingly obvious connection between parents' experiences with discrimination, beliefs about barriers, and views about education, these concepts are conceptually and empirically distinct; experiencing discrimination does not necessarily mean that one will consider his/her race as an albatross or will view education as pointless. Therefore, in testing the notion that black parents are indeed an influential force in precipitating an antipathy toward school among black youth, one must consider which set of factors—discriminatory experiences, beliefs about barriers, or views about education—mediate this process.

I address the aforementioned questions by assessing whether parents' experiences and beliefs have implications for the value youth attribute to school, their educational aspirations and expectations, the barriers they anticipate in the future, and their academic achievement.[6] I present these findings in a series of minigraphs in Figure 3.5. I show the youth averages on various

Figure 3.5: Implications of Parents' Perceptions of Discrimination and Value of
School for Selected Youth Outcomes

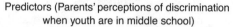

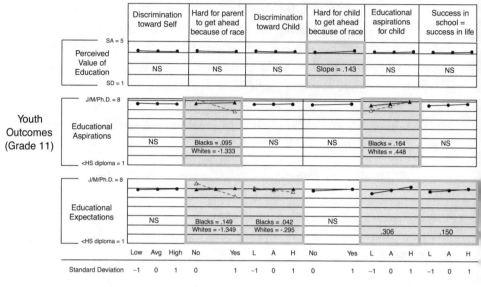

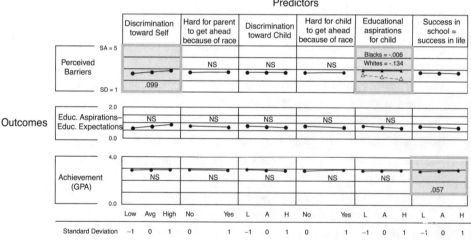

outcomes for parents who are low, average, and high on the measures for parents' perceptions of discrimination, beliefs about barriers, and views about education. Graphs that represent a statistically significant relationship are highlighted, and those that do not are labeled "NS" for "not significant."

The top panel shows that only one parental indicator is associated with the value youth attribute to education. Parental concern over the potential barriers to upward mobility their child will encounter due to race has a *positive* association with the value youth attribute to school. Thus, youth with parents who believe race will make it harder for them to succeed (labeled as "no/yes" along the bottom of the figure) attribute more value to school than those whose parents do not view race as an obstacle for their child.

The next two panels show that parents' perceptions of racial barriers are not significantly related to black children's educational aspiration or expectations. Instead, it is white youth for whom parental beliefs in barriers and expectations of discrimination for their child seem to have an adverse consequence. In general, parents with greater educational aspirations for their child have children with higher educational aspirations and expectations than parents with lower educational aspirations. Also, parents' beliefs about the value of schooling are positively associated with their children's educational expectations. Basically, in the three pairings (out of twelve) for which parents' negative experiences and beliefs have adverse consequences for children, the declines are observed only in the outcomes for whites.

Figure 3.5 also contains findings for the links between parents' experiences and beliefs regarding the opportunity structure and the barriers youth anticipate, as well as their academic achievement. The anticipation of bar-

Note: Several points of clarity are warranted with regard to Figure 3.5. First, each minigraph shows the slope or changes in the youth outcome—listed along the left side of the figure—associated with increases in the parental indicator listed across the top of the graphs. Each panel represents one equation; all slopes for each outcome were obtained from the same statistical regression model that includes race, sex, all parental beliefs listed across the top of the figure, and socioeconomic background (family income, parental education, and family structure). Second, in order to convey both youths' averages on the outcomes and how they are associated with the parental factors, I graph the slopes through the mean of the youth outcomes. Third, each minigraph displays the association as the average score for youths at two levels of the parental indicator: one standard deviation (or the average difference of each parent from the mean of all parents on the parental indicator) below and above the mean of the parental indicator, passing through the mean of the youth outcomes. Fourth, in cases where the slope differs by race, the slope is graphed separately for blacks and whites. Finally, whereas graphs that show no significant association are labeled "NS" for *not significant*, those that display a significant association at the .05 level of significance are highlighted (see the methodology presented in Appendix C for further details).

riers is high among youths whose parents experience more discrimination. I also estimate youths' perception of barriers by an indicator I call "perceived limited opportunities for upward social mobility"—the discrepancy between aspired and expected educational attainment. Greater discrepancy between the amount of schooling students *wish* to attain (that is, educational aspirations) and the amount of schooling they believe they will attain (educational expectations) reflects greater perceptions of limited opportunities. The findings show that none of the parental indicators is associated with this outcome.

Finally, the findings for academic performance suggest that only one parental indicator is associated with achievement. Achievement is higher for youth whose parents believe their child cannot be successful in life without being successful in school. Supplemental findings also show that increases in parents' educational aspirations for their child and belief that schooling is important for their child's success are associated with an increase in the odds of college enrollment for youth. More importantly, parental perceptions of racial discrimination and barriers—for themselves or their child—have little connection to youths' academic success.

Do Racial Differences Exist in How Children Are Socialized about the Opportunity Structure?

In the analysis above I focus on parents' experiences and beliefs about the opportunity structure. Although the findings provide some information on the intergenerational transmission of beliefs about the opportunity structure, parents' experiences and beliefs are not directly indicative of their socialization practices. It does not necessarily follow that parents will disclose instances of discrimination or transmit their beliefs about barriers to their children. Nevertheless, since children might learn about these experiences and beliefs by simply observing their parents, overhearing conversations, or through some other indirect means, it is important to examine the implications of these experiences for academic investment.

In order to provide a better assessment of how children are socialized around the opportunity structure, it is necessary to examine the direct messages they receive about schooling. I determine whether black and white children are socialized differently in Figure 3.6. Since youths' peers are important socializing agents (Davis-Kean and Eccles 2005), I show comparisons of messages about the value of schooling received from both parents and peers. In addition to parental messages about the value of schooling

Figure 3.6: Academic Socialization from Parents and Peers (means)

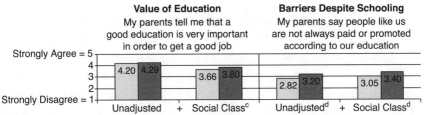

Parent Messages (MADICS)

Value of Education
My parents tell me that a
good education is very important
in order to get a good job

Barriers Despite Schooling
My parents say people like us
are not always paid or promoted
according to our education

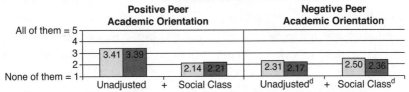

Peer Schooling Messages (MADICS)[a]

**Positive Peer
Academic Orientation**

**Negative Peer
Academic Orientation**

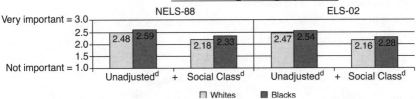

Peer Schooling Messages (National)[b]

NELS-88   ELS-02

☐ Whites   ■ Blacks

Note: The social class comparisons account for family income, parental education, family structure, and youths' sex.

[a] Positive Peer academic orientation is measured as youths' average response to the following questions: How many of the friends you spend most of your time with: 1) do well in school? 2) plan to go to college? 3) like to discuss schoolwork or other intellectual things with you? 4) think it is important to work hard on schoolwork? Negative peer orientation is measured as the average response to the following questions: 1) think working hard to get good grades is a waste of time? 2) cheat on school tests? 3) don't like having to come to school? 4) think being popular with friends is more important than getting As in school? 5) think it's okay not to do their homework if their friends want to do something else instead?

[b] Peer academic orientation is measured as the average of youths' assessment of the importance their friends place on the following: 1) regular class attendance, 2) getting good grades, 3) studying, 4) completing high school, and 5) continuing education beyond high school.

[c] Racial difference is significant at the .05 level.

[d] Racial difference is significant at the .01 level.

and the barriers present within the opportunity structure, I employ indicators of both the positive and negative messages youth attain about schooling from their peers.

The findings in the top panel suggest that black and white youth receive messages about the value of education to similar degrees. This contradicts the notion that black parents convey the importance of schooling to their children less than white parents. If the comparison is made after accounting for socioeconomic factors, black youth receive messages about the value of school slightly more than whites. However, findings on the right-hand side of the top panel suggest that black youth also receive more messages from their parents about barriers than their white counterparts both before and after accounting for social class. The findings in the second panel of Figure 3.6 are not consistent with the resistance model; there are no racial differences reported in positive peer academic orientation. Similarly, whereas the resistance model predicts that black children have lower achievement due in part to having fewer academically engaged peers than whites, the findings show that blacks have fewer peers with a negative academic orientation than whites.

It is important to assess the robustness of analyses based on the MADICS whenever possible. Earlier I showed that the finding of greater educational aspirations and expectations for black parents relative to their white counterparts in the MADICS is also present in the NELS and ELS, two national datasets. In the bottom panel of Figure 3.6 I replicate the analysis for peer academic orientation based on the MADICS using peer academic orientation from the NELS and ELS. Similar to the findings for group differences in parents' educational aspirations and expectations, analysis of peer orientation based on both the NELS and ELS yields patterns nearly identical to those observed in the MADICS displayed in the second panel of Figure 3.6. In fact, the MADICS understates the black advantage on positive peer orientation; the national data show slightly larger group differences than the MADICS.

I determine the extent to which children internalize these messages in Figure 3.7 using the same youth outcomes and analytic plan from Figure 3.5. The findings show that youth who receive more messages about the value of education from their parents attribute more value to schooling and have higher educational aspirations and expectation than those who receive fewer messages about the value of schooling. In contrast, parental messages about barriers are unrelated to these three outcomes. However, parental

Figure 3.7: Implications of Messages about Opportunities for Youths'
Perceptions of Opportunities

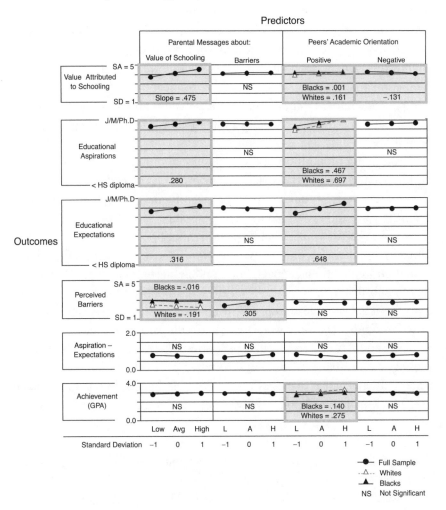

Note: All slopes for each outcome were obtained from the same statistical regression model that included race, sex, the parental and peer messages listed across the top of the figure, and socio-economic background (family income, parental education, and family structure). These graphs were constructed using the same strategy employed for Figure 3.5. Graphs that show no significant association are labeled "NS" for *not significant*. Those that display a significant association at the .05 level of significance are highlighted.

messages about barriers are positively related to youths' own perceptions of barriers. With regards to messages from peers, positive peer orientation is associated with significant increases in youths' educational aspirations and expectations and in academic achievement. Negative peer orientation is related to only one outcome: youth with more negative peers attribute slightly less value to schooling than those with fewer negative peers. In supplemental analysis, a reassessment of the implications of parents' aspiration and peer academic orientation for youths' beliefs about the importance of education using the NELS yields similar patterns to those observed in the MADICS.

Given that a proposition of the oppositional culture theory is that black children navigate a social space that compromises academic investment due to its overwhelming disparagement of education, the findings in Figure 3.7 are rather temperate. The resistance model predicts that messages about barriers and negative peer orientation should lead to large declines in four of the six outcomes (value attributed to schooling, educational aspirations, educational expectations, and achievement). Instead, it seems that the positive messages youth receive are important for more outcomes than the less favorable messages. Specifically, out of the six outcomes assessed in Figure 3.7, more were associated with parents' messages about the value of school (four) and positive peer orientation (four) than with parents' messages about barriers (one) and negative peer orientation (one). More importantly, negative messages from parents and peers do not appear to be consequential for academic achievement.

Chapter Summary

The findings I present in this chapter show that although black parents expect their children to experience racial discrimination, they also attribute more value to education than white parents. The findings from this chapter are not consistent with the claim that the larger black community has an antagonistic relationship toward education. Specifically, black parents believe education is essential for their children's future success, and they have higher educational aspirations for them than white parents have for their children. More relevant to the claims of the resistance model, the findings do not support the notion that black parents are catalysts for the cultural norm attributed to black adolescents that undervalues education and leads to educational disengagement. Figure 3.5 shows that parents' beliefs regarding discrimination and the challenges connected with race—for themselves or their children—were associated with youths' educational outcomes in a manner consistent with the resistance model in only four of the twenty-four minigraphs in which these relationships were assessed (twenty-eight minigraphs if I include the analysis for college enrollment). Furthermore, three of these associations were applicable only for whites and not blacks. Similarly, a systematic association between negative messages about school from parents and peers and the youth outcomes appears in only two of the twelve minigraphs that assess these links in Figure 3.7. Overall, negative beliefs (and messages) about the opportunity structure among youths' socializing agents were systematically related to youths' educational outcomes in a manner consistent with the resistance model in only 17 percent of the assessments made in this chapter (or 8 percent if the assessments were limited to blacks).

In contrast, parents' beliefs about the importance of education were associated with improvements in youth outcomes in five of the twelve minigraphs that display these connections in Figure 3.5. Positive messages from parents and peers were beneficial in eight of twelve pairings examined in Figure 3.7. Thus, the favorable beliefs and messages about education from key socializing agents showed a positive association with the educational outcomes in nearly 60 percent of the assessments made between these factors in this chapter. More surprising, black youth seem to have an advantage over whites with regard to favorable beliefs and messages about education they receive from parents and peers. This pattern is confirmed in all three datasets used in this chapter. I return to this finding, which may seem counterintuitive to supporters of the resistance model, in Chapter 5.

Although the finding that parental perceptions of discrimination and racial barriers do not compromise the academic measures I assessed above might come as a surprise to proponents of the resistance model, they are consistent with the research literature on racial socialization. Research on racial socialization suggests that in addition to instilling group pride and exposing their children to the culture, history, and heritage of their group, black parents attempt to make children aware of and prepare them for racial bias (Bowman and Howard 1985; Cross, Parham, and Helms 1991). The transmission of views regarding race and ethnicity by parents has been found to help children cope with racial discrimination and is predictive of positive youth outcomes (Bowman and Howard 1985). This suggests that while minority parents may make their children aware of the potential racial barriers facing them in the future, they also transmit messages of racial pride, which leads to higher self-efficacy and a sense of personal mastery that prevents minority children from disinvesting in school.

In sum, the findings show that black parents hold more negative perceptions about the opportunity structure yet attribute more value to education than their white counterparts. Whereas the former finding supports the resistance model, the latter finding runs counter to the framework. Additionally, parents' and peers' beliefs and messages regarding the importance of academic achievement have greater relevance for children's academic outcomes than their negative experiences or beliefs about the opportunity structure and schooling. The findings confirm that parents and peers are important influencing agents, though not in the manner predicted by the resistance model.

Based on the findings from this chapter, I provide an updated version of the resistance model in Figure 3.8. Findings did show support for the portion of the framework represented by path *a*; black parents differ from white parents in perceptions of discrimination, barriers, and value associated with education. However, only parents' views about the importance of education are consequential for youths' perceptions of opportunity (path *b*) and academic outcomes (path *c*). Since parents' experiences of discrimination and perceptions of barriers are not associated with declines in the youth outcomes I examined as predicted by the theory, there are no paths emanating from those indicators. Instead, it is the positive beliefs about the opportunity structure that seem to be consequential for youths' academic outcomes.

In Chapter 1, I noted that each component of this diagram is critical to the oppositional culture hypothesis. A pivotal point that I mentioned was

Figure 3.8:   Framework Revisited I

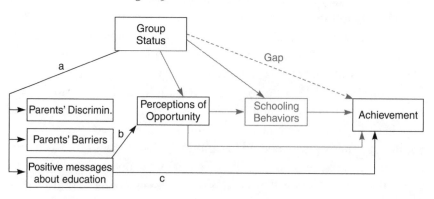

that if any of these causal links does not hold, then the oppositional culture theory is compromised. Thus, the findings from this chapter strike a major blow to the framework. Despite having a legitimate basis to be cynical about fairness within the opportunity structure (which I discussed in Chapter 2), and their greater belief in barriers, black parents do not transmit these beliefs to their children in a manner that compromises their beliefs about the importance of schooling. The parental beliefs about schooling that are related to youth perceptions about the importance of schooling and academic achievement are positive messages. This finding is not inconsistent with the oppositional culture theory, as positive messages about schooling should lead to an increase in youths' academic investment. However, negative messages about schooling should lead to a decline in youths' academic investment. It is the lack of an association between parents' and peers' negative beliefs and messages with the youth outcomes, coupled with greater positive beliefs and messages about schooling among blacks, that deals the major blow to the theory. That is, although we would expect that negative beliefs and messages from parents and peers should compromise investment, and that blacks' parents and peers should have less favorable beliefs and messages about schooling than whites, this is not the case.

Proponents of the oppositional culture theory can point out that these findings might not be enough to invalidate the resistance model. Finding that messages about barriers from parents do not compromise educational outcomes does not mean that negative beliefs about future opportunities are inconsequential. It could be that the beliefs of parents and peers examined in this chapter are too distal from youths' academic outcomes. Perhaps the focus should be placed on youths' own perceptions about opportunity rather than on how they are socialized vis-à-vis future opportunities. The analyses presented in this chapter do not speak to whether racial differences in perceptions about the opportunity structure exist among youth and whether their own beliefs about school as a mechanism for upward mobility are related to academic investment. I explore this portion of the framework in the next chapter.

4

EFFECTS OF YOUTH PERCEPTIONS OF
OPPORTUNITY ON ACADEMIC ACHIEVEMENT

In Chapter 3, I showed that parental perceptions of discrimination and racial barriers do not compromise blacks' academic orientation. However, this says nothing about youths' own perceptions regarding the opportunity structure. Youths' perceptions about upward mobility are an important component of Ogbu's framework. Although this aspect of the framework has been examined by others (Ainsworth-Darnell and Downey 1998; Mickelson 1990; O'Connor 1999), there is a dearth of quantitative research on whether blacks' perceptions of barriers in particular are consequential for their academic investment. I argue that previous studies have not adequately assessed youths' beliefs about the opportunity structure (schooling as a mechanism for upward socioeconomic mobility) because researchers have conflated youths' perceptions of the returns on education with their belief in barriers to upward mobility, which has resulted in an incomplete understanding of the implication that perceptions about the system of social mobility have for schooling behaviors.

Investigating youths' views about opportunity is important because the resistance model posits that belief in the achievement ideology (that is, that education leads to status attainment) is the primary predictor of academic investment. Indeed, it is those who believe in the connection between education and socioeconomic mobility the most who decide to pursue schooling beyond the compulsory level. In this chapter, I extend the resistance model literature by outlining a conceptual distinction between different beliefs about the opportunity structure—benefits of education versus barriers to upward mobility—and assessing the potential implications of these beliefs for academic outcomes.

I provide a visual illustration of this portion of the framework in Figure 4.1 (the diagram is based on the original version of the theory introduced in Chapter 1). Specifically, path d denotes that black and white youth have different perceptions about the opportunity structure. In Chapter 3, I showed that black and white parents differ in their perceptions about the opportunity structure and noted that parents are a major conduit through which youth develop these perceptions. In this chapter, I examine whether differences in these perceptions exist among black and white youth and whether these perceptions are important for both academic investment (as indicated by schooling behaviors and denoted by path *e*) and academic outcomes (denoted by path *f*). Below I provide a summary of the research literature corresponding to path *d*, followed by a similar discussion for paths *e* and *f*.

Perceptions of the Opportunity Structure, Race, and Schooling

Given that black youth have lower academic achievement than their white counterparts, and that academic investment should be partially driven by the belief that schooling facilitates upward mobility, it seems reasonable to expect that black youth are doubtful about the value of schooling. If so, then black underachievement can be attributed to blacks' perceptions of barriers to advancement and their belief that schooling will not enable them to overcome such barriers. However, the issue of whether blacks view education as a means for upward socioeconomic mobility is not straightforward.

Studies that document blacks' pessimistic views about "getting ahead" in the United States suggest that blacks who are most inclined to perceive barriers to advancement are those who have invested the most in schooling. Specifically, Cose (1993) and Feagin and Sikes (1994) document a high belief in barriers among blacks who have already attained success in both schooling and the labor market. Similarly, Hochschild (1995) notes that

Figure 4.1:   Chapter in Focus: Youths' Perceptions of Opportunity and Academic Investment

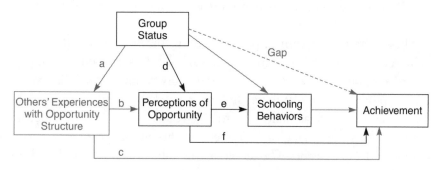

relative to whites and disadvantaged blacks, affluent blacks perceive more racial discrimination and greater barriers to success. Moreover, she shows that, paradoxically, the belief in education and hard work as mechanisms for upward mobility is most strongly held by poor blacks. She notes that poorly educated blacks, more than any other racial/class group, express a great deal of confidence in schools despite their skepticism of other American institutions. Thus, contrary to Ogbu's suggestion, these scholars note blacks generally believe in the achievement ideology but begin to question this belief once their investment in education has already occurred.

The research literature is mixed on the link between beliefs about the opportunity structure and schooling investment. Survey-based inquiries support the notion that students who believe in the achievement ideology experience academic successes, while those who challenge this belief do not (Ford and Harris 1996; Mickelson 1990). However, other studies show blacks are capable of maintaining high academic orientation despite beliefs in structural barriers within the opportunity structure for members of their group (Akom 2003; MacLeod 2009; O'Connor 1999; Tyson, Darity, and Castellino 2005). Thus, some studies find that black youth do attribute value to education while other studies show that blacks disinvest from schooling because they do not consider education as an effective mechanism for overcoming barriers to upward mobility. Furthermore, the finding that black youth have more positive beliefs about schooling than whites despite their lower achievement is quite common. Further research is needed to gain a better understanding of both racial differences in beliefs about the importance of education and the link between these beliefs and academic investment. Can students believe in barriers yet maintain an achievement ideology? What should be made of studies that show blacks express greater belief in educational returns than whites despite their lower academic achievement (Ainsworth-Darnell and Downey 1998; Cook and Ludwig 1997)? Which set of beliefs matters more for achievement: perceived educational returns or belief in barriers?

These questions remain in part because within the research literature, achievement ideology combines aspects of both beliefs about the importance of schooling and the existence of barriers to upward mobility. Since Ogbu's model is a popular theory linking societal conditions to individuals' schooling behaviors via beliefs, he may have inadvertently contributed to the lack of research that clearly delineates between these concepts. He often merged the concepts of beliefs about the value of school with beliefs in barriers despite schooling into his analysis of perceived returns to education. For instance, Ogbu (1991:53) writes that "[blacks] have come to view the inadequate and unequal reward of education as a part of the institutionalized discrimination structure which getting an education cannot eliminate." Describing blacks' beliefs about the extent to which they will be rewarded (value of school) as part of the barriers schooling cannot overcome leaves no clear distinction between these two concepts. Instead, they appear substantively equivalent; perceptions of low rewards must be accompanied by perceptions of high barriers.

The failure of previous studies to clearly account for the diverse nature of people's beliefs is a critical deficit in the endeavor to understand how perceptions of the prevailing system of social mobility influence students' schooling behavior. It is also important for social scientists to consider beliefs and affective attitudes as conceptually and empirically distinct. Strategies for academic improvement might differ if beliefs are more important for achievement (for example, placing greater emphasis on the value of education) than if attitudes are more important (for example, incorporating material that students find more interesting into lesson plans).

Rosyln Mickelson's (1990) study was among the first and most influential studies to address this lack of conceptual clarity, which she attributed to be the root of the attitude-achievement paradox—blacks strong belief in the value to education while simultaneously having low academic achievement. She argued that researchers often do not distinguish between theoretical (that is, abstract) and practical (that is, concrete) attitudes about schooling. Abstract attitudes reflect dominant ideology regarding the ideal role of education. These are the attitudes that correspond to the clichés that people give when someone asks about their views on education. Examples include "education is good" and "school is cool," and other generic slogans used to promote the idea that education is important among children. These are the responses that most young people know should be given when asked about the value of education.

On the other hand, concrete attitudes are rooted in life experiences. Mickelson (1990:58) writes that "concrete attitudes shed needed light on the process by which the structure of opportunity (in terms of race and class) shapes academic achievement and thereby help explain why so many black students do not do well in school." It is these attitudes that I assessed among parents in Chapter 3. Mickelson focused her attention on adolescents. Using data from high school seniors in the Los Angeles area, she found that 1) abstract attitudes have no effect on grades, 2) concrete attitudes have a positive effect, and 3) blacks hold less positive concrete attitudes towards education than whites, which she attributes to the material realities they experience that "challenge the rhetoric of the American Dream" (1990:59).

While Mickelson's research is important in identifying *which* attitudes are consequential for achievement, several questions remain regarding the role of youths' beliefs about the opportunity structure for schooling. Previous research shows that blacks value school more than whites (Ainsworth-Darnell and Downey 1998; Cook and Ludwig 1997; Harris 2006), even if the analysis is limited to low-income youth (MacLeod 2009). Blacks also attain higher levels of education than whites with comparable family socioeconomic backgrounds, even without accounting for wealth (Mason 1997, 2007). This phenomenon could be related to the greater value attributed to education by black parents, which I discussed in Chapter 3. Black parents are more likely than whites to call their child's teacher, attend school meetings and events, and help their children with homework net of socioeconomic factors (Cook and Ludwig 1997). Similarly, poor black parents are more likely than their Latino/a, Asian, and white counterparts to discuss their children's school experiences and plans, restrict television on school nights, set rules about grades, and help with homework (U.S. Department of Education 1992). Despite the material realities blacks encounter, blacks seem to attribute value to schooling, and according to the accounts provided by historians, this appears to have always been the case (Anderson 1988; Litwack 1998; Williams 2005).

According to the resistance model, as well as Mickelson's (1990) findings, belief in barriers should lead to academic disinvestment, which explains why blacks have lower achievement than whites despite any reverence toward education they might espouse. Based on the discussion in Chapter 2 and the findings from Chapter 3, we also know that a substantial proportion of blacks believe that blacks encounter racial barriers. If concrete attitudes are rooted in material realities, and blacks hold less positive concrete attitudes than whites because they encounter barriers, then blacks should invest in schooling less than whites net of socioeconomic factors, not more. Do beliefs in barriers really compromise achievement?

I addressed this issue in a study published in the *Social Science Quarterly* (Harris 2008). I suggested that important questions remain because scholars have conflated two separate beliefs about upward mobility: *value of school-*

ing and *perceived barriers despite schooling.* The former concept refers to beliefs about the potential for schooling to improve one's life chances. This is similar to perceived returns to education, which is often the focus of studies on the achievement ideology. The latter belief—perceived barriers—refers to belief in the existence of barriers to upward mobility despite one's level of education. Neither concept is intended to capture the extent to which students like school (affective attitudes), a factor that occupies less importance than beliefs about the opportunity structure within the resistance model.

Value of schooling and *perceived barriers despite schooling* are not synonymous with the abstract and concrete attitudes assessed by Mickelson (1990, 2001). The former measures are intended to capture students' beliefs about school with regards to *their* future experiences with the opportunity structure. Mickelson's measure of abstract attitudes assesses students' more general outlook on education, whereas the scale I use tracks the value students believe they themselves will receive from education. For example, Mickelson's abstract attitudes scale includes items that ask youth whether education can end poverty, enable poor people to become middle class, and create a path to a better life. Rather than partially relying on youths' estimates about what school can do for society in general, the value of schooling scale that I employ is comprised of items that ask youth about whether education is beneficial for them or children like them (for example, "I have to do well in school if I want to be a success in life," or "getting a good education is the best way to get ahead in life for the kids in my neighborhood").

Mickelson's concrete attitudes were intended to partially capture the intergenerational transmission of oppositional culture—or how students are socialized with regard to the future payoff of school. Of the six items included in the concrete attitudes scale, three asked students about the barriers members of their family have experienced, and two other items asked youth whether their friends do homework and whether reading, writing, and making change is all they need to learn for their future. I measure belief in barriers as whether youths anticipate fair treatment based on their educational attainment. Therefore, although measures in this chapter are similar to those employed by Mickelson (1990, 2001), they are used differently to reflect the aforementioned distinctions between beliefs. I capture the socialization of these beliefs separately using the same measures from the previous chapter (that is, messages from parents and peers). I argue that the value/barriers beliefs distinction is an improvement on the abstract/concrete attitudes distinction because the former is more aligned with how people conceptualize the importance of schooling and barriers to upward mobility.

Do Black and White Adolescents Differ in Their Perceptions of Opportunity?

Below I present the findings from my research on this issue. Once again, I employ data from the Maryland Adolescence Development In Context Study (MADICS). In addition to its richness, the longitudinal design of the MADICS provides a good opportunity to make clear delineations between beliefs and affective attitudes and to examine their connection to academic outcomes net of prior academic success. Additionally, the MADICS contains questions similar to those used by Mickelson (1990, 2001), which allows for the use of measures on perceptions about the system of mobility rooted in previous research.

Figure 4.2 contains racial comparisons for adolescents in middle school on the value they attribute to schooling and the barriers they believe that they will encounter despite the level of schooling they attain, using the same indicators from Chapter 3. The findings suggest that black students attribute more value to schooling and perceive more barriers than whites. It appears that blacks make nuanced distinctions about education as a means for upward mobility and for attaining racial equality. In Chapter 2, I highlighted the empirical evidence that shows blacks have a legitimate basis for perceiving an unfair opportunity structure. However, they also have a legitimate basis for believing in the value of schooling; for example, recall that Figure 2.1—which graphs the relationship between educational attainment and income using census data—shows blacks receive an increase in earnings for each additional level of education they complete.

The key component for making sense of this seeming contradiction in beliefs—blacks' greater belief in both the value of school and the barriers school cannot help them overcome—is the reference group. Within the context of Mickelson's development of the notion of abstract and concrete attitudes, it is unclear who the relevant comparison group is. Racial discrimination as an obstacle skews blacks' returns to schooling downward relative to whites, but any individual black person generally will do better economically than his or her fellow counterpart with less schooling. So comparisons across racial groups rather than within racial groups may dis-

Figure 4.2: Perceptions of School as a Mechanism for Upward Mobility

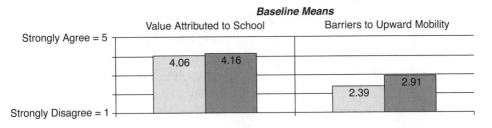

Baseline Means

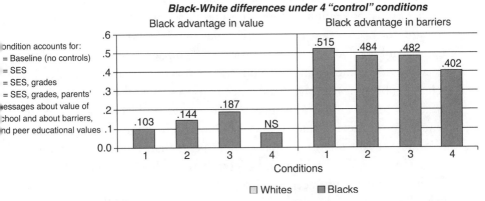

Black-White differences under 4 "control" conditions

Note: The SES (socioeconomic status) condition shows the black-white difference after accounting for family income, parental education, and family structure. Sex is also included as a control for conditions 2–4. The difference in baseline estimates between the top and bottom panel reflects rounding. NS denotes that the difference is not significant at the .05 level. All differences not labeled "NS" are statistically significant at the .01 level with the exception of the baseline difference for value attributed to school, which is significant at the .05 level of significance. See Appendix C for the analytic plan and Appendix D for a description of measures used in this analysis.

courage blacks from believing in schooling as a mechanism for overcoming barriers (although this might not necessarily be the case, as there could be an overcompensation effect as discussed in Chapter 3), but within-group comparisons should serve as encouragement. Mickelson never considers the relevance of the within-group comparison in the construction of a rational calculation of opportunity among blacks.

In the bottom panel of Figure 4.2, I display four estimates for each indicator. Changes in the estimates across the bars can be attributed to the factors taken into account, which are labeled next to the graph. The first bar simply shows the average baseline difference between black and white youth observed on the measures in the top panel, which was obtained by subtracting the average score for whites from those of blacks. The second estimate for each indicator shows that black students attribute more value to schooling and perceive more barriers than whites, even when comparisons are made between blacks and whites with similar socioeconomic backgrounds. The estimates remain similar after also accounting for youths' prior academic achievement (displayed in the third bar for each measure).

Finally, the fourth bar shows the estimated racial differences after accounting for how youth are socialized in relation to the opportunity structure using the same measures displayed in Figure 3.7. Numerous scholars note that messages about education provided by family and friends are critical to youths' perceptions about the value they attribute to education for upward socioeconomic mobility (Fordham and Ogbu 1986; Mickelson 1990; Steinberg, Dornbusch, and Brown 1992), a pattern that I examined in Chapter 3. The racial difference on perceptions of the value attributed to schooling becomes nonsignificant once messages about the value of school are taken into account. This suggests that the reason black youth have an advantage on this indicator is because they receive more messages about the value of education from parents and peers than their white counterparts. However, the final bar for belief in barriers shows that even after all factors are taken into account, black youth still perceive more barriers toward upward mobility than whites. Thus, there are factors that contribute to blacks' advantage on this indicator beyond their socioeconomic backgrounds, academic achievement, and the messages they receive from their parents and peers.

Do Youths' Perceptions of Opportunity Have Implications for Their Academic Outcomes?

Youths' perceptions of opportunity matter only to the extent that they are consequential for academic outcomes. In the top panel of Figure 4.3, I show the estimated increase in GPA during grade 11 associated with one-point increases in students' responses on the indicators measuring the value they attribute to school, their perceptions of barriers, and their affective attitudes toward school. Findings suggest that students' achievement is positively influenced by their beliefs about the value of school and their affect toward schooling and *not* by beliefs about future barriers they might encounter. Specifically, the average increase in GPA associated with a one-unit increase on the 5-point scale along which youths' belief about the value of school is measured is .16 for both whites and blacks. Although this "effect" may seem modest, the average difference between a student who scores a 1 on the scale measuring value of schooling and a student who scores a 5 is slightly over two-thirds of a point in GPA. This is equivalent to the difference between having a GPA of 2.4 versus slightly over 3.0. When GPA is assessed against students' affective attitudes toward school, the gain in GPA is larger for white youth; for blacks, affective attitudes are only slightly less related to achievement than their belief about the value of schooling. However, the perception of barriers is not systematically related to achievement for either group. The difference in GPA between students at the opposite extremes of the scale for perceived barriers is 0.14 for whites and 0.05 for blacks.

Figure 4.3: Implication of Beliefs and Attitudes for Grades and College Enrollment

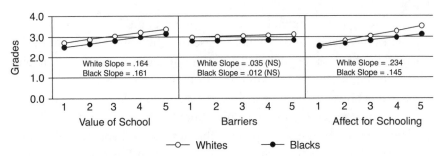

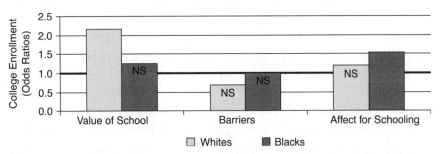

Note: The slopes for each group were obtained from statistical regression models that account for socioeconomic background (that is, family income, parental education, and family structure), sex, prior grades, peer values toward school, and parents' messages about both the value of school and barriers despite schooling. For the purpose of graphing, the slope for each group was subtracted from (and added to) the group-specific mean GPA twice. The odds were obtained from logistic regression models that account for the same aforementioned factors. NS denotes that the slope is not significant. All slopes for value of school and affect for schooling in the top panel are significant at the .01 level. In the bottom panel, value of school for whites is significant at the .01 level and affect for schooling for blacks is significant at the .05 level. See Appendix C for the analytic plan and Appendix D for a description of measures used in this analysis.

The bottom panel of Figure 4.3 contains estimates for how students' beliefs and attitudes predict the odds of college enrollment. Only the belief about the value of school is associated with college enrollment for whites; for these students, the average increase in the odds of college enrollment associated with an increase of one unit on the scale measuring the value attributed to school is over 100 percent. Thus, on average, a white student who scores a 5 on the scale measuring value of schooling is over four times more likely to enroll in college than a student who scores a 1 on the scale. For blacks, neither set of beliefs are associated with their odds of enrolling in college. However, blacks at each successive level along the scale for affect toward schooling are on average 50 percent more likely to enroll in college than those at each previous level along the scale. More importantly, belief in barriers appears inconsequential for the odds of college enrollment for both groups.

The finding that parental beliefs in barriers are unrelated to many youth outcomes in Chapter 3 makes more sense in light of the findings from this chapter; youths' own belief in barriers is not related to their academic outcomes. It might seem counterintuitive to some readers that a belief in barriers, or that one will experience obstacles to success in a particular domain, does not necessarily compromise investment within that domain. These findings show that groups who perceive barriers can still believe in the value of schooling. Perhaps the indicators for barriers that I have examined thus far are not capturing perceptions of barriers proximal enough to what students might consider as a target for them to be discriminated against. The notion that students will invest in education with the belief that the benefits to them will be less than advertised requires further investigation, using less general measures of barriers to upward mobility.

A Closer Look at Perceived Barriers through Gender and Race
As I discussed in Chapter 2, some people debate whether racial discrimination still exists within the United States. Let us assume for a moment that many black youths believe that while some barriers do exist, their effects are minimal compared to what they once were, and thus these black youths do not allow these beliefs to impact their academic investment. This might account for the findings that I have presented relative to this point. However, few people will debate the reality that women continue to experience gender discrimination. Therefore, as a group that continues to experience barriers to upward mobility, we would expect females to be disillusioned about

the future and doubt the value of schooling. Given women's lower educational returns (Joy 2003), it seems plausible that girls would lower their educational and occupational expectations to be more consistent with the realities they encounter. Thus, further discussion of gender differences within the opportunity structure and females' responses to these differences could shed more insight into the link between barriers and academic investment.

Several scholars emphasize the importance of considering the intersection of gender and race in sociological research on systems of stratification (for a review, see Browne and Misra 2003 and Chafetz 1997). Browne and Misra (2003:488) write, "Race is 'gendered' and gender is 'racialized,' so that race and gender fuse to create unique experiences and opportunities for all groups." For example, a focus exclusively on women's disadvantage in economic relations without taking race into account misses the complex interconnections between some groups. In many cities, white women earn more than black men (McCall 2000). Also, since black women represent two social subordinate groups, they are vulnerable to a "race" penalty in addition to the "gender" penalty experienced by white women. O'Connor's (1999) study provides another example of this intersection. She finds that black boys perceive that a stigma is attached to them for ostensibly having a greater potential for violence and incarceration, which affects their educational experiences in ways distinct from that of the "white kid" or "black girl." Thus, research on perceptions about future opportunities should consider both race and gender.

The inequality experienced by women in the labor market is persistent and pervasive. For example, following rapid declines in the gender earnings gap during the 1980s, convergence in the gap has stalled since 1990. Today, women earn about seventy-seven cents for every dollar earned by men (Cotter, Hermsen, and Vanneman 2004). College major accounts for only about one-tenth of the gender wage gap (Joy 2003; Marini and Fan 1997). Even within similar fields of study, women earn less than men (see top panel of Figure 4.4). Joy (2003) finds that if women enter the job force with similar educational credentials and labor market preferences as men, the labor market would still value them less. She estimated that if women received similar returns to their qualifications as men, their salaries would be 25 percent higher.

Despite their unfavorable experiences within the opportunity structure, compared to males, females hold an advantage in grade point average in high school (Marini and Fan 1997) and college (Buchmann and DiPrete 2006). Girls also repeat grade levels less, have higher graduation rates

(Jacobs 1996), and outpace boys in the number of college preparatory courses and advanced placement examinations they take in high school (Bae et al. 2000). Furthermore, trend statistics reveal that over the past half century women have made significant gains in educational attainment relative to men; whereas 65 percent of all bachelor's degrees in 1960 were awarded to men, by 2004, 58 percent of all bachelor's degrees were awarded to women (Buchmann and DiPrete 2006). The greater increases in four-year degrees for women relative to men are occurring across a wide range of majors (see bottom panel of Figure 4.4).

Figure 4.4:   Earnings and Educational Attainment by Gender

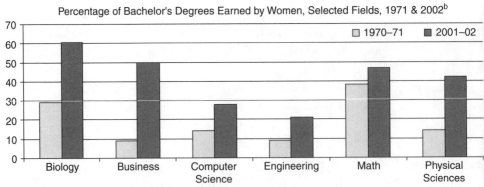

[a] Source: Peter and Horn 2005, U.S. Department of Education, Institute of Education Sciences (IES), NCES 2005–169.

[b] Source: Livingston and Wirt 2004, U.S. Department of Education, IES, NCES 2004–076. Percentages are based on data from all degree-granting institutions.

This seemingly paradoxical pattern—girls' greater investment in school despite women's lower educational returns—has been referred to as "the anomaly of women's achievement" (Mickelson 1989). The female achievement advantage despite the persistent sex inequality in wages within the labor market seems to violate the resistance model's premise that persistent experiences or perceptions of barriers to success with regard to future employment and earnings compromise academic investment. This pattern suggests that even in the case of gender, it seems that the clear existence of barriers does not subvert educational achievements.

It is important to note that the resistance model is intended for understanding racial differences in school achievement. However, this portion of the resistance model can (and should) be explored along the dimensions of gender and race for two reasons. First, the resistance model is perhaps the preeminent framework that links the prevailing system of social mobility with students' schooling behaviors. The framework posits that those facing an unfair system of social mobility will disinvest from schooling. Therefore, the case of gender falls within the parameter of these assumptions and provides another opportunity to investigate the link between perceptions of barriers and academic investment in general. Second, it is possible that perceptions of barriers are more consequential for academic outcomes if barriers are considered along the dimensions of both gender and race, or more specifically, race by gender. The previous findings based solely on race—with sex as a control—could be masking the impact of barriers; the scores for each racial group averaged the responses of males and females.

Beliefs in Barriers Based on Gender and Race

The richness of the MADICS allows me to examine perceptions of barriers by race and gender. In Figure 4.5, I show the percent of eighth graders who anticipate barriers in the labor force and in education because of their gender and race for four groups: white males, white females, black males, and black females. The findings show that a much greater proportion of girls believe they will experience discrimination based on gender in the labor force than boys. Sixty percent of black females and nearly half of white females believe this to be the case. Interestingly, one-third of black males and less than one-tenth of white males anticipate gender barriers in the labor force.

The patterns for the next three indicators of perceived barriers are the same. A greater proportion of both black females and black males expect

Figure 4.5:   Percent of Youth that Expect Discrimination Based on Sex and Race

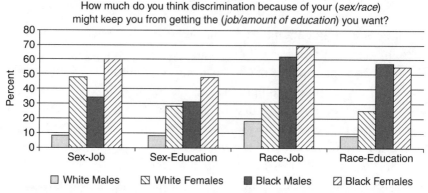

How much do you think discrimination because of your (*sex/race*) might keep you from getting the (*job/amount of education*) you want?

☐ White Males   ◩ White Females   ■ Black Males   ▨ Black Females

Note: Percentages displayed are unadjusted. All differences are statistically significant at the .05 level for "sex-job" and "race-job." For "sex-education," all groups differ from white males and black females at the .05 level (the difference between white females and black males is not significant). For "race-education," with the exception of black males and females, who are statistically similar, all groups differ from one another at the .05 level.

gender discrimination to affect their education and anticipate their race to be a barrier in both the labor force and in education. For the indicators of discrimination based on race, a much larger proportion of blacks, both male and female, expect to face barriers. Over a quarter of white females anticipate discrimination described by the last three indicators. Finally, less than one-tenth of white males anticipate discrimination as described by all but one indicator: race discrimination in the labor force, though they still perceive this less than the other groups. This finding suggests that white boys feel more "protected" or have a greater sense of privilege that comes from being both male and white than do members of the other groups.

In Figure 4.6, I display findings for the extent to which these groups believe that both their sex and race will make it harder for them to get ahead in life. The findings suggest that girls view their gender as a barrier more than boys; the mean scores on this indicator by gender are nearly identical across race. The findings for racial barriers fall along racial lines; blacks anticipate more racial barriers in "getting ahead" than whites, regardless of gender. I now turn to whether perceptions of barriers due to race and gender are related to youths' academic investment.

Figure 4.6: Youths' Perceptions of Barriers Based on Sex and Race (means)

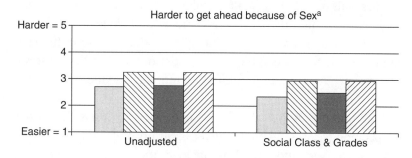

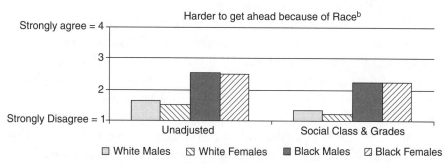

☐ White Males ☒ White Females ■ Black Males ▨ Black Females

Note: The social class and grades condition shows the group averages after accounting for family income, parental education, family structure, and grades in school. Statistical differences ($p < .05$) in the top panel fall along gender lines; there is no difference between white males and black males and no difference between white females and black females, but both groups of males differ from both groups of females. This pattern exists with regards to race in the bottom panel.

[a] Do you think it will be harder or easier for you to get ahead in life because you are a (boy/girl)?

[b] Average response to the following two questions: (a) Because of your race, no matter how hard you work, you will always have to work harder than others to prove yourself; (b) because of your race, it is important that you do better than other kids at school.

Implications of Beliefs in Barriers Based on Gender and Race

I provide an even richer examination of the implications of beliefs in barriers for academic investment in Table 4.1. I show the results for analyses that assess whether the beliefs charted in Figures 4.5 and 4.6 are related to three sets of educational outcomes: psychological investment, behavioral investment, and academic outcomes (or grades). Psychological investment is measured by students' educational aspirations, educational expectations, and their belief that effort in school leads to job success. Behavioral investment is measured by the frequency with which students seek help to improve academically, and the amount of time they spend on school activities/

clubs (for example, student government), homework, and educational activities outside school. Finally, analyses are conducted for two academic
outcomes: achievement (that is, grades) and college enrollment. One
should expect that youth who anticipate discrimination in the labor force
and in education because of their gender or race should put less stock in
education as a mechanism for upward mobility and therefore fare worse on
these indicators.

The findings show that only five of fifty-four pairings have a systematic
association (see highlighted estimates). Surprisingly, only two show a negative association; students who anticipate more gender discrimination in
education have lower educational aspirations than those who expect less
gender discrimination, and those scoring at the top of the scale for the indicator of race as a barrier for getting ahead have a GPA about a third of a
point lower than those at the bottom of the scale (-.084 x 3). However, youth
who view their gender as an obstacle in the labor force have higher school
achievement than those who do not. Also, students who anticipate more
racial discrimination in education spend more time on educational activities and have nearly twice the odds of enrolling in college as those who do
not see race as an obstacle. Supplemental analysis shows these associations
do not differ across groups.

It is important to note that girls and black youth are not entirely pessimistic about education as a mechanism for upward mobility. I show this in
Figure 4.7 using both the MADICS (grade 11) and the Education
Longitudinal Study of 2002 (ELS) (grade 10). The first set of bars in the top
panel based on the MADICS illustrate that a greater proportion of girls
believe that doing well in school is important for success in the labor market than boys. A comparable indicator from the ELS suggests that a greater
proportion of black youth believe education in general is important for future job attainment. Similarly, more girls attribute importance to good
grades than boys. Interestingly, white males score the lowest proportion on
all indicators while black females score toward the highest. The findings in
the bottom panel of Figure 4.7 show the differences across the groups relative to white males on their views of education as necessary for future success and stability and on their grades. The findings suggest that girls regard
education as more important to their future than boys. They also have better grades than their male counterparts after accounting for social class.

Table 4.1: The Implication of Perceptions of Discrimination for Academic Investment Predictors *(Mid. School)*

Outcomes (HS)	Sex as Barrier for:		Race as Barrier for:		Harder to Advance:	
	Job	Educa.	Job	Educa.	Sex	Race
Psychological Investment						
Educational Aspirations	NS	−.420	NS	NS	NS	NS
Educational Expectations	NS	NS	NS	NS	NS	NS
Effort in school = Job success	NS	NS	NS	NS	NS	NS
Behavioral Investment						
Seek help for trouble in school	NS	NS	NS	NS	NS	NS
Time on school activities/clubs	NS	NS	NS	NS	NS	NS
Time on homework	NS	NS	NS	NS	NS	NS
Time on educational activities	NS	NS	NS	.365	NS	NS
Academic Outcomes						
Achievement	.162	NS	NS	NS	NS	−.084
College Enrollment (Odds)	NS	NS	NS	1.908	NS	NS

Note: Numbers represent slopes obtained from statistical regression models (OLS) that account for socioeconomic background (i.e., family income, parental education, and family structure) and the perceptions of barriers listed across the top of the table. NS denotes that the association is not significant. The significance level for all associations is based on $p < .05$. See Appendix C for the analytic plan and Appendix D for a description of measures used in this analysis.

Figure 4.7: Belief in the Value of Education by Sex and Race

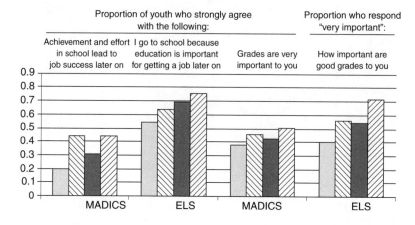

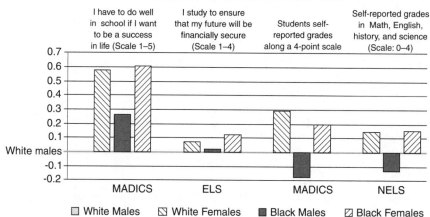

□ White Males   ⊠ White Females   ■ Black Males   ▨ Black Females

Note: The means for white males on the questions in the bottom panel, in order of presentation, are 3.91, 2.64, 1.90, and 1.99. The high number on the scales for the first two questions in the bottom panel corresponds to "strongly agree." The mean differences for self-reported grades account for socioeconomic background (family income, parental education, and family structure). See Appendix C for the analytic plan and Appendix D for a complete description of measures.

Chapter Summary

In this chapter, I set out to provide a better understanding of how beliefs about the system of social mobility affect students' academic investment. I find that beliefs in barriers are not associated with the academic outcomes assessed in this chapter. I also conducted an analysis that accounts for the intersection of race and gender. The anticipation of discrimination in the labor force, school, and life in general because of both gender and race does not compromise students' investment in schooling. It seems that students do not dwell on the negative aspects of the system of social mobility.

The findings in this chapter also show that blacks simultaneously attribute value to schooling and believe in barriers despite schooling, which is consistent with findings others have reported (for example, Hochschild 1995; Young 1999). This is also the case for females, who perceive greater barriers—even within education—but yet attribute more importance to schooling than boys. Because blacks as a whole have lower achievement than whites, this finding yields a paradox among blacks similar to that addressed by Mickelson in 1990. Specifically, blacks attribute more value to education yet have lower achievement than whites. I have addressed this "paradox" previously (Harris 2008) by employing the logic given by Ainsworth-Darnell and Downey (1998). They note that it would be difficult to determine whether blacks are overestimating the value of schooling or whether whites are underestimating the value of schooling. The same question could be asked about whites: why do they have lower proschool beliefs/attitudes despite their higher levels of school achievement? Outcomes for blacks are typically assessed *relative to* whites, which results in the inconsistency between beliefs/attitudes and school achievement among whites to be overlooked and among blacks to be framed as a paradox.

Blacks' beliefs and attitudes seem less paradoxical when one considers academic outcomes not based on achievement. As I noted earlier, a report by the U.S. Department of Education (1992) shows that black parents are more likely to discuss their children's school experiences and plans, restrict television on school nights, set rules about grades, and help with homework than are poor Latino/a, Asian, and white parents. Consideration of these outcomes brings blacks' greater belief in the value of schooling and affective attitudes into closer alignment with their behaviors. More importantly, as I discussed in Chapter 2, there was a time when blacks risked their lives for the pursuit of education, a challenge that never confronted whites. When considered in this context, it would be paradoxical if blacks had lower regard for schooling than whites. Similarly, blacks' greater belief in barriers is not surprising given that the American Dream remains elusive for many blacks, who often express the view that they must work harder than whites to receive similar rewards (Cose 1993; Hochschild 1995). Therefore, blacks' beliefs about the role of schooling for upward mobility appear to be relatively accurate.

Similarly, the notion that girls are more invested in schooling despite anticipating more obstacles than boys should also not be considered a paradox. Mickelson (1989) notes girls' achievement advantage is not an anomaly if considered within the more fluid boundaries that separate women's public and private lives, which exist along a continuum rather than a dichotomy. Drawing on feminist theory, she notes that women weave public and private roles into a single tapestry and are more likely to seek educational returns suitable for both spheres. Mickelson (1989) argues that differently from men, women do not perform comparative cost benefit analyses of educational returns when investing in school. Considering girls' achievement advantage an anomaly assumes there is only one measure for educational returns. Furthermore, Lopez (2003) shows that despite the discrimination that young Caribbean women experience in the workforce, they remain optimistic. O'Connor (1999) finds that high achievers are highly attuned to structural barriers to opportunity.

It is important to note that although women earn less than men, when the comparison is made between individuals similarly situated with regard to educational attainment and occupation, women actually experience greater returns to education than men (DiPrete and Buchmann 2006). In a study of gender-specific trends in educational returns using national data, DiPrete and Buchmann (2006) find that the difference in earnings between individuals with a four-year college degree and those with a high school diploma is greater for women, which indicates that women experience greater value from additional educational attainment than men. They also find that women experience greater returns to education in standard of living (that is, on gross family income adjusted for family size) and insurance against poverty than men, and these findings are more pronounced for blacks than whites. However, DiPrete and Buchmann caution that these patterns might not account for the female advantage in educational attainment. They note that it is unclear whether the lag between the increasing trend in returns to college for women and their increased enrollment patterns is "big enough to conclude that the trend in outcomes was feeding back through the perceptions of young people to affect their [college] enrollment decisions" (2006:18). Furthermore, as the findings from this chapter suggest, females still perceive greater barriers to upward mobility than males.

Findings reported in this chapter highlight the importance for researchers studying the racial achievement gap to maintain conceptual clarity between different types of beliefs. Group differences in perceived barriers are typically assessed as differences in perceptions of educational returns. However, the focus on perceptions about the rewards of further schooling presents a partial assessment of how societal conditions in the labor market influence schooling behavior. Instead, to refine our understanding of the implications that the labor market has for academic investment, perceptions of *barriers* to upward socioeconomic mobility need to be examined rather than estimated based on perceptions of educational returns. Doing so yields findings that support Ogbu's thesis that beliefs are mechanisms by which the opportunity structure influences students' academic investment, though not in the manner Ogbu expected.

I present a revised version of the resistance model that considers the findings from Chapters 3 and 4 in Figure 4.8. Accounting for the multidimensionality of beliefs about the opportunity structure provides greater clarity about the intergenerational transmission of beliefs regarding the value of schooling, as denoted by paths b_1 and b_2. The modifications that stem from this chapter are highlighted and illustrate that racial differences exist in both the value that youth attribute to schooling and the barriers they anticipate within the opportunity structure. Therefore, the original path d, which pointed to youths' perceptions about opportunity, has been adjusted to account for these differences (paths d_1 and d_2). The figure also illustrates that whereas perceptions about the value of schooling matter for achievement, belief in barriers do not. Since perceived value of schooling is associated with achievement, I bypassed path e for values. However, the overall pattern of results in this chapter shows that beliefs in barriers are not related to schooling behaviors or achievement. Thus, young people do not allow negative perceptions about the opportunity structure to compromise their schooling.

Similar to Chapter 3, the findings from this chapter provide a major challenge to the resistance model. Black youth express a greater belief in barriers than their white counterparts, which the theory predicts. However, beliefs in barriers are not related to academic investment, which contradicts perhaps the most fundamental aspect of the theory. Instead, it is the value that youth attribute to schooling—for which blacks hold an advantage over whites—that is related to academic achievement. Thus, it is the direction of the racial difference in the belief in the value of schooling (that is, the black advantage relative to whites) and the lack of association between barriers and academic investment that breaks a major link in the causal structure of the framework. Figure 4.8 represents my earnest attempt to reconstruct the framework, though the oppositional culture theory is severely compromised as several key causal links do not hold, or hold in the opposite direction than the theory predicts.

Can the oppositional culture theory still be used to explain why blacks have lower achievement than whites? While many proponents of the resistance model might point to a culture of disinvestment from schooling among blacks (denoted by the *Gap, g, h* triangle in Figure 4.8), Chapters 3 and 4 show that if such a culture exists it is detached from negative perceptions about the opportunity structure (that is, belief in barriers) or anti-schooling messages from parents and peers. The finding from Chapters 3 and 4 suggest that negative beliefs about the opportunity structure are not the culprits of the racial achievement gap. Instead, it is the favorable beliefs that matter for achievement, and blacks are not disadvantaged on these types of beliefs. Is the resistance model simply a bad theory of academic disinvestment?

Thus far I have explored the *reasoning* behind the culture of resistance (or academic disinvestment) attributed to blacks, which relies on perceptions about the opportunity structure and attributions about the value of schooling, all stemming from a historically evolving hierarchical societal structure within a seemingly meritocratic society. While the elaborate configuration of concepts (such as voluntary/involuntary minority, cultural inversion, identity oppositional to the dominant group) gives the theory great richness and depth, these factors might not be necessary for a group to simply disinvest from schooling. Essentially, the oppositional culture theory attaches a rich story to the *"gap, g, h"* triangle of Figure 4.8. While some ele-

Figure 4.8:   Framework Revisited II

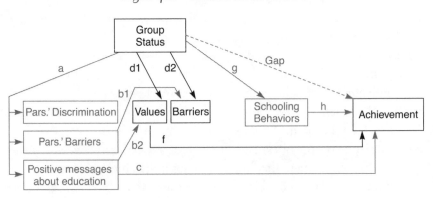

ments of this story seem to be supported by data (for example, racial differences in beliefs, greater belief in barriers among blacks, perceptions of values linked to achievement), a casual observer could still maintain that blacks resist schooling simply by observing "*gap, g, h.*" In fact, one can argue that the components exogenous to "*gap, g, h*" are more important to academicians than to the casual observer, who might attach a different set of factors to "*gap, g, h*" that correspond to an entirely different theoretical framework. In other words, perhaps proponents of the theory are really focusing on the behavioral components of culture (students' attitudes toward school and schooling behaviors), which are separate from perceptions about school as a mechanism for upward mobility and might stem from some other source. Students' day-to-day behaviors might differ by race in a manner consistent with the resistance model, which could lead to the conclusion that some adolescents really do not care about school, regardless of whether they know it will be beneficial to them in the future. I address this general academic orientation—path *g*—in the next chapter.

5

RACIAL DIFFERENCES IN
ACADEMIC ORIENTATION OF YOUTH

Most studies that capture teachers' perspectives with regard to black students' academic investment tend to focus on teachers' perceptions or treatment of black youth (Bol and Berry 2005; Delpit 1995; Diamond, Randolph, and Spillane 2004; Downey and Pribesh 2004; Ferguson 2000; Ferguson 2003; McKown and Weinstein 2008; Morris 2005, 2007; Neal et al. 2003; Tyler, Boykin, and Walton 2006). In general, these studies show that teachers attribute a culture that opposes schooling to black students. However, a theme that fails to emerge is whether teachers believe blacks oppose schooling because of their perceptions about the opportunity structure. Rather, the emphasis tends to be on the stereotypes teachers have about different racial groups and their attitudes about students' effort, behavior, and dress.

It is unlikely that a casual observer who is a proponent of the notion that black youth resist schooling would incorporate components of the opportunity structure into their explanation of this resistance. Figure 5.1 helps to illustrate this point. Essentially, teachers are aware of the gap, represented by the dashed line, and many believe that black students have a ubiquitous "culture" of underachievement, represented by path g. However, the paths that precede path g do not appear to be part of their assessments. Perhaps these paths are merely an Ivory-tower preoccupation with little real-world relevance. While this might render the oppositional culture theory as specified by Ogbu less viable, blacks' poor achievement relative to whites keeps the notion that they resist education plausible, regardless of the reasons behind their resistance.

In this chapter, I examine whether the negative schooling orientation (that is, the psychological and behavioral stance toward education) attributed to black students exists, and if so, whether it reflects a purposeful resistance to schooling. In other words, do black students actually attempt to (put forth effort to) fail? My emphasis on *purposeful* resistance is important to the discussion of oppositional culture because there is a tendency to invoke culture to explain persistent patterns of inequality in academic outcomes. However, it would be a mistake to attribute a culture of resistance to blacks based upon their academic achievement. A racial achievement gap can still exist without the presence of a pervasive oppositional culture among blacks. Similarly, black youth can display an oppositional culture even if they do not have lower levels of achievement than whites. Oppositional culture is not synonymous with poor academic achievement; rather, it is an explanation of poor achievement.

To be clear, I am not arguing that (nor assessing whether) blacks do not have an approach to schooling that is counterproductive; their lower academic achievement suggests that the manner in which they approach school is ineffective given the current standards and modes of evaluation. However, students can have a positive academic orientation—a favorable disposition toward schooling—yet have an inefficient (or simply a counterproductive) approach to schooling. Academic orientation should be used to determine whether poor achievement and counterproductive approaches to schooling represent a *purposeful* culture of opposition toward education. If the evidence fails to support the notion that black youth have lower academic orientation than whites, then the counterproductive approach to schooling observed among blacks by proponents of the resistance model would not reflect a *deliberate* attempt by black youth to sabotage their own academic achievement (that is, resistance to schooling). An alternative explanation for blacks' poor academic achievement and counterproductive (rather than consciously oppositional) approach to schooling would be war-

Figure 5.1:   Chapter in Focus: Youths' Academic Orientation

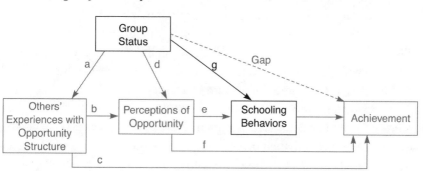

ranted. Black youth might want to succeed academically but simply not know how.

This discussion corresponds to path g in Figure 5.1. As shown in the previous two chapters, black youth are clearly aware that education is important for upward mobility. However, are blacks underperforming academically because they are not invested in education? And if they are not invested, is it because they simply find school boring or the subject matter difficult to relate to? Might there be some other reason that dissuades black youth from performing well academically, even when they believe that education is important? Although Chapters 3 and 4 suggest that the reasoning derived from the oppositional culture theory to explain the disengagement attributed to blacks is not consistent with the evidence, black students might still display behaviors that could be interpreted as resistance to school—or as disinvestment; black youth might have a more negative academic orientation than their white counterparts regardless of their beliefs about school as a mechanism for upward mobility.

Despite work by numerous scholars challenging the notion that an oppositional culture is prevalent among blacks (Ainsworth-Darnell and Downey 1998; Akom 2003; Carter 2005; Cook and Ludwig 1998; MacLeod 2009; O'Connor 1997; Tyson 2002; Tyson, Darity and Castellino 2005), the link denoted by path g continues to receive attention within the framework. However, these studies typically focus on select aspects of the framework while neglecting other, equally significant ones. For example, behavioral resistance in the form of negative peer sanctioning for good performance—an idea proposed by anthropologist Signithia Fordham (2008) and commonly known as the "acting white" hypothesis—generally receives most of the attention. Quantitative assessments of the full range of factors within the theory can be challenging because of data limitations or the restrictive length of articles in scientific journals.

In an attempt to move beyond these limitations, I conducted a study that examined five major tenets of the resistance model (Harris 2006), the results of which are included in this chapter. Specifically, I examined whether relative to whites, black children 1) perceive fewer returns to education and more limited opportunities for upward social mobility; 2) have less favorable affect toward school; 3) exhibit greater resistance to school; 4) have peer groups with greater countereducational orientation; and 5) receive greater negative sanctions from their peers for high academic achievement. Whereas the third tenet corresponds closely to path g, the other tenets reflect general academic orientation or disposition toward school. Therefore, in this chapter, I examine racial differences in general academic orientation, which includes both attitudes and behaviors.

Although some of the aforementioned tenets have been examined in previous quantitative studies (most notably Ainsworth-Darnell and Downey 1998 and Cook and Ludwig 1997), I extend this work by using three datasets to employ a more extensive set of measures of academic orientation. I provide racial comparisons on over thirty outcomes consisting of both traditional survey items and time diaries. I also examine racial differences in academic orientation using a nationally representative sample of youth in England. My aim here is to search for any substantial empirical evidence that might support the notion that blacks purposefully resist school. Path g corresponds to the only aspect of the oppositional culture theory that can actually be visually observed among students. Paths prior to g are assumed; they are used to explain the visually observable patterns of behavior denoted by g. Since path g might represent the primary link responsible for the cultural deficiency narrative among blacks, it is important to consider it carefully. I begin my assessment by focusing on students' schooling beliefs and attitudes; I then address their schooling behaviors. I also provide an assessment of the "acting white" hypothesis.

What Students Say

The aforementioned claims can be assessed by comparing black and white youths' views on indicators that capture the five claims, using survey data obtained from the MADICS. The first of these comparisons is conducted on questions that indicate the value students attribute to education, their desire for further schooling, and their affect toward schooling.[1] Recall that Ogbu (1978) notes that the expected gains from education held by children and their parents or community serve as an important determinant of orientation toward schooling. Therefore, black children should perceive fewer returns to education and should have lower educational aspirations and expectations than white children. Another way to assess black youths' perceptions of opportunities relative to whites is to determine whether there is greater discrepancy between their aspired and expected educational attainment. Presumably, the educational level youth *wish* to attain (educational aspiration) should be similar to the level of education they expect to complete (educational expectation), unless they perceive limited opportunities with regard to upward mobility.

These racial comparisons are displayed in Figure 5.2. The names of the survey indicators are listed on the side of the expected "effect" as posited by the resistance model; indicators for which blacks should score lower than whites are labeled on the negative side of the graph, while those on which blacks should score higher are labeled on the positive side of the graph. Since variation exists on the scale along which the indicators are measured, the effect sizes should not be interpreted across indicators. Rather, the focus should be on the location of the estimates—whether they are on the negative or positive side of the graph. I display two estimates for each indicator.[2] The first shows the black-white difference on the indicator (open circle) and the second shows this difference once social class is taken into account (full circle). That is, the full circle represents how black youth would differ from their white counterparts if they had similar family income, parental education, and family structure. The standard errors are represented by the tails on both sides of the estimates.[3]

The findings for the indicators of youths' perceptions of educational returns and their desired and expected educational level show no support for the first claim that black children perceive fewer returns to education. Specifically, black students report greater perceptions of educational returns (.091) and higher educational aspirations (.123) than whites, even prior to accounting for socioeconomic background factors. The black-white difference on how far they expect to go in school is not significant, which means that the estimate is within the margin of error for random variation and should be treated as a black-white difference of zero. However, when the estimate is adjusted to account for background factors, it moves to the right-hand side of the graph, indicating that among blacks and whites with similar socioeconomic backgrounds, blacks expect to go farther in school. In fact, accounting for socioeconomic factors will usually result in estimates tilting toward a black advantage because the estimate is now for the average group difference among black and white youth with similar socioeconomic standing. Thus, the black disadvantage on socioeconomic factors is removed. This also leads to an increase in blacks' advantage on perceived returns to education of 27 percent (to .116), and their advantage on educational aspirations nearly doubles (.239).

Analysis for the fourth outcome in Figure 5.2, however, shows blacks believe they will not attain their desired level of education more than whites. This might indicate that they perceive greater limited educational opportunities than whites. This difference declines by 41 percent when blacks are compared to whites with similar socioeconomic standing (from .193 to .114). Nevertheless, the discrepancy between the educational attainment students would like to reach and the educational attainment they believe they will reach is greater for blacks, even after accounting for background factors. It seems that something other than socioeconomic factors contributes to their greater belief that they will not reach their educational goals. This is consistent with the pattern observed for belief in barriers in Chapter 4.

Despite the fact that blacks perceive greater returns to education and desire further schooling than whites, it is unclear whether black students differ from whites on attitudes toward education. In Chapter 4, I noted that Mickelson (1990) separated attitudes toward education into abstract and

Figure 5.2: Racial Differences in Perceptions of Educational Returns and Affect toward Schooling

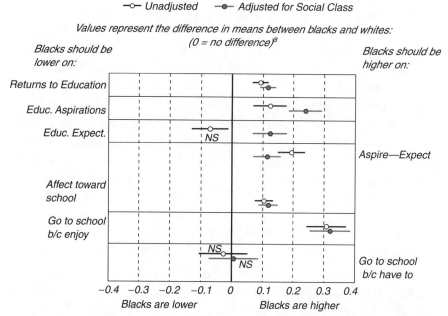

[a] The graph displays the estimate (circle) and standard error (tails). The means on the measures for whites (unadjusted) and in order of presentation are 4.13, 7.62, 6.95, 0.66, 3.60, 4.16, and 5.02. Changes in these means are negligible after adjusting for social class. Adjusted estimates illustrate the group differences after accounting for parents' education, family income, family structure, youths' sex, and grade in school. NS denotes not significant (p-value is set to .05). Values were obtained from pooled cross-sectional regression models (OLS) using robust standard errors. See Appendix C for the analytic plan and Appendix D for a description of measures.

concrete attitudes. Her discussion of these attitudes is similar to my discussion of beliefs about the value of school and barriers despite education in Chapter 4. Since these indicators are intended to capture what children believe to be true with regard to the role that education can have in their future, I refer to them as beliefs, which is separate from favorable or unfavorable affective feelings toward school; one can believe education is important for success yet dislike school. Schooling attitudes need to be assessed in a manner that does not require youth to estimate future educational returns.

I provide an assessment of whether black children have less favorable affect toward school than whites in the bottom portion of Figure 5.2, using indicators that tap into students' affective feelings toward school without asking them to estimate the future payoff of schooling. Specifically, I compare black and white youth on the indicator for affect toward school used in Chapter 4 and on whether they attend school because they enjoy their classes or because school attendance is mandatory. According to the resistance model, black children should have lower affect toward schooling than whites and should be less inclined to report enjoyment of classes as a reason for their school attendance; rather, they should report more than whites that they attend school because of mandatory attendance policies.

The findings, however, show that blacks have greater affect toward school and rate enjoyment of classes as more important for their school attendance than whites. There is no racial difference on the importance students attribute to mandatory attendance policies as a basis for their school attendance (the estimates for this indicator are within the margin of error). These findings are the same whether socioeconomic factors are taken into account or not.

What Students Do

Although the previous analyses suggest that blacks do not perceive fewer educational returns nor have less favorable affect toward schooling than whites, Ogbu (1991:446) cautions that black Americans' greater proschool attitudes merely reflect "wishful thinking . . . [because blacks] simply do not match their aspirations with effort." He asks us to consider if "it [is] logical to expect that blacks and whites would exert the same energy and perform alike in school when the caste system, through the job ceiling, consistently underutilizes black training and ability and underrewards blacks for their education" (1978:195). He argues that using students' attitudes toward school to measure school resistance is inadequate because "direct questions will generally elicit responses similar to those given by white Americans" (1991:444). Instead, school resistance is better gauged by assessing students' behavior—what they do or fail to do to improve academically. According to Ogbu, blacks' repudiation of schooling is marked by truancy, delinquency, and lack of serious effort. Therefore, I assessed the third claim—that blacks resist schooling more than whites—by determining whether blacks fare worse than whites on behavioral indicators for students' academic investment and school resistance. These findings are displayed in Figure 5.3.

Academic investment is measured by five indicators: the frequency with which youth seek help when they are having trouble in school; time spent on school activities/clubs, time on homework, time on learning activities outside of school; and the importance youth attribute to academic activities. School resistance is measured as the frequency with which youth skip school or cut classes, the number of times they have been suspended from school, and the importance they attribute to nonacademic activities. Ogbu cited sports as an important nonacademic activity. He notes, "one major issue in prioritizing was deciding between sports and academics" (2003:28). Recall that Ogbu (1978) argues the American caste system encourages a dual system of social/status mobility leading ethnic minorities to disinvest from academics and focus on perceived nonwhite domains such as sports, which they perceive will be more rewarding. Therefore, according to the resistance model, blacks should score lower on indicators that measure academic investment and higher on the indicators of school resistance.

The top portion of Figure 5.3 shows little support for the claim that blacks exert less effort to improve academically than whites. Findings show blacks seek help when they are having trouble in school more than whites. They also spend the same amount of time on homework and educational activities as whites. Although blacks spend less time on school activities/clubs, the adjusted estimate suggests that this can be attributed to their lower socioeconomic status; the estimate moves into the margin of error once background factors are taken into account. Blacks actually place greater importance on academic activities than whites (a black advantage of .416 in both unadjusted and adjusted estimates). The bottom portion of Figure 5.3 shows that although blacks do not skip school/cut classes more than whites, they are suspended more often than whites. Only a little more than one-third of their higher suspension levels can be attributed to socioeconomic differences (from .375 to .232). Finally, they also place greater importance

Figure 5.3:   Racial Differences in Academic Investment and School Resistance

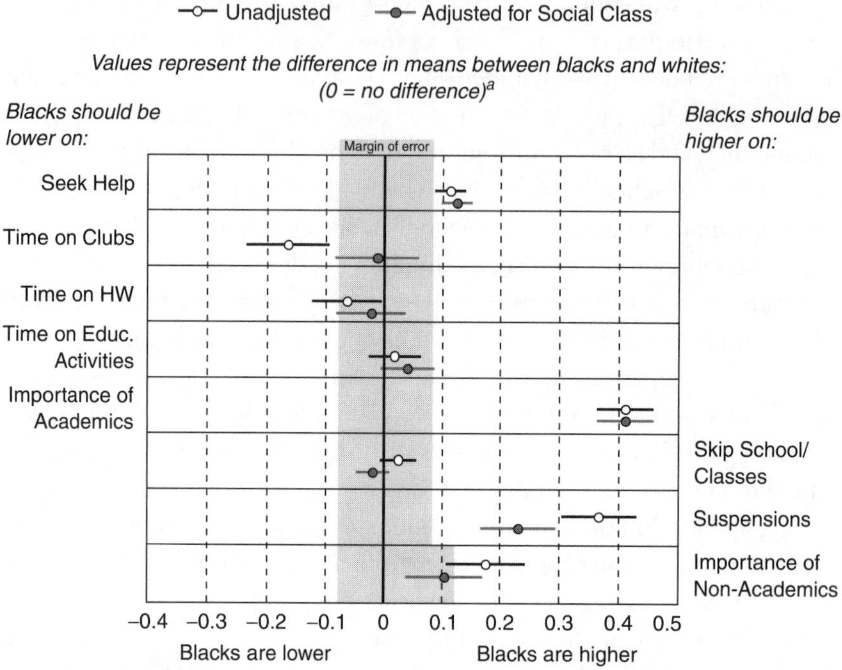

—○— Unadjusted   —●— Adjusted for Social Class

Values represent the difference in means between blacks and whites:
(0 = no difference)[a]

Blacks should be lower on:
- Seek Help
- Time on Clubs
- Time on HW
- Time on Educ. Activities
- Importance of Academics

Blacks should be higher on:
- Skip School/ Classes
- Suspensions
- Importance of Non-Academics

Margin of error

−0.4 −0.3 −0.2 −0.1 0 0.1 0.2 0.3 0.4 0.5

Blacks are lower   Blacks are higher

[a] The graph displays the estimate (circle) and standard error (tails). The means for whites (unadjusted) are as follows: *seek help* (2.87), *time on clubs* (1.81), *time on HW* (4.70), *time on educational activities* (3.03), *importance of academics* (4.95), *skip school or classes* (1.52), *suspension* (0.33), and *importance of nonacademics* (4.26). Changes in these means are negligible after adjusting for social class. Adjusted estimates illustrate the group differences after accounting for parents' education, family income, family structure, youths' sex, and grade in school. Values within the margin of error suggest that the racial difference is not significant (p is *not* less than .05). Values were obtained from pooled cross-sectional regression models (OLS) using robust standard errors. All indicators are self-reported. See Appendix C for further details on the analytic plan and Appendix D for a description of measures.

on sports, though not when compared to whites of similar socioeconomic status.

It is important to note school suspension is not necessarily equivalent to school resistance. Several studies on blacks' differential disciplinary rates suggest school practices are partially to blame (see, for instance, Delpit 1995; Ferguson 2000; Lewis 2003; Morris 2005; Tyson 2002, 2003). Specifically, these studies find that cultural discontinuity between black families and the institutionalized structure of schools, which value cultural norms and standards of "mainstream" white middle-class society, results in school personnel placing greater emphasis on black children's behavior. For example, Ferguson (2000) finds school personnel view the dress and behavior of black males as recalcitrant and oppositional, and as a consequence tend to exert strict control over black male students. She notes that culturally based assumptions about black males lead them to face constant regulation of their dress, behavior, and speech. Similarly, Morris (2005) finds whereas white and Asian American children are viewed as nonthreatening, black (and Latino/a) children are considered dangerous and therefore face constant surveillance and greater discipline for behavioral infractions. In sum, these studies show "schools react to students based on perceptions of race and gender and use these concepts as a basis for specific patterns of regulation" (Morris 2005:28). Thus, suspension might reflect differential treatment black children experience in schools. The causal ordering might be reversed; receiving a suspension could be an effect of being a target of school personnel.

In order to further assess the claim that blacks resist schooling, I move beyond typical survey data and employ data from time diaries contained in the Child Development Supplement (CDS) to the Panel Study for Income Dynamics (PSID). The PSID began in 1968 as a nationally representative study of five thousand American families who were interviewed every year until 1997, after which data collection occurred biannually. In 1997, the PSID added the CDS, which sampled 3,563 children between the ages of zero and twelve from PSID families. A follow-up study was conducted in 2002–2003 among 2,908 children—then between the ages of five and eighteen—whose families remained active in the PSID panel. I use the time diaries from CDS-II because it contains data on youth through the entire school cycle (grades 1 through 12).

The time diary is a chronology of events over a twenty-four-hour period beginning at midnight of the designated day. Two time diaries were collected for each child, one that was completed within three days of a randomly designated weekday and the other within one week of a designated weekend day. Children were able to record both the primary activity in which they were engaged, the start and finish time of the activity, and whether any other activity was taking place simultaneously. I used the time diaries to obtain an estimate for how much time black and white youth spend on academic activities outside of school, which I coded into three activities: homework, general educational activities, and leisure reading. Educational activities include being tutored, nonschool professional classes or lectures, studying/research/reading, library activities, reviewing homework with parents/caregiver, and other similar activities. Leisure reading includes looking at or reading books, magazines, reviews, pamphlets, newspapers, other nonschool related reading, and being read to/listening to a story. Academic activities were included only if they were the primary activity in which the child was engaged.

The time diary findings are displayed in Figure 5.4. The first two bars suggest that white and black youth spend about the same amount of time on academic activities during weekdays (51 minutes for whites and 50 minutes for blacks). However, the next two bars suggest that blacks spend less time on academic activities during weekends. Specifically, black youth spend only half as much time (17 minutes) on academic activities as white youth (34 minutes). It is important to note that these findings do not account for socioeconomic background. Therefore, the average difference of 34 minutes during typical weekends (the difference of 17 minutes multiplied by two) might not be a race "effect," but rather an artifact of racial difference in background factors.

Figure 5.4:   Time on Academic Activities for Youths in Grades 1 through 12: CDS Time Diaries

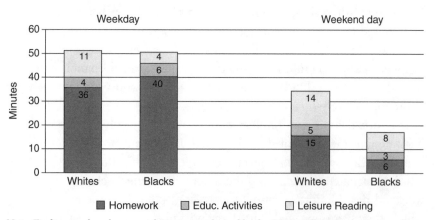

Note: Findings are based on a weighting system devised by the PSID staff to account for the effects of the initial probability of being sampled and attrition over time — which is generally low — and incorporates a poststratification factor to ensure the data are nationally representative. (For a detailed description of the CDS weight construction, see http://psidonline.isr.umich.edu/CDS/weightsdoc.html.) Unweighted sample size is 2,016 for the weekday (1,078 whites and 938 blacks) and 1,994 for the weekend day (1,069 whites and 925 blacks). Estimates are rounded to the nearest minute. With the exception of total time spent on academic activities during the weekday, all racial differences in the figure are statistically significant at the .05 level of significance. See Appendix C for further details on the analytic plan and Appendix D for a description of measures.

To determine how much of the black disadvantage on time spent on academic activities during the weekends can be attributed to background factors, I show how the estimated difference of 34 minutes changes as various background factors are taken into account in Figure 5.5. The first bar represents the unadjusted 34-minute baseline difference, which does not account for any background factors. The second bar shows that the estimate remains relatively unchanged after accounting for sex and grade in school. However, the baseline difference declines by one-third after accounting for family income (down to 23 minutes), and further declines to just under 20 minutes after accounting for parents' education. Controlling for family structure and number of books in a household, two additional factors indicative of a youth's socioeconomic status, further reduces the estimate to under a 10-minute black-white difference. Finally, accounting for youths' reading ability brings the estimate to roughly 4 minutes, which is a little over 10 percent of the original baseline difference. This means that nearly 90 percent of the black disadvantage in time spent on academic activities during weekends relative to whites can be explained by the factors listed across the top of Figure 5.5.

The finding that black and white children spend a similar amount of time on academic activities during weekdays might contravene many people's beliefs. I was both surprised and skeptical of this finding. My distrust was not due to the data, but rather to my analytic plan; perhaps conducting the

Figure 5.5: Black Disadvantage in Time on Academic Activities during Weekends (Minutes)

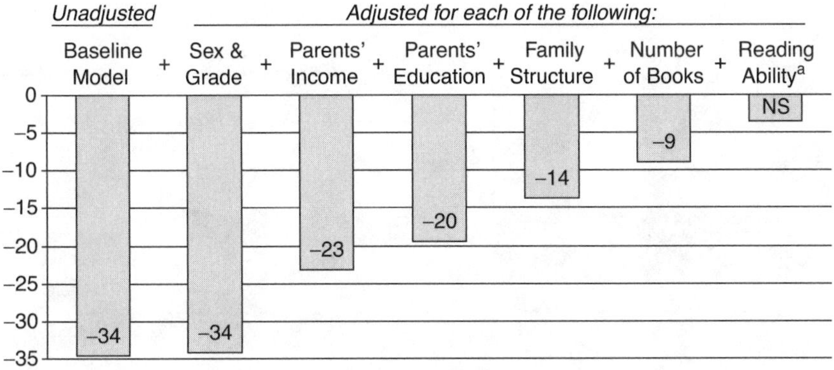

Note: Findings are based on weighted data. Unweighted sample size is 1,994. Estimates are rounded to the nearest minute.
[a] NS denotes that the racial difference is not significant ($t = -1.71$, $p = .087$).

analysis on the full sample—students in grades 1 through 12—might conceal a pattern of school resistance among adolescents. Therefore, I conducted the analysis for students in grades 7 through 12. These findings, shown in Figure 5.6, suggest that black adolescents spend less time on academic activities during both weekdays and weekends. White and black youth spend an average of 58 and 48 minutes per weekday on academic activities, respectively, which totals an average difference of 50 minutes on weekdays during a typical week. On the weekend day, the average time spent on academic activities is 42 minutes for whites and 17 minutes for blacks. This discrepancy of 25 minutes suggests an average black-white difference of 50 minutes on weekends.

The findings in Figure 5.6 are consistent with what one would expect given the racial achievement gap. However, it is important to determine whether this pattern is spurious. That is, the racial differences on the time students spend on academic activities can only be attributed to deliberate academic resistance among blacks if the black disadvantage remains after accounting for socioeconomic background factors. Otherwise, interpreting the black disadvantage as black youths' resistance to schooling could lead educators to respond to blacks based on their perceptions of a *false positive* oppositional culture—counterproductive schooling behaviors and achievement assumed to be premeditated or viewed as deliberate academic resistance when the poor results are actually driven by alternative factors. I discuss this further in Chapter 7.

I examine whether the black-white differences in time spent on academic

Figure 5.6: Time on Academic Activities among Adolescents (Grades 7–12): CDS Time Diaries

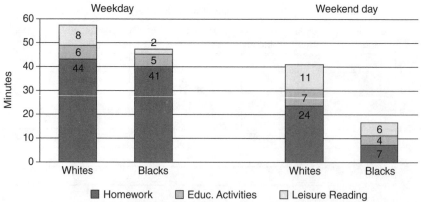

Note: Unweighted sample size is 953 for the weekday (509 whites and 444 blacks) and 943 for the weekend day (505 whites and 438 blacks). Estimates are rounded to the nearest minute. All racial differences are statistically significant ($p < .05$).

activities during both weekdays and weekends among adolescents can be attributed to socioeconomic factors in Figure 5.7. The top panel shows that the 50-minute black-white difference on weekdays reduces to an average of 19 minutes when the comparison is made between blacks and whites who are similar with regard to family income. However, there is no difference when parents' education is taken into account. Thus, black and white adolescents with similar socioeconomic backgrounds spend the same amount of time on academic activities during weekdays. Black adolescents who are similar to whites on all factors listed across the top of the figure actually have an advantage of 18 minutes per week on academic activities relative to white adolescents. The bottom panel shows that socioeconomic factors explain 92 percent of the black disadvantage on weekends; that is, the gap reduces from 51 to 4 minutes. In sum, the analysis of time diary data does not yield results consistent with the belief that black youth resist schooling.

Figure 5.7: Black Disadvantage in Time on Academic Activities during Adolescence (Minutes)

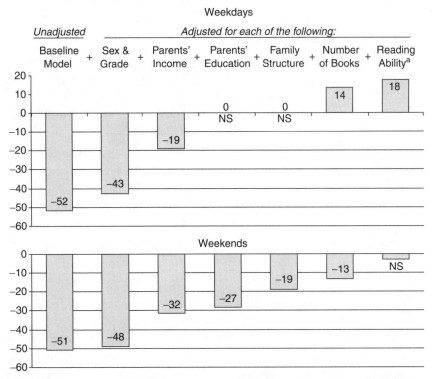

Note: Findings are based on weighted data. Unweighted sample size for weekdays and weekends is 953 and 943, respectively. Estimates are rounded to the nearest minute.
[a] NS denotes that the difference is not statistically significant at the .05 level.

The "Acting White" Hypothesis

The most widely known tenet associated with the oppositional culture theory is the "acting white" hypothesis (Fordham and Ogbu 1986). Recall that Ogbu (1994) notes subordinate groups define achievement as inappropriate for them because they regard schooling as within the domain of their oppressors. Therefore, academic success is equated to "acting white" (Fordham and Ogbu 1986). I assess this assertion by determining whether high-achieving blacks receive greater negative sanctioning from their peers than white students.

The MADICS contains a series of indicators of youths' level of confidence within the social domain. Specifically, students were asked to rate their ability in making friends, the trouble they have getting along with other children, their perception of how popular they are among their peer groups, and their satisfaction with the number of friends they have. These indicators were not collected within an academic context; they were asked in a section of the survey intended to collect information on youths' social lives. Therefore, there is no reason to believe that youths' academic identity would be more salient during that time than their identity across other domains (for example, athletic skill, physical appearance, musical or artistic ability). However, if youth are navigating a social environment in which good academic performance is negatively sanctioned, then higher-achieving students should fare worse on these social measures. Specifically, they should report having more difficulty in making friends, having greater trouble getting along with other children, feeling less popular than their peers, and having lower satisfaction with the number of friends they have. In contrast, low-achieving students should report having greater social standing than their higher-achieving counterparts. I stratified the sample of adolescents in the MADICS into three groups based on academic performance (GPA): low achievers, average achievers, and high achievers. Low achievers are students in the bottom quarter of the achievement distribution, and high achievers are those in the top quarter of the achievement distribution. I compared students in these two groups to their counterparts in the middle of the achievement distribution, which includes average achievers.

The findings for the first two indicators of social status displayed in Figure 5.8 show that students' level of school performance is not related to their ability to make friends nor, more importantly, get along with their peers, which is a better illustration of whether good performance is negatively sanctioned. The means on these indicators are similar across achievement levels for both blacks and whites. With regard to racial differences, the difference on the indicators of social standing within each achievement level is less important than the slopes for both blacks and whites. If black students must pay a greater social cost for academic success, then one would expect a greater decline in the slope estimating youths' ability to make friends for blacks relative to the slope for whites. Alternatively, blacks' slope connecting the estimates for the trouble children have getting along with peers should increase to a greater degree than their white counterparts. However, the racial differences in slopes for both indicators of social standing are not significant. Thus, well-performing blacks do not have more difficulty making friends nor greater trouble getting along with their peers than well-performing whites.

The bottom panel of Figure 5.8 suggests that academic achievement also appears to be unrelated to popularity. Popularity is constant across school

Figure 5.8:   Social Cost for Good Academic Performance

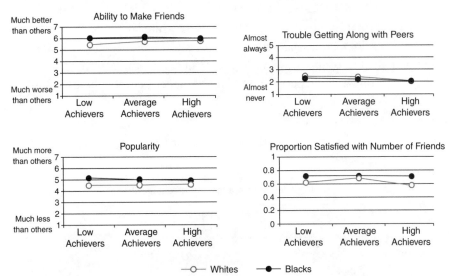

Note: Low and high achievers are students in the bottom and top quartile of the GPA distribution, respectively. Average achievers are students in the second and third quartiles of the GPA distribution. The averages for the achievement groups on the indicators of social standing were obtained after accounting for socioeconomic background (family income, parental education, and family structure), and youths' sex. The question about the *ability to make friends* and *trouble getting along with peers* were asked only in grade 7. However, the findings for *popularity* and *proportion satisfied with number of friends* are pooled cross-sections and account for grade level (that is, grades 8 and 11). There are no racial differences in this figure (*p* is *not* less than .05).

performance, and this pattern is similar for blacks and whites. The graph on the right shows that the proportion of blacks satisfied with the number of friends they have is similar across levels of academic performance. However, for whites, a lower proportion of high-achieving students are satisfied with the number of friends that they have than average-achieving students. In fact, though not significant, the difference in proportions between average achievers and high achievers is greater for whites than blacks, which runs counter to the notion that blacks experience a greater social cost for high achievement than whites.

Although these indicators of social standing provide an assessment of whether students experience a social cost for high academic performance, they do not tap into students' perceptions regarding whether good school performance is "acting white." In order to provide a more direct assessment of the "acting white" hypothesis, I compared blacks with low achievement to those with high achievement in grade 7 on whether they regard education as a "white" domain. Figure 5.9 shows an overwhelming proportion of blacks do *not* equate academic success with whiteness. However, about 17 percent of black youth believe getting good grades is "acting white." The more important finding regarding the "acting white" hypothesis is that the percentages do not differ significantly across achievement groups, which suggests that the fear of appearing white as a result of performing well in school is not the reason for differences in school performance between these groups.

Figure 5.9:   Direct Assessment of the "Acting White" Hypothesis (Blacks Only, Grade 7)

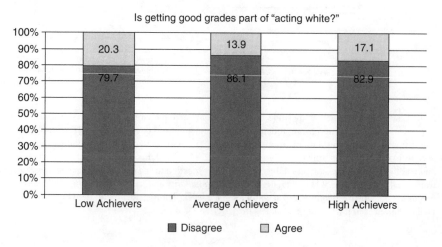

The hypothesis that blacks view academic success as "acting white" and negatively sanction high-achieving students suggests they negotiate a social space with a culture counterproductive to academic pursuits. Therefore, black youth should have peers with a negative culture in general, which might lead to more opportunities for resisting school. However, Figure 5.10 suggests that black students do not have peers that engage more in negative behaviors or have greater negative values than whites; the differences between these groups are within the margin of error. These measures address the general cultural deficiency argument commonly attributed to black youth. Black children's peers do have modestly higher positive values toward school after adjusting for socioeconomic status. The final indicator suggests blacks are surrounded by peers who hold *less* negative values toward school than white youth.

Does Blacks' School Resistance Increase over Time?

It is possible that school resistance among blacks relative to whites might become more apparent if racial differences are assessed over time. That is, rather than focusing on racial difference on the aforementioned indicators

Figure 5.10: Racial Differences in Peer Orientation

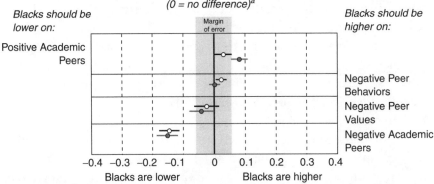

ᵃ The graph displays the estimate (circle) and standard error (tails). The means for whites (unadjusted) are 3.40, 1.23, 2.52, and 2.29 for *positive academic peers, negative peer behaviors, negative peer values,* and *negative academic peers,* respectively. Changes in these means are negligible after adjusting for social class. Adjusted estimates illustrate the group differences after accounting for parents' education, family income, family structure, sex, and youths' grade in school. Values within the margin of error suggest that the racial difference is not significant at the .05 level. Values were obtained from pooled cross-sectional regression models (OLS) using robust standard errors. See Appendix C for further details on the analytic plan and Appendix D for a description of measures.

during adolescence, perhaps the focus should be on whether the scores for blacks on the indicators increasingly diverge from those of whites as they move closer to adulthood. Ogbu suggests that blacks *develop* perceptions that their educational efforts are undervalued within society. As they transition into adulthood, they gain awareness of minorities' misfortunes with the opportunity structure and system of social mobility. In his most recent analysis of poorly achieving blacks in the affluent suburb of Shaker Heights, Ohio, Ogbu (2003:20) describes their academic efforts as decreasing markedly from elementary to high school. He notes that although lack of effort "might not be serious in the early grades, it became more serious as students got older and began to think that they, too, would have difficulty in the opportunity structure . . . just because they were black" (2003:154). He suggests they did not try hard despite believing in American ideals (such as success through education and hard work) because they were "mistrustful, ambivalent, and skeptical, especially as they got older and moved up in their school career" (2003:41).

Since school resistance over time is an often-overlooked component of the theory, previous studies provide limited assessments of the theory's maturation component. Although studies have examined school resistance across multiple age groups (for example, Downey and Ainsworth-Darnell 2002; Farkas, Lleras, and Maczuga 2002), they use cohorts comprised of different children. Tyson (2002, 2003) examines the development of oppositional schooling attitudes among blacks in elementary school. In general, she finds that black children begin school very much engaged and achievement-oriented and that the rejection of school norms does *not* characterize the larger black culture. However, she finds that the schooling experience plays a central role in the development of negative schooling attitudes, an issue I address in Chapter 7. However, since her aim was to examine these issues among younger students, her sample consisted of children in elementary school.

I have addressed the dearth of research on school resistance across adolescence in another study (Harris 2006). I assessed whether blacks fared increasingly worse than whites on the following outcomes as they progressed from middle to high school: their perceived returns to education; their educational aspirations and expectations; their affect toward school; the extent to which their school attendance is based on enjoyment of classes or because it is mandatory; whether they seek help when having trouble at school; time they spend on school clubs, homework, and educational activities; the importance they attribute to academics; the number of times they skipped school and were suspended; the importance they attribute to nonacademics; and the influence of peers and friends on their attitudes toward schooling (relying on the measures of positive and negative peer culture used earlier in this chapter). In that study, the findings showed that all differences in the aforementioned outcomes remained similar from grades 7 through 11 with one exception: positive peer orientation toward school. While positive peer values on school declined for both groups toward the end of middle school and through grade 11, the decline over time is greater among the peers of blacks than those of whites.[4] This finding is consistent with the resistance model. However, this decline is not synonymous with an increase in negative peer values toward schooling. Recall that black children's peers have less negative values toward school than the peers of whites and they maintain lower levels of negative values toward schooling than the peers of whites over time.

Overall, my analysis suggests that declines in academic orientation occur among all youth as they matriculate through school. For example, perceived returns to education decreased over time for both groups. Since group differences remain constant over time, blacks maintain their advantage relative to whites on this indicator. Both groups also experienced similar rates of decline in educational expectations, school affect, rating of class enjoyment as important for their school attendance, and an increase in feeling that they attend school because it is required. Whites' greater achievement leads researchers to overlook this phenomenon. Ogbu (2003) emphasizes that affect toward school declines over time for blacks. However, he builds a theory of group differences based on observations of one group. The findings in Figure 5.2 suggest that the black-white achievement gap results from factors other than affective schooling attitudes.

Are the Findings Based on the MADICS Generalizable?

As I mentioned earlier, the advantage of using the MADICS is that it contains a richer collection of measures relevant to the resistance model than those found in the NELS. Although the MADICS was not designed to draw inferences relative to the national population, I am unaware of theoretical models positing that the underlying causal mechanisms of school resistance vary by social class or geographic area (such as east/west or urban/suburban). The resistance model attributes an oppositional cultural frame of reference to the wider "black community" (for further elaboration, see

Tyson 2002:1166–1167). To underscore this notion, Ogbu (2003) attempted to show that an oppositional culture exists among black youth in the affluent school district of Shaker Heights, Ohio. In reference to his first visit to Shaker Heights, Ogbu (2003:xiii) noted: "One possible reason that came to our attention during our first visit was the disengagement of Black students from academic work." This conclusion—made on the first visit—framed the objective of that study, which was to discover why blacks were disengaged from academic work. Thus, black academic disengagement is posited to be so prevalent that it can be identified almost instantly, even among affluent blacks.

Another reason for my lack of concern about the validity of the MADICS is that the results described above yield similar conclusions to studies that use national data (that is, Ainsworth-Darnell and Downey 1998; Cook and Ludwig 1998). Again, this is not surprising given that there is no prior theoretical or empirical basis for expecting the processes and parameters underlying school resistance to vary by region or social class. Studies using data based on a national sample of students also find that blacks perceive greater returns to education than whites and that no differences exist in educational expectations between these groups (Ainsworth-Darnell and Downey 1998; Cook and Ludwig 1997; Voelkl 1993). The decline in academic orientation among adolescents—regardless of race—I discussed above was also found five decades ago by Coleman (1961) and more recently by Steinberg (1996).

Similar support from national data exists for several findings I report above in ways that again seem to contradict expectations. Specifically, the finding that shows no racial differences on the time children spend on homework is consistent with other nationally representative studies (Cook and Ludwig 1997; Thernstrom and Thernstrom 2003). Studies finding group differences generally show only a modest disadvantage for blacks (Ainsworth-Darnell and Downey 1998; Cook and Ludwig 1998). This does not suggest blacks are efficient with their time on homework, however. In an analysis of fifteen affluent school districts, Ferguson found black students were 20 percent less likely to complete their homework than whites (see Thernstrom and Thernstrom 2003:143). The lack of racial difference on skipping school or class in the MADICS is also consistent with analysis based on the National Educational Longitudinal Study, in which Cook and Ludwig (1997) find similar frequency of skipping class among black and white tenth graders.

With regard to the "acting white" hypothesis, the finding that black students receive no greater social penalty for good school performance than whites is also consistent with studies that use national data (Ainsworth-Darnell and Downey 1998; Cook and Ludwig 1998). In fact, differences between these groups favor blacks. Ainsworth-Darnell and Downey (1998) show high-achieving blacks are more popular than their white counterparts regardless of whether achievement is measured using standardized test scores or grades. Marryshow et al. (2005) administered psychological tests presenting various racialized scenarios to students between the ages of ten and twelve, one involving a black high achiever with a white (or mainstream) cultural orientation and the other a black high achiever with a black cultural orientation. There was a clear preference among the students for high achievers to exhibit a black cultural orientation. These results were replicated by Sankofa et al. (2005) among low-income black children between the ages of eight and eleven, who also predicted that both their parents and peers would hold more favorable attitudes toward high achievers with an African American cultural orientation than toward the mainstream cultural high achievers.

Horvat and Lewis (2003) introduce a framework that helps reconcile Fordham and Ogbu's findings with those that show no support for the "acting white" hypothesis. They found students "navigated and negotiated multiple friendship groups within the African American peer group." They further observed that "there were some cases of students modifying or downplaying their academic success . . . [and also] instances in which students share their academic success with peers who are supportive of their academic endeavors" (2003:266). Thus, the resistance displayed by some may be conditional on the peers present within a particular setting; they can "camouflage" their success around low-achieving blacks as Fordham and Ogbu (1986) observe, and they can also "discuss freely and receive applause for their academic achievements and aspirations" among high-achieving blacks as Horvat and Lewis find (2003:266).

Several qualitative studies also fail to find a pervasive antischooling culture among blacks (Akom 2003; Carter 2005; MacLeod 2009; O'Connor 1997; Tyson, Darity, and Castellino 2005). MacLeod (2009) shows that this is the case even among low-income youth. He finds that the black youth in his study—the Brothers—believe that "American society is open; equality of opportunity is perceived as a reality." He adds, "Schooling is regarded by the Brothers as the means to economic success; consequently, they care about school, [and] accept its norms and standards" (2009:102). Interestingly, MacLeod finds that it is the white low-income youth—the Hallway Hangers—who exhibit an oppositional culture toward schooling. He states, "Their unwillingness to partake of the educational system stems from an assessment of the cost and benefits of playing the game . . . Given this logic, the oppositional behavior of the Hallway Hangers is a form of resistance to an institution that cannot deliver on its promise of upward social mobility for all students" (2009:108).

Although the consistency in the findings between analyses based on the MADICS and those based on national data is reassuring, the advantage of using the MADICS is that it contains a wealth of measures not available in most national datasets. This richness provides a good opportunity to assess many nuanced aspects of the resistance model. It also has a panel longitudinal design that allows for an assessment of whether development from middle school to high school leads to greater opposition toward schooling among blacks than whites. My purpose of employing the MADICS is to extend the assessment of the major tenets of the oppositional culture theory further than national datasets allow. My reason for this is that many (if not most) of the previous studies on the theory fail to yield support for many of its tenets, because the data available in national datasets simply lack the depth necessary to detect patterns that support the framework. The MADICS suggests that one fails to hit the bedrock of oppositional culture even if one digs deeper into the soil of students' cultural disposition toward schooling.

Rethinking the Implications of Marginalization for Educational Engagement

My research on the racial achievement gap began with an assessment of the resistance model. My motivation has been to provide a serious and comprehensive analysis of the oppositional culture theory. Despite the skepticism among some research scientists about the framework's viability, the acceptance of the framework as common sense within the nonacademic community warrants giving the theory such serious consideration. In this process I have uncovered an interesting pattern with implications for the study of social stratification: belonging to a marginalized group does not necessarily result in disengagement from the system of social mobility. This pattern challenges the general notion that actual or perceived marginalization compromises social (or educational) engagement. The consistency of the findings across datasets has led me to question whether there is something particularly unique about the U.S. context—the history of the civil rights movement, for example—that produces this seemingly paradoxical pattern.

The connection between group status—marginalized versus nonmarginalized—and academic investment requires greater inquiry. Specifically, are the patterns observed within the United States a universal indication of how groups marginalized within any given society orient themselves toward education? This question is important for stratification research in general, particularly considering that education is increasingly becoming the primary mechanism for upward mobility in industrialized and postindustrialized countries. Therefore, I examine whether evidence exists for the oppositional culture theory within a non-U.S. context.

Searching for Oppositional Culture beyond the United States

Although the findings I have presented thus far show little support for the resistance model, perhaps something can be learned by assessing the framework outside of the United States. Ogbu (1978) published a comparative assessment of racial and ethnic differences in school achievement in six countries (Britain, India, Israel, Japan, New Zealand, and the United States). However, the cross-cultural dimension of the framework has received little attention, which is surprising given that the theory was intended to provide a cross-cultural framework for understanding how members of marginalized groups orient themselves toward education. Below I provide an assessment of the resistance model within the United Kingdom.[5]

The United Kingdom is an ideal setting in which to examine the resistance model. Ethnic minorities in the United Kingdom have historically faced difficulties in utilizing education to become upwardly mobile. For example, Bernard Coard's (1971) classic study on the educational experience of West Indian children in England identified a process of programmed retardation of black youth in British schools. A report by the Parliamentary Select Committee (1973:38) documents that in 1971, of the more than five thousand youth enrolled in special schools—particularly for "mentally retarded" children—in England and Wales, 70 percent were West Indian. This is startling considering that West Indians comprised less than 1 percent of the national population. Mortimore et al. (1988) found that a large proportion of black youth in the Inner London Education Authority were placed in schooling tracks lower than those prescribed by their test scores rather than the "band one" level that leads to entry into secondary school. Similar to British blacks, Asians in the United Kingdom can be considered as involuntary minorities. Over four-fifths of British Asians are descendants from India, Pakistan, or Bangladesh (British National Statistics 2001). Since India was under British rule until 1947, along with the territories that now comprise Pakistan and Bangladesh, most British Asians belong to a group that was incorporated into the United Kingdom via colonization.

It is not surprising that Britain was one of the six countries highlighted by Ogbu (1978) in his early work to underscore the cross-cultural applicability of his framework. Despite the introduction of state-sponsored comprehensive schools in the late 1960s to allow all students access to postsecondary education (Kerckhoff 2000, 2003), the British education system is more stratified than the U.S. system (Modood 1993). Furthermore, ethnic minorities with similar qualifications to whites have experienced higher rates of unemployment (Smith 1981). Therefore, it is reasonable to expect that ethnic minorities—both Asian and black—within the United Kingdom are less likely to regard education as a mechanism for upward mobility than whites.

I assess the resistance model in the United Kingdom using the Longitudinal Study of Young People in England (LSYPE), which contains data on 13,529 whites, 981 Asians, and 381 blacks born in England between September 1989 and August 1990. The LSYPE was developed to understand the factors affecting young people's transition from the later years of compulsory education, through any subsequent education or training, and into the labor market. Data have been collected annually since the respondents were in year 9 or the equivalent on February 2004.

Figure 5.11 displays findings for ethnic comparisons among youth on four indicators of academic orientation: the frequency with which they read for pleasure, how happy they are at school, the value they attribute to school, and their academic disengagement. Three estimates are shown for each indicator. The first represents how each group differs from whites. The next two estimates show the group differences after accounting for 1) social class (measured according to parents' occupation) and 2) social class and perceived discrimination. The LSYPE measure of discrimination is specific to discrimination based on ethnicity, race, or religion from teachers within the school setting. Recall that indicators for which ethnic minorities are posited to fare worse than whites are labeled on the negative side of the graph and vice versa.

The first three indicators suggest that ethnic minorities do not have lower proschool orientation than whites. The unadjusted estimates show that relative to whites, black youth read for pleasure more often, Asians are hap-

Figure 5.11:   Racial Differences in Academic Orientation among British
                 Adolescents

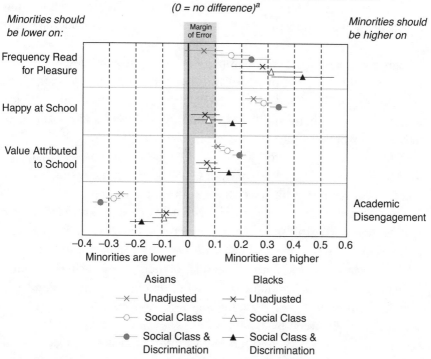

Values represent the difference in means between minorites and whites:
(0 = no difference)[a]

^a The graph displays the estimate (x, circle, or triangle) and standard error (tails). The means for whites (unadjusted) are 4.32, 3.01, 3.30, and 2.28 for *frequency read for pleasure, happy at school, value attributed to schooling,* and *academic disengagement,* respectively. Changes in these means are negligible after adjusting for social class and discrimination. Estimates adjusted for social class illustrate the group differences after accounting for parents' occupation. Discrimination is measured as youths' yes/no response to the following question: "Do you think you have ever been treated unfairly by teachers at your school because of your skin, ethnicity, race, or religion?" Values within the margin of error suggest that the racial difference is not significant at the .05 level. Values were obtained from regression models (OLS). See Appendix C for further details on the analytic plan and Appendix D for a description of measures.

pier at school, and both groups attribute greater value to school. These advantages become greater when the comparison is made between youth with similar socioeconomic background. Doing so shows that Asian youth also read for pleasure more than whites. The third estimate shows that accounting for discrimination further widens ethnic minorities' proschool orientation relative to whites. Since greater perceptions of discrimination lead to declines in the frequency with which youth read for pleasure, happiness at school, and value attributed to schooling, accounting for discrimination will lead to changes in the estimates that favor ethnic minorities because they perceive more discrimination than whites. Estimates for the final indicator suggest that ethnic minorities are *less* disengaged from academics than whites.

Figure 5.12 displays group comparisons on indicators of school resistance. Specifically, I compare the groups on the odds of *not* desiring post–compulsory education and on two indicators that gauge behavioral resistance to schooling: whether a youth's parent(s) was contacted about his/her behavior and whether the youth has ever been suspended or expelled. The bold line is intended to provide a basis by which to compare the estimates for Asians and blacks to those of whites; an estimate of 1.0 would indicate that the group is just as likely as whites to affirm the indicator.

The bars for the first indicator show that both Asians and blacks have lower odds of *not* desiring post–compulsory education than whites. However, only Asians have lower odds than whites on the behavioral indicators of school resistance. Blacks have higher odds of their parents being contacted by their schools for behavioral issues and of ever having been suspended or expelled from school, and these findings remain even when the comparisons are made between blacks and whites with similar socioeconomic status. These findings are consistent with those found among black youth

Figure 5.12:   Odds Ratios for School Resistance among British Adolescents

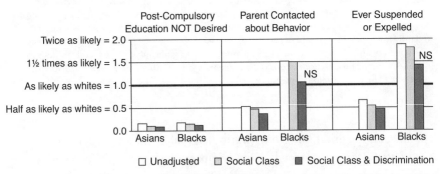

Note: Estimates adjusted for social class illustrate the group differences after accounting for parents' occupation. NS denotes that the racial difference from whites is not significant at the .05 level. Post–compulsory education not desired is youths' yes/no response to whether they want to continue schooling beyond age 16 (reversed coded). See Appendix C for further details on the analytic plan and Appendix D for a description of measures.

within the United States. The third estimate for blacks shows that they do not differ significantly from whites on these indicators after discrimination is taken into account. This suggests that discrimination explains why black youth fare worse on these indicators than whites, which is also consistent with the findings from several studies among U.S. samples that attribute blacks' differential disciplinary rates partially to school practices (for example, Delpit 1995; Ferguson 2000; Lewis 2003; Morris 2005; Tyson 2002, 2003).

Thus far, the analysis of the experience of British youth parallels the findings I presented earlier based on youth within the United States. In addition, I do not find that ethnic minorities in the United Kingdom face greater negative sanctioning for good academic performance than their white counterparts. Figure 5.13 shows that youth who attribute more value to schooling do not have a lower frequency of visits to their home from friends nor of going out with their friends than those who attribute less value to schooling. More importantly, the parallel slopes suggest these findings are

Figure 5.13: The "Acting White" Hypothesis among British Adolescents

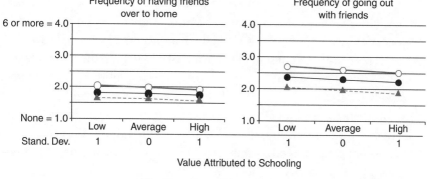

Note: Value attributed to schooling is measured as the average of three items along a 4-point scale (1 = strongly disagree and 4 = strongly agree). Estimates are adjusted for social class (that is, parents' occupation), sex, and youths' perceptions of discrimination by teachers based on skin, ethnicity, race, or religion. The association between value attributed to school and the social standing outcomes are displayed as the average score for youths at two levels of value attributed to school: one standard deviation (or the average difference of each person from the mean of all people on the indicator for value of school) below and above the mean of value of school, passing through the mean of the outcomes. This conveys both youths' averages on the outcomes and the association between the value attributed to school and the outcomes. Slopes do not differ significantly by race (p is not less than .05). See Appendix C for further details on the analytic plan and Appendix D for a description of measures.

the same across race. I also repeated this analysis substituting reading and math achievement for value attributed to schooling. The slopes for each group were completely horizontal on both outcomes, regardless of whether achievement was measured as reading or math.

Chapter Summary

The evidence I present in this chapter relies on three datasets, spans two countries, and consists of thirty-four indicators to assess academic orientation. No single indicator is a perfect measure of the dimension of academic orientation it is intended to capture. Therefore, the basis on which the resistance model is assessed should not rest with the finding for any one particular indicator. Each indicator provides a separate snapshot of academic orientation. Rather, what should be interpreted is the overall pattern that the indicators yield as a whole.

Blacks fared worse than whites on five indicators. First, blacks had a greater difference between their aspired and expected educational attainment than whites, which indicates their greater beliefs in limited opportunities than whites. The findings that I present in Chapter 4 show that these beliefs do not compromise academic investment. Second, blacks within the United States spend less time on academic activities during weekends than whites, although over three-fourths of this difference can be attributed to socioeconomic background. The final three indicators on which blacks fared worse were measures of in-school behavior. Blacks in both the United States and the United Kingdom were suspended from school more than whites, and black parents were more likely to be contacted by school officials about their child's behavior more than their white counterparts within the United Kingdom. However, given that the findings for the other twenty-nine indicators do not support the resistance model, it is unclear whether the findings for in-school behavior reflect *purposeful* resistance to schooling among blacks or differential treatment black children experience in schools as several studies suggest (e.g., Delpit 1995; Ferguson 2000; Lewis 2003; Morris 2005; Tyson 2002, 2003). In sum, the findings from Chapters 3 through 5 suggest that the ineffective (or counterproductive) schooling behaviors partially responsible for blacks' lower achievement relative to whites reflect a lack of academic skill sets necessary for academic success rather than a purposeful culture of resistance to schooling.

The advantage held by blacks relative to whites on many measures presented in this chapter (even prior to adjusting for socioeconomic status) should not be attributed to positive bias in their response patterns. The findings based on time-use data also yield minimal support for the resistance model. Time diaries are less subject to social desirability bias than survey-based estimates of time expenditures (see Hofferth and Sandberg 2001). Substantial methodological research has established the validity and reliability of time diaries (Juster and Stafford 1991). Furthermore, as Ainsworth-Darnell and Downey (1998) eloquently note, determining whether blacks are overestimating or whites are underestimating the value of schooling is a nonresolvable debate. It is quite possible blacks have a greater academic orientation than whites because they base their assessments on a more disadvantaged reference group than whites. If black students overstate their academic orientation because of social desirability, why would they not understate their negative behaviors such as suspensions from school and time on academic activities during the weekends?

Despite the impreciseness of each measure, if a culture of academic resistance permeates through the community of blacks or other caste-like minorities, one would expect at least half (seventeen) of the thirty-four outcomes to yield findings consistent with the resistance model. Such findings would contribute to uncertainty regarding the viability of the framework, as arguments could be made for or against the theory. However, it is unlikely that only five indicators would produce findings consistent with the theory if a pervasive oppositional culture exists among minorities, even if by chance. Nevertheless, many educators and public intellectuals—John McWhorter, Shelby Steele, Bill Cosby—have expressed that black youth must overcome the larger black community's negative orientation toward academics. In Chapter 6 I examine whether blacks who are less connected to their race have better academic orientation toward schooling. In other words, since it is posited that blacks who "act white" tend to be more academically successful, in the next chapter I assess whether distancing oneself from race is an effective strategy for black youth to attain academic success.

6

SHOULD BLACKS BECOME RACELESS
TO IMPROVE ACHIEVEMENT?

In Chapters 3 through 5, I examined various aspects of the oppositional
culture theory. The components that I assessed in those chapters, all major aspects of the framework, were proposed by Ogbu. However, scholars
other than Ogbu have introduced assumptions now associated with the resistance model. Signithia Fordham made nuanced connections about the
black schooling experience that are consistent with the resistance model,
yet distinct enough to comprise a separate theoretical framework. Aspects of
her framework, including fear of "acting white" and the need to separate
oneself from an Ebonics-laden black culture, are now part of the discourse
about the achievement gap in the popular media (promoted by individuals
such as Bill Cosby, John McWhorter, and Shelby Steele).[1] Whereas the
former concept of "acting white" highlights a problem, the latter concept—
separation from black culture or "racelessness"—is more of a prescription
for improving achievement. Fordham (1988, 1996) suggested high-achieving
blacks typically employ a strategy of minimizing "their relationship to the
black community and to the stigma attached to 'blackness'" by adopting a
raceless identity, which enables them to pursue academic success and upward socioeconomic mobility (1988:57).

Interestingly, Fordham's notion of racelessness has received limited consideration from (and influence on) the research community, perhaps due to
the scant empirical evidence provided in support of this phenomenon.
Also, the connection between racelessness and the idea that high-achieving
black students behave "white" has probably led many researchers to con-
flate these concepts. In the study that introduced the "acting white" hypothesis (Fordham and Ogbu 1986), Fordham noted that a black culture
antithetical to mainstream American society, a culture that negatively sanctions those who attempt to perform well in school, was a major reason for
the low academic achievement of black youth. The study documented how
high-achieving blacks often choose between either adopting behaviors that

reinforce black culture and thereby compromise their achievement (for example, by reducing effort, skipping school or cutting classes, using "Ebonics") or risk having their black peers question their legitimacy as members of the black community and accuse them of being "brainiacs," or what Fordham labeled "acting white." However, racelessness is different conceptually from "acting white," as seeking distance from a racial identity is not synonymous to "acting white." This distinction can easily be missed. Both concepts, however, emphasize black youths' cultural frame of reference for understanding their schooling experiences and posit that the academic success of black youths is contingent upon how they orient themselves toward the black community.

In this chapter, I step away from the resistance model to examine whether adopting a raceless persona is an effective strategy for academic success among black youth. Fordham's notion of racelessness seems like an appropriate strategy devised directly to address many of the pitfalls to achieving academic success for black youth posited by the oppositional culture theory. Therefore, an examination of racelessness provides an assessment (albeit indirect) of some assumptions inherent within the resistance model. Below I lay the groundwork for understanding the concept of racelessness.

The Black Fictive Kinship System

Fordham (1988, 1996) provides an anthropological concept useful for understanding blacks' social identity and cultural frame of reference: fictive kinship. She describes fictive kinship as a kinship-like connection between a group of people within a given society not related by blood or marriage yet who maintain a sense of peoplehood or collective social identity resulting from their similar social, political, and/or economic status. The term thus accounts for "the idea of 'brotherhood' and 'sisterhood' of all Black Americans" (Fordham 1988:56).

Being black does not necessarily grant membership into the fictive kinship system. Fordham (1988:56) writes: "One can be black in color, but choose not to seek membership in the fictive kinship system. One can also be denied membership by the group because one's behavior, attitudes, and activities are perceived as being at variance with those thought to be appropriate and group-specific, which are culturally patterned and serve to delineate 'us' from 'them.'" Fordham offers as an example of this cultural exclusivity "the tendency for Black Americans to emphasize *group loyalty* in situations involving conflict or competition with Whites" (1988:56). Thus, membership into the fictive kinship is primarily determined by the larger black community's judgment regarding whether an individual adequately practices the fundamental elements of "black culture."

The implication of Black Fictive Kinship for Schooling

Similar to Ogbu, Fordham (1988, 1996) suggests that the black community's culture of resistance towards education within the United States is a conduit for the academic underachievement of blacks relative to whites. She notes that "high-achieving students find that commitment to the achievement ideology is contested, opposed, and frequently thwarted by the limitations endemic to membership in the Black community" (1996:248). Fordham (1996) argues that school failure is a mechanism by which blacks demonstrate their distinctiveness from dominant "white" culture; black youth deem it necessary to fail since, according to the resistance framework, they must negotiate a social space that negatively sanctions high-achieving students (Fordham and Ogbu 1986). Therefore, it seems logical that distancing oneself from the black community (that is, becoming raceless) should be associated with higher academic achievement.

Numerous behavioral aspects of the black fictive kinship are incompatible with schooling. A reason often given for blacks' lower school achievement is the cultural discontinuity between black families and the institutionalized structure of schools—which value cultural norms of "mainstream" white middle-class society. Fordham (1988, 1996) notes that the collective ethos that characterizes the black fictive kinship system conflicts with the individualistic ethos sanctioned by most schools. She writes that black children who enter school are forced to "unlearn or, at least, to modify their own culturally sanctioned interactional and behavioral styles and adopt those styles rewarded in the school context if they wish to achieve academic success" (1988:55). Recent studies have demonstrated convincingly that blacks experience greater difficulty in converting cultural resources into cultural capital in schools (Lareau and Horvat 1999; Roscigno and Ainsworth-Darnell 1999). Lareau and Horvat (1999) find the possession and activation of capital—both social and cultural—in schools vary by race, which leads to variation between groups in the extent to which they are socially included (that is, behaviors are recognized and legitimated) and excluded (that is, members are marginalized and rebuffed) from the academic setting.

It is important to note that schools sometimes exacerbate the effects of this cultural incompatibility. Lewis (2003) notes schools are racially coded spaces where racialization—the assignment of persons to racial categories with symbols, attributes, and other meanings viewed as primordial to those categories—occurs. She finds racial categorization in schools is not a neutral or benign process, but one imbued with power; racial boundaries are created as persons are simultaneously included and/or excluded from a range of resources and opportunities based on how they are labeled. Perceptions that the black fictive kinship system does not value schooling coupled with the cultural discontinuity between blacks and the structure of schools can result in pejorative symbols/meanings being attached to "blackness," particularly in academic settings.

Numerous studies show the effect of this process (for example, Delpit 1995; Ferguson 2000; Lewis 2003; Morris 2005; Tyson 2002, 2003). Specifically, they find that school personnel place greater emphasis on regulating black children's behavior. Tyson (2002, 2003) finds that although black children begin school very much engaged and achievement-oriented, their positive feelings decline over time because school officials place strong emphasis on transforming many aspects of black children's culture, which inadvertently communicates inadequacy associated with "blackness." Nevertheless, since schools react to students based on perceptions of race, which in turn influences patterns of regulation (Morris 2005:28), blacks who aspire for high achievement must find strategies for circumventing the adverse consequences associated with membership in the black fictive kinship system.

Establishing Cognitive Distance from the Fictive Kinship System: Becoming Raceless

Fordham (1988, 1996) posits that a strategy employed by blacks who wish to maintain academic success and achieve upward socioeconomic mobility is to distance themselves from the fictive kinship system. She notes that in contrast to "students who seek to maintain their identification and affiliation with the indigenous culture, students who assimilate seek to maximize their success potential by minimizing their relationship to the Black community and to the stigma attached to 'blackness'" (1988:57). Fordham (1988, 1996) finds this is typically accomplished through the adoption of a raceless identity, which she defines as a conscious or unconscious effort to disaffiliate from the black fictive kinship system.

A raceless identity is posited to be an important mechanism for blacks in academic settings to circumvent *stereotype vulnerability* (Spencer and Steele

1992; Steele 1988)—the need to consistently disavow group-based negative feedback. Steele (1997) notes increased reminders of barriers and stereotypes compromise academic performance. He refers to this phenomenon as stereotype threat, which occurs when individuals fear their behavior(s) may confirm stereotypes (often negative) about a group to which they belong. Steele and Aronson (1995) found that black college students whose race was not made salient outperformed those whose race was made salient on academic tasks. Thus, stereotype threat has important consequences for identity construction, making self-protection an important focus for black Americans (Crocker and Major 1989; Oyserman, Gant, and Ager 1995). Becoming raceless and committing to the ideology of the dominant social system should diminish the adverse effects of persistent negative stereotypes about black Americans and allow black adolescents to freely adopt and activate mainstream cultural norms.

Although adopting a raceless identity is posited as a strategy for academic success, research suggests racelessness may be detrimental to psychological health. For example, while raceless students modulate their speech and behaviors and disaffiliate from "black" activities sanctioned by the fictive kinship system to gain approval from their teachers, they experience increased psychological isolation and feelings of depression; they find themselves marginalized as a result of being rejected by their black peers but yet not fully accepted by their white high-achieving peers (Fordham and Ogbu 1986; Fordham 1988, 1996; Tatum 1992). As such, many high-achieving blacks perceive academic success as a pyrrhic victory (Fordham 1988; Ogbu 2003). They expend psychological resources, "juggling their school and community personae in order to minimize the conflicts and anxieties generated by the need to interact with the various competing constituencies represented in the school context" (Fordham 1988:80). The anxiety created by this psychological tug-of-war leads them either to sabotage (for example, by exerting little effort or procrastinating) (Ford 1996; Ogbu 2003; Ogbu and Simons 1998) or to camouflage their academic abilities (Fordham and Ogbu 1986). For black Americans, high academic achievement and psychological stress are seen as inextricably commingled.

An Alternative Response: Feeling a Connection to Race

In contrast to the raceless identity discussed by Fordham, several studies suggest adopting a strong racial identity promotes academic success and educational attainment for blacks (see, for instance, Anderson 1988; Edwards and Polite 1992; Weinberg 1977). Children whose parents practice positive racial socialization—who convey the importance of ethnic pride, group af- filiation, self-development, and an awareness of racial barriers and strategies for dealing with them—attain significantly higher grades than those not given these messages (Bowman and Howard 1985). Previous research also shows that academically successful black students express positive racial identities (Sanders 1997). Chavous et al. (2003) find that high racial central- ity (that is, viewing race as important to one's self-definition), strong group pride, and a positive perception of society's regard for blacks are related to positive academic beliefs; their research also demonstrates that a strong group connection is related to discrimination awareness in ways that pro- mote academic success. In fact, Sellers, Chavous, and Cooke (1998) find that ideologies deemphasizing race (that is, that have a humanist orienta- tion) and emphasizing a connection to the mainstream (that is, that en- courage assimilation) are not associated with academic success, though their sample consists of black college students.[2]

A strong racial identity seems to be beneficial for blacks' school achieve- ment for several reasons. First, a strong racial identity is associated with a greater awareness of racial barriers. Cross, Parham, and Helms (1991:328) posit that racial identity—the perception one shares a common racial heri- tage with a group and the extent to which that group serves as a salient refer- ence group—serves as a mechanism "to defend and protect a person from psychological insults, and, where possible, to warn of impending psycho- logical attacks that stem from having to live in a racist society." A positive sense of racial identity and awareness of current or potential racism and discrimination—particularly in education and employment—are impor- tant contributing factors for a positive achievement ethos among many black Americans (Bowman and Howard 1985; Edwards and Polite 1992). According to O'Connor (1997), students aware of such injustices identify their "collective struggle" as the factor that leads them to continue to ex- cel. Sanders (1997) found that among eighth-grade black students—at all achievement levels—who had a high awareness of racial discrimination, there was a tendency to respond to discrimination in ways that were condu- cive rather than detrimental to academic success.

Second, a positive racial identity appears to promote positive mental health. Students displaying greater racial pride have fewer psychological problems (Hemmings 1998). Fordham (1988:81) herself acknowledges that a raceless persona "is marked by conflict and ambivalence." Arroyo and Zigler (1995) likewise suggest that distancing students from their culture breeds psychological problems. In essence, Hemmings (1998) and Arroyo and Zigler (1995) argue that attitudes stressing a positive construction of race and ethnicity are related to positive psychological outcomes, and these positive outcomes can lead to positive educational achievement outcomes. Smith (1989) argues race creates a bond and feeling of peoplehood and that positive regard for one's race is important to racial minorities' psychological health.

Oyserman, Gant, and Ager (1995) note that identity negotiation for black youth should involve the dual task of assembling a positive sense of self while discrediting negative identities attributed to black Americans. However, they posit that in contrast to becoming raceless, cultivating a sense of self as part of kin and community and interacting with the group are important components of black identity that provide a sense of meaning and purpose. These forms of identification also tie the self to normative strategies for goal attainment, particularly school achievement. Therefore, in addition to discrediting negative stereotypes about the black community, it is important for blacks pursuing academic success—while having positive psychological health—to maintain attachment to the fictive kinship system and to associate positive meaning to this membership.

In sum, the child development literature suggests ethnic identity has a protective function enabling black youth to have positive school achievement and psychosocial health (Chavous et al. 2003; Miller 1999; Sanders 1997; Wong, Eccles, and Sameroff 2003). Thus, whereas the racelessness perspective views race as a debilitating factor that inhibits academic success, this perspective posits that blacks with a positive racial/ethnic identity perform better in school because they maintain high self-esteem as a result of their superior ability to manage negative environments and deal with discrimination (see Miller 1999). There is a dearth of research that examines the effectiveness of racelessness as a strategy for maintaining academic achievement/ethos among blacks.[3] Below I explore whether adopting a raceless identity is an effective strategy for attaining various educational outcomes compared to other non-raceless profiles for blacks in high school.

The Implication of Racelessness for Achievement among Black Youth

In collaboration with Kris Marsh (Harris and Marsh 2010), I used the MADICS to assess the racelessness perspective—the notion that racelessness is a strategy employed by black youth who wish to pursue and maintain academic success. The black community's negative orientation toward schooling—an orientation that Fordham argues makes a raceless identity important for individuals striving for academic success—is attributed to the wider "black community" (for further elaboration, see Tyson 2002:1166–1167). This tendency is underscored by Fordham's (1988, 1996) assessment of her framework in a high school on the east coast. Therefore, data from the MADICS is appropriate for testing these claims.

A test of the racelessness perspective is not synonymous with testing the "acting white" hypothesis, which proposes good school performance is denigrated and labeled as "acting white" (see, for example, Fordham and Ogbu 1986 and Tyson, Darity, and Castellino 2005). Instead, this chapter examines whether a raceless persona among blacks in high school is associated with positive academic orientation. In researching this question, I used two pairs of indicators to create five profiles intended to capture blacks' connection to race. The first pair is intended to capture black youths' feelings of similarity to other blacks: 1) I have a strong attachment to other black people and 2) being black is an important reflection of who I am. The second pair is intended to capture feelings of dissimilarity to other blacks: 1) I feel different or unique from other blacks and 2) I feel that being black has little to do with how I feel about myself. Each indicator was dichotomized and coded "yes" if respondents affirmed the statement (agreed or strongly agreed) and "no" if respondents did not affirm the statement (disagreed, strongly disagreed, or neither).

The five profiles are illustrated in Figure 6.1. I am particularly interested in the four definitive profiles depicted in the corners of the cross-tabulation. Specifically, these race profiles describe students who 1) do not affirm any measure (*race neutral or raceless*), 2) affirm both similarity measures and *neither* dissimilarity measure (*race similar*), 3) affirm both dissimilarity measures and *neither* similarity measure (*race dissimilar*), and 4) affirm both the similarity and dissimilarity measures (*race ambivalent*). The final profile, *mild ambivalent*, includes all other possible combinations (that is, those who affirm at least one of each type of measure or affirm only one of the four measures), as supplemental analysis reveals groups within this profile are relatively similar across outcomes. Blacks in the race-neutral profile should have higher academic orientation than those in the other race profiles, indicating that blacks with a raceless persona have a more effective strategy for academic success than their nonraceless counterparts.

The race profiles provide categories that reasonably capture how black youth orient themselves toward their race. To determine whether the profiles

Figure 6.1:   Cross-tabulation of Race Similarity and Race Dissimilarity

Race Similarity Measures

		Affirm None	Affirm One	Affirm Both	Total
	Affirm None	44 Neutral	66	122 Similar	232
Race Dissimilarity Measures	Affirm One	41	358 Mild Ambivalent 81	127	249
	Affirm Both	31 Dissimilar	43	50 Ambivalent	124
	Total	116	190	299	605

are related to racial attitudes in the expected manner, I compare the students in each profile on four indicators that capture attitudes toward race in Figure 6.2. The first two attitudes capture an affective component to race — whether the students are 1) happy to be black and 2) regret being black. The next two attitudes capture students' racial beliefs about shared fate — the extent to which 1) their success helps other blacks and 2) they benefit from the success of other blacks.[4]

Figure 6.2 shows that only 39 percent of black youth in the race-neutral profile and 32 percent of those in the dissimilar profile strongly affirm that they are happy to be black. In contrast, a much greater percentage of blacks in the mild-ambivalent (65 percent), ambivalent (85 percent), and similar (90 percent) profiles report that they are happy to be black. The findings for the next attitude show that the race-neutral profile contains the greatest percentage of blacks who do not strongly disavow that they regret being black (46 percent), followed closely by those in the dissimilar profile. Only 13 percent of blacks in the similar profile report that they regret being black. Over three-fourths of blacks in the race-ambivalent and similar profiles believe that their success will help other blacks, compared to roughly half for blacks in the dissimilar profile and about one-third for those in the race-neutral profile. This pattern is similar for the final indicator of shared fate, with over four-fifths of blacks in the ambivalent and similar profiles believing that they benefit from the success of other blacks. Less than a third of

Figure 6.2: Racial Attitudes across the Race Profiles

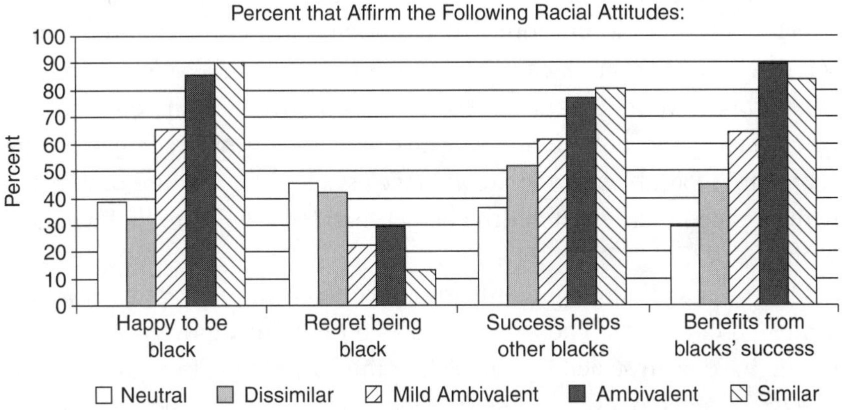

Percent that Affirm the Following Racial Attitudes:

Note: All racial attitudes are measured on a 0–1 scale: I am happy to be black (1 = strongly agree, scored by 68 percent of the sample); I often regret that I am black (1 = strongly disagree, scored by 24 percent of the sample); It will help other blacks if I am successful (1 = agree or strongly agree, scored by 64 percent of the sample); It helps me when other black people are successful (1 = agree or strongly agree, 67 percent of the sample).

those in the neutral profile and less than half in the dissimilar profile believe this to be the case. In sum, it appears that blacks in the neutral profile fare worse on the racial attitude measures, followed closely by those in the dissimilar profile.

To test whether racelessness is an effective strategy for academic success, I use four measures of academic orientation: achievement, educational aspirations, value attributed to schooling, and detachment from schooling. There are two advantages to including the latter three measures in this analysis. First, variations in individual aptitude may preclude some students who give maximum effort and whose academic behaviors resemble those of high achievers in many facets of schooling from being high achievers themselves. Second, high educational aspirations reflect a desire for upward socioeconomic mobility, which is associated with the dominant society. Therefore, since racelessness is posited as a strategy for circumventing negative sanctioning for pursuing goals within a "white" domain, raceless blacks should at least have higher educational aspirations, value school more, and be less detached from school than their nonraceless counterparts.

As discussed earlier, the oppositional culture theory describes the prevailing thought held by the black fictive kinship community regarding upward socioeconomic mobility. Specifically, black Americans believe they will experience barriers to success with regard to future employment and earnings, which leads them to put forth less effort and have lower commitment to schoolwork. However, since racelessness is posited to be a typical strategy by which black youth circumvent the black fictive kinship community's counteracademic culture and negative sanctioning of academic success (Fordham 1988), blacks who are *not* raceless should fare worse on the academic outcomes assessed in this chapter than those who are in the neutral profile.

Figure 6.3 contains the comparisons between the race profiles on the academic outcomes. The average scores on the outcomes for the neutral profile have been scaled to zero so that the bars can be interpreted as the average distance between these students and those in the nonneutral profiles. The findings show that blacks in the nonneutral profiles have higher achievement than those in the neutral profile. They also have higher educational aspirations and attribute more value to school than those in the neutral profile. This pattern extends to findings for profile differences in detachment from schooling; all students who have nonneutral profiles are less detached from schooling than students in the race neutral profile. In sum, the findings in Figure 6.3 suggest that adopting a raceless persona is not an effective strategy for academic success. In a separate set of analyses, I compared the race profiles across numerous other outcomes of academic orientation contained within the MADICS. However, there were no significant differences between the profiles, further suggesting that adopting a raceless persona is not an effective strategy for academic success.

Another manner in which to assess the racelessness perspective is to determine whether the aforementioned racial attitudes relate to academic orientation. If a connection to being black has adverse consequences for academic orientation, then blacks who are happy about their race should score lower on indicators of academic engagement. The same should be true about blacks who perceive that a relationship exists between their success and the success of other blacks. However, the findings in Table 6.1 suggest that this is not the case.

Table 6.1 shows that the only racial attitude that is associated with declines in achievement, educational aspirations, and value attributed to school is regret for being black. Feeling happy to be black and beliefs of shared fate are associated with increases in these outcomes. In contrast, re-

Figure 6.3: Academic Orientation by Race Profiles *Relative* to Youth in the Race-Neutral Profile

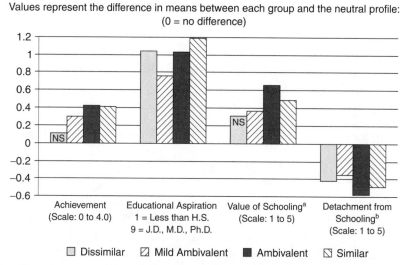

Values represent the difference in means between each group and the neutral profile:
(0 = no difference)

Achievement (Scale: 0 to 4.0)	Educational Aspiration 1 = Less than H.S. 9 = J.D., M.D., Ph.D.	Value of Schooling[a] (Scale: 1 to 5)	Detachment from Schooling[b] (Scale: 1 to 5)

☐ Dissimilar   ▨ Mild Ambivalent   ■ Ambivalent   ◩ Similar

Note: The estimates are unadjusted. The means for youth in the neutral profile are 2.51, 6.92, 3.77, and 2.26 for achievement, educational aspirations, value of schooling, and detachment from schooling, respectively. NS denotes not significant at the .05 level.

[a] Value of schooling is measured as the average of youths' responses to the following questions on a 5-point scale (5 = strongly agree): 1) I have to do well in school if I want to be a success in life, 2) getting a good education is the best way to get ahead in life for the kids in my neighborhood, 3) achievement and effort in school lead to job success later on, and 4) education really pays off in the future for people like me.

[b] Detachment from schooling is measured as the average of youths' responses to the following questions on a 5-point scale (5 = strongly agree): 1) schooling is a waste of time, 2) I don't really care about schooling, 3) schooling is not so important for kids like me.

gret about being black is the only racial attitude associated with an increase in detachment from school; youth who affirm the other racial attitudes are less detached from school than those who do not affirm those attitudes. Overall, feeling happy to be black, believing that one's success helps other blacks, and believing that one benefits from the success of other blacks are associated with greater academic orientation. Even more telling is that blacks who believe that they benefit from the success of other blacks—a belief that clearly requires feeling a connection to other blacks—fare better on all four measures of academic orientation than those who do not hold this belief.

Table 6.1: The Implication of Racial Attitudes for Academic Orientation

	Averages for Youth Who:		
Achievement	Do not affirm	Affirm	Difference
Happy to be black	2.70	2.86	.16
Regret being black	2.89	2.57	−.32
It will help other blacks if I am successful	2.69	2.87	.18
It helps me when other black people are successful	2.61	2.90	.29
Educational Aspirations	Do not affirm	Affirm	Difference
Happy to be black	7.54	7.84	.30
Regret being black	7.84	7.46	−.38
It will help other blacks if I am successful	7.39	7.93	.54
It helps me when other black people are successful	7.40	7.90	.50
Value of School	Do not affirm	Affirm	Difference
Happy to be black	3.90	4.26	.36
Regret being black	4.27	3.75	−.52
It will help other blacks if I am successful	3.97	4.25	.28
It helps me when other black people are successful	3.83	4.30	.47
Detachment from School	Do not affirm	Affirm	Difference
Happy to be black	2.18	1.75	−.43
Regret being black	1.76	2.31	.55
It will help other blacks if I am successful	2.04	1.80	−.24
It helps me when other black people are successful	2.15	1.76	−.39

Note: Raw means are displayed. All differences are statistically significant ($p < .05$). Estimates that show declines in the outcome are in *italics*. Achievement ranges from 0 to 4.0. Educational aspirations ranges from 1 = less than high school to 9 = J.D., M.D., Ph.D. Value of school and detachment from school range from 1 = strongly disagree to 5 = strongly agree.

Chapter Summary

The goal of this chapter was to determine whether blacks with a raceless identity—those with weak or no attachment to their race—have better educational outcomes than blacks who do not have a raceless identity. Specifically, I examined whether the connection black adolescents have to their race is associated with school achievement, educational aspirations, value attributed to schooling, and detachment from schooling. In addition, I examined whether blacks' affective feelings toward their race and their beliefs about the extent to which their success helps other blacks (or to which they benefit from the success of other blacks) have implications for the aforementioned outcomes.

Findings do not show that racelessness is an effective strategy for achieving favorable academic outcomes among black youth. Blacks in the race-neutral profile do not have higher achievement than those in the other race profiles. Blacks in the ambivalent and similar profiles have higher achievement, educational aspirations, attribute more value to schooling, and are less detached from schooling than those in the race-neutral profile. Affective feelings toward being black and feelings of having a shared fate with other blacks relate to the outcomes differently than the racelessness perspective posits. For example, it seems that blacks who are happy to be black and believe that a connection exists between their own success and the success of other blacks have a more favorable academic orientation than those who do not affirm these feelings and beliefs about their race. Moreover, feelings of regret about being black are associated with lower academic orientation. These findings are consistent with several studies that find a positive or strong racial identity is associated with better academic outcomes (see, for example, Bowman and Howard 1985; Edwards and Polite 1992; Sanders 1997; Sellers, Chavous and Cooke 1998).

Several studies provide possible explanations for the pattern found in this chapter. For example, McCreary, Slavin, and Berry (1996) find that blacks with high racial identity are more successful at coping with stress and have lower rates of participation in problem behaviors, both of which can be helpful in academic domains. Wong, Eccles, and Sameroff (2003) find high ethnic connectedness diminishes the adverse effect perceived discrimination has on black students' beliefs of self-competence, school achievement, and perceptions of friends' positive school characteristics. They also find ethnic connectedness diminishes the positive effect perceived discrimination has on problem behaviors. Smith and Lalonde (2003), whose study examined black youth in a Canadian context, also find that a strong affinity to race among blacks is psychologically protective.

Meanings attached to identities can be both self-ascribed and designated by others (Gecas and Burke 1995). Burke (1991) notes individuals experience stress when there is inconsistency between one's self-ascribed and "other-ascribed" identities. A raceless identity is an attempt to take control of one's identity by resisting the other's altercasting; within an educational context, it is a disidentification from the black fictive kinship system (and problems endemic to the system) in an attempt to construct a positive identification of someone academically oriented. As such, it can be described as a "Not Me"—a self-disidentification enacted by individuals to resist identities imputed by others (McCall 2003). However, the findings in this chapter suggest racelessness operates in the same manner discussed by Pyke and Johnson (2003), who found that Asian American women who distanced themselves from the stigmatized image of Asian women as subservient reinforced the notion that Asian women are inferior. In contrast, rather than distancing themselves from the black fictive kinship, blacks in the race-similar profile seem to be rehabilitating their black identity to include the domain of achievement in the fictive kinship system. This suggests it is possible for black youth to enact a "Not Me" identity that disidentifies with black academic failure without compromising their identities as members of the black fictive kinship system.

Oyserman, Gant, and Ager (1995) provide a framework of identity development that accounts for the experiences of youth who must struggle to find a means of conceptualizing plausible paths toward academic success in a context unfavorable to members of their group. They propose a triadic identity structure in which individuals connect the self to the group, find a path toward academic achievement as a group member, and make sense of stereotypes and structural limitations imposed by one's group membership. Otherwise, academic success may be viewed as co-opted by the white middle class. The finding that blacks in the raceless identity profile fare worse than those in the race-ambivalent and race-similar profiles on the outcomes in this chapter suggests it is possible for blacks simultaneously to maintain some connection to other blacks and have favorable academic characteristics. Research by Horvat and Lewis (2003) and Datnow and Cooper (1997) suggests black peer groups are not monolithic; they allow space to affirm academic identity and racial identity.

It is important to note that although a strong racial identity appears to enhance schooling outcomes, a black nationalistic ideology, which emphasizes that the black experience is unique and that blacks should control their own destiny with minimal input from or contact with other groups, can be maladaptive. Studies by Sellers et al. (1998) and Oyserman et al. (2003) find that a more multicultural or minority identity—an ideology that emphasizes similarities between oppressed groups, recognition that one's in-group must overcome obstacles, and a positive connection to the in-group and larger society—is more adaptive for academic success.

The findings presented in Chapters 3 through 6 suggest that shifting the focus away from beliefs about opportunity and from the belief that a purposeful antiacademic orientation exists among blacks would lead to a more fruitful discussion about the racial achievement gap. They also show that children belonging to a marginalized group do not necessarily adopt a culture antithetical toward education, which raises a key question: If negative beliefs about school as a means for upward mobility are inconsequential for achievement, and blacks do not have a decidedly more negative academic orientation than whites, why do proponents of the theory report observing an "oppositional" culture among black students? In Chapter 5, I suggested that whereas the observations of these proponents might be accurate—since black youths' lack of high achievement suggests that they do engage in counterproductive schooling behaviors—their interpretations of black students' behaviors are not accurate. Essentially, kids do not want to fail. An approach that leads to failure could be independent of the intent to fail. In Chapter 7, I discuss why a culture of purposeful school resistance is not the origin of the racial achievement gap and cannot be responsible for the gap observed among adolescents. I also discuss where educators and policy makers should focus their attention in lieu of oppositional culture.

7

SHIFTING THE FOCUS AWAY FROM CULTURE
AND TOWARD PRIOR SKILLS

Perhaps the most important component of the resistance model is the portion that attributes racial difference in achievement to racial differences in students' observable academic culture. Despite the scientific evidence that blacks do not have lower academic orientation than whites, proponents of the resistance model remain unconvinced. They point to observable concrete behavioral aspects of being a student, such as effort, attentiveness, comportment, and other indicators of academic motivation, which appear to be worse among black students. The lack of alternative explanations and a counterproductive behavioral approach to schooling that repeatedly leads to poor achievement makes it easy to interpret black students' academic behavior as a purposeful resistance to schooling. Even among research scholars, the focus has been on examining whether blacks have a culture of underachievement. The tenet of the framework receiving the most research attention has been whether blacks equate academic success with "acting white" (see, for example, Akom 2003; Carter 2005; Cook and Ludwig 1997; Fordham and Ogbu 1986; Harris 2006; Horvat and Lewis 2003; O'Connor 1999; Tyson, Darity, and Castellino 2005).

The notion that blacks' poor achievement stems from behaviors observed within the classroom suffers from a flawed assumption. It assumes that black youth have the academic skills to be successful but choose to not employ them in favor of academic failure. What is often forgotten is that both learning and achievement are longitudinal and complex processes; we cannot jump to an examination of adolescence, investigate achievement gaps and their immediate correlates, and then arrive at the answers to inequality, because achievement is a cumulative process. Although some educators might point to what appear to be negative attitudes toward learning among blacks, previous research suggests that prior achievement plays a central role in the development of academic attitudes and behaviors early in the schooling process (Tyson 2002). To the extent oppositional behaviors are driven by prior academic skills, failure to account for prior skills could lead scholars and laypeople alike to overestimate the effects of behaviors.

In collaboration with Keith Robinson (Harris and Robinson 2007), I examined whether the resistance model suffers from omitted variable bias—a term used to describe a key component missing from a theory, which if taken into account would lead to different results. In that study, we argued that oppositional culture as a theory cannot adequately explain racial differences in achievement if it is not adapted to account for how achievement and behaviors are intertwined over the course of a student's educational trajectory (from elementary school through high school). Therefore, omitting prior skills from the story can lead to erroneous interpretations about students' motivation for academic success. Since this had not been considered prior to our study, it remained unclear to what extent students' school behavioral responses to beliefs about the system of social mobility explain racial differences in achievement or even predict achievement once prior skills are taken into account. We argued that hypothesized and estimated effects of oppositional school behaviors might be overestimated.

The omission of prior skills creates both a methodological and conceptual gap within the resistance model literature. From a methodological standpoint, research on current skills or achievement deficiencies generally accounts for past academic skills. However, within the context of the oppositional culture theory, the emphasis is placed on culture, or what I have been referring to as academic orientation. Past quantitative studies attempt to establish whether black students enact resistance to education more than whites by conducting black-white comparisons on a series of attitudes and behaviors. Blacks' advantage on negative schooling attitudes or behaviors reflects a finding consistent with the theory. Another common strategy uses various analytic approaches to assess whether blacks experience a greater social cost than whites for high academic achievement. Thus, studies on oppositional culture test for the existence of a culture of resistance against schooling among blacks rather than the extent to which an oppositional culture explains the achievement gap. Prior academic skills often do not enter the conceptual equation because achievement generally does not serve as a measure of culture; the spotlight is on the contextual climate that promotes a culture of underachievement rather than achievement itself.

The oppositional culture theory is often tested using samples of students in high school. From a conceptual standpoint, this makes sense because of the assumptions about the role of perceptions students may hold about the opportunity structure in relation to race. Students in high school are expected to have a more developed understanding of the opportunities available to members of their racial/minority group within the system of social mobility (see, for example, Ainsworth-Darnell and Downey 1998; Carter 2005; Cook and Ludwig 1997; Fordham and Ogbu 1986; Mickelson 1990; Ogbu 2003). It is this understanding that is purported to be the basis for the emergence of · an oppositional culture among blacks. Therefore, group comparisons of beliefs about the opportunity structure are often conducted among adolescents because studying resistance during this stage fits within the assumptions underlying the resistance model. However, the failure of these studies to grasp the importance of prior skills reflects a conceptual gap in the framework.

I illustrate this proposed adjustment to the resistance model in Figure 7.1. The Figure shows that prior skills are related to race (racial groups differ in their academic skills during preadolescence) and that behaviors during adolescence are endogenous to—or determined by—skill levels prior to adolescence (represented by path i). Given its immediate proximity to achievement, it is understandable that the "effect" of schooling behaviors—denoted by path h—receives much of the attention. However, the focus in previous research on beliefs about the opportunity structure and the sanctioning of peers for good achievement has resulted in a lack of examination of path h after accounting for paths i and j. Students' skill level prior to adolescence might explain a greater proportion of the racial achievement gap and reduce the emphasis that has been placed on the effect of schooling behaviors on achievement. For example, the portion of the achievement gap attributed to racial differences in schooling behaviors might actually be driven by preadolescent skill sets.[1] This is not to say that early skill deficits lead to later skill deficits, but that early skill deficits severely compromise the viability of the resistance model.

It is important to account for students' academic skill levels prior to high school for two reasons. First, as observed by Karolyn Tyson (2002) in a study of two all-black elementary schools, schooling experiences—particularly early achievement outcomes—play a central role in developing schooling behaviors. She notes that "children's negative statements about school reflected a desire to avoid further experiences of failure" (2002:1184). Tyson shows that negative schooling behaviors among some adolescents reflect the masking of other feelings that can result from poor school achievement, such as fear, hurt, or embarrassment, and she provides narratives of the onset of this pro-

Figure 7.1: Framework Revisited III: The Inclusion of Prior Skills in the Resistance Model

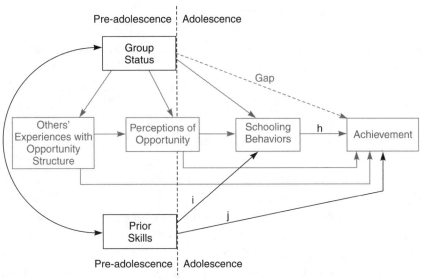

cess. Second, research shows students begin to sort into cognitive trajectories as early as first grade (Entwisle and Alexander 1992; Fryer and Levitt 2004). Farkas and his colleagues find that most students who read below grade level by the end of the third grade read so far below grade level by middle and high school that they have difficulty with the curriculum (Farkas 1993, 1996; Farkas et al. 1990). This finding suggests that the acquisition of academic skills is a cumulative process.

It is not surprising that blacks display less productive schooling behaviors than whites, even if they believe education is important for future success. A student with strong academic preparation should have better study skills and engage academic material more efficiently than those with weaker preparation. Thernstrom and Thernstrom (2003) discuss how black students are often bewildered by their homework and classroom lessons. They note black youth often lack the prerequisite skills to efficiently complete academic tasks and as a result fall further behind. Similarly, Ogbu's (2003) own data suggest that skill deficiencies contribute to a lack of effort. He recalls that after asking students why some blacks did not work hard, one student responded that "some black students believed that it was cute to be dumb." Obgu reported that "when pressed for an explanation, [the student] said that it was because they couldn't do well and that they didn't want anyone else to do well" (Ogbu 2003:25). However, Ogbu ignored preadolescent skill development in all of his studies.

Ogbu (2003) also notes that countereducational attitudes expressed by some black students are not entirely free from self-doubt about abilities to succeed. He described several instances in which black students did not enroll in honors and AP classes because they were afraid that they would not succeed. However, Ogbu still did not treat prior skills as a central component of his framework. Therefore, preadolescent academic skills have received far less attention than the findings presented in this chapter suggest they warrant. The accounts described above do not validate the notion that blacks are eager to resist schooling. Instead, they suggest some black students may fail to try at times because they lack the necessary skills to succeed. Interpreting this as deliberate school resistance seems unproductive.

In this chapter, I present research on the contention that prior skill levels are an important omission to the resistance model (Harris and Robinson 2007). The analyses I offer assess whether the counterproductive behaviors often labeled as oppositional in high school explain a greater proportion of racial differences in twelfth-grade achievement than students' academic skills prior to high school. I also display findings for the extent to which schooling behaviors remain important for predicting future achievement after accounting for students' prior skills. Accounting for pre–high school skills seems important for a theory in which the behavior-achievement link during high school is a key component. The analyses are from the first three waves of the data from the National Education Longitudinal Study of 1988 (NELS), in which the students were in grades 8 (1988), 10 (1990), and 12 (1992). The sample consists of 5,950 whites, 764 blacks, and 597 Asian Americans (n = 7,311).[2] Whites, blacks, and Asian Americans represent three groups that are perceived by educators and the general public in distinctly different ways. Whereas blacks are regarded as oppositional toward education, Asian Americans are often dubbed the model minority. These three groups also correspond to the dominant, involuntary, and voluntary groups in the United States as defined by the oppositional culture theory.

Difference in Schooling Behavior by Race

Figure 7.2 displays racial differences on six indicators of schooling behavior assessed when students were in the tenth grade. The top panel shows findings for three counterproductive schooling behaviors: teachers' estimates of the frequency with which the student is disruptive in class, the number of times the student was in trouble for not following school rules during the first half of the school year, and students' estimate of whether other students see them as a troublemaker.[3] The bottom panel shows findings for three productive schooling behaviors: the amount of time youths spend on homework each week out of school, teachers' view of whether the student usually works hard for good grades, and teachers' estimate of how often the student is attentive in class.[4]

Asian Americans score lower on two of the three counterproductive schooling behaviors (blacks score lower on being a troublemaker) and engage in all three productive schooling behaviors more than whites and blacks. This finding supports the contention that voluntary minorities are more academically engaged than members of the dominant and involuntary minority groups. Blacks score lower on two of the three counterproductive schooling behaviors than whites—in getting into trouble for not following rules and being a troublemaker. However, they engage in productive schooling behaviors *less* than whites and Asian Americans. Specifically,

Figure 7.2:   Schooling Behaviors among Whites, Asians, and Blacks: NELS

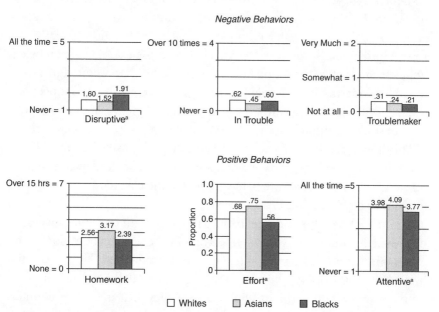

Note: Estimates are unadjusted. The differences between all of the bars are statistically significant.
   [a] Based on teachers' report.

black youth spend less time on homework, and teachers report that they are more disruptive and less attentive in class and that they put forth less effort for good grades.

Although the findings in Figure 7.2 are consistent with the resistance model, they should not be considered contradictory to those presented in Chapter 5 for several reasons. First, the findings in Figure 7.2 do not account for students' social-class background. Since five of the six indicators capture behaviors *within* the classroom, I decided to display the unadjusted group averages. Teachers and other school personnel typically do not cognitively adjust for social class when they develop perceptions about students based on their observations within the classroom or school. I believe it is important to display these findings because they lend credibility to teachers' real-time assessments of the schooling behaviors of whites, Asian Americans, and blacks. This approach also helps to clarify the incongruence between the findings in Chapter 5 that blacks do not have lower academic orientation than whites and the observations and conclusions many teachers make about students.

Second, three of the four behavioral measures on which blacks fare worse than whites and Asian Americans are teacher-reported: *disruptive, effort,* and *attentiveness.* Recall from the discussion in Chapter 5 that numerous studies find school personnel place greater emphasis on regulating black children's behavior (see, for example, Delpit 1995; Ferguson 2000; Lewis 2003; Morris 2005; Tyson 2002, 2003). Therefore, the extent to which blacks hold less productive schooling behaviors on the teacher-reported measures might be overestimated. As mentioned above, it is unrealistic to expect that teachers will cognitively adjust for social-class background in their observations of students and might therefore be conflating race and social class.[5]

Third, whereas the indicators used in Chapter 5 assessed general academic orientation, five of the six schooling behaviors displayed in Figure 7.2 are indicators that capture behaviors *within* the classroom (homework is the lone exception). A student can have a favorable academic orientation toward schooling—for example, believe it is important for future success or not view education as a "white" endeavor—but yet display behaviors in the classroom that could be interpreted as counterproductive. Thus, given the findings from Chapters 3 through 6, which suggest that black children are no more oppositional toward school than whites, blacks' greater counterproductive schooling behaviors displayed in Figure 7.2 should not be interpreted as *deliberate* academic resistance. Rather, the question that should be asked is whether teachers are indentifying *false positive* resistance to schooling—counterproductive schooling behaviors viewed as deliberate academic resistance when the poor results are actually driven by other factors, such as fear of failure, poor academic preparation, or lack of student/ study skills.

Schooling Behaviors versus Prior Skills

Before we can attribute the racial achievement gap to racial differences in schooling behaviors, we must consider differences in prior skills as an alternative explanation. The findings in Figure 7.3, which show the unadjusted achievement for whites, Asian Americans, and blacks, suggest that prior academic skills cannot be eliminated as the source of the racial achievement gap during adolescence. Specifically, the top panel shows that blacks have lower test scores in reading and math, and have lower grades than whites and Asian Americans prior to entering high school.[6] Thus, blacks' lower academic skills prior to high school might be a major factor in their lower achievement toward the end of their K-12 schooling career, which is shown in the bottom panel of Figure 7.3. Below I examine whether schooling behaviors account for a greater proportion of the racial achievement gap than prior academic preparation.

Figures 7.2 and 7.3 show, respectively, that black youth have more counterproductive schooling behaviors during high school and lower levels of academic skills prior to high school. Which of these factors accounts most fully for the racial achievement gap observed toward the end of the K-12 schooling cycle? Even if we assume that blacks' greater counterproductive behaviors stem from deliberate academic resistance, how consequential are these behaviors for blacks' lower academic achievement compared to whites?

Figure 7.4 presents findings for paths *h* and *j* in Figure 7.1. All findings account for students' socioeconomic background factors (family income, parental education, and family structure) and youths' sex. As used in this chapter, then, the label "unadjusted" indicates that the estimate represented by the first bar does not account for students' schooling behaviors or prior academic skills. Since my interest is in the achievement gap, white students' achievement is scaled to zero so that achievement for Asian Americans and blacks can be interpreted as relative to whites; thus, the bars represent achievement gaps.

The top panel displays the findings for reading achievement. The first bar for reading shows that blacks have lower reading scores than whites. After

Figure 7.3:   Prior Skills and Twelfth-Grade Achievement among Whites, Asians, and Blacks: NELS

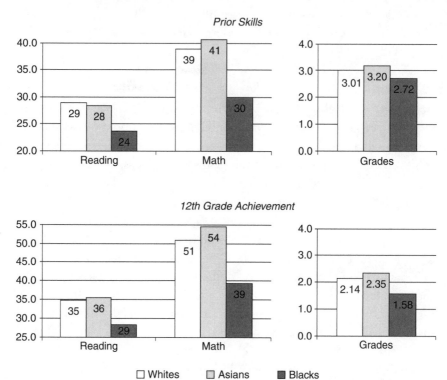

Note: Estimates are unadjusted. Reading and math test scores are the item response theory (IRT) scores from standardized tests that were administered to students in the NELS. The IRT scores for an individual reflect an estimate of the number of items that person would have answered correctly if s/he had answered all of the items that appeared in any form of the test (NELS:88 Psychometric Report). The IRT model uses the pattern of right, wrong, and omitted responses to the items in a test form, and also takes into account the difficulty of each item, the degree of discrimination required to respond to it, and its "guessability," to place each test taker at a particular point on a continuous ability scale (NELS:88 Psychometric Report). The objective of the IRT model is to put the scores each student records from grades 8 to 12 (in each subject) on the same vertical scale so that the scores can have a consistent interpretation. Grades in twelfth grade are not GPAs; they are combined grades in reading, math, science, and social studies. Although this measure ranges from 0 to 4.0, it is not equivalent to grade point average. All racial differences are significant at the .05 level with the exception of the Asian-white gaps in reading.

accounting for schooling behaviors, the black disadvantage in reading declines from 4.8 to 4.18 points. Thus, schooling behaviors explain only 13 percent of the black-white achievement gap in reading. In contrast, accounting for reading skills prior to high school reduces the gap to 1.34 points, a 72 percent decline from the original gap of 4.8 points. The next bar shows

Figure 7.4: Percent of Twelfth-Grade Achievement Gaps Attributable to Schooling Behaviors and Prior Skills: NELS

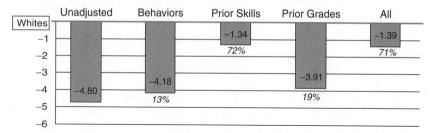

Reading Achievement

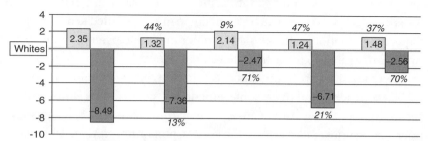

Math Achievement

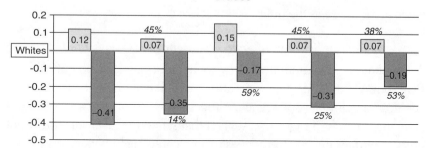

Grades

☐ Asians   ▣ Blacks

Note: "Unadjusted" refers to schooling behaviors and prior skills; all bars show estimates after accounting for parents' education, family income, family structure, and youths' sex. Values were obtained from regression models (OLS) using robust standard errors. Behaviors represent those displayed in Figure 7.2. All measures of achievement (twelfth-grade reading, math, and grades, and prior skills and grades) are the same measures of achievement displayed in Figure 7.3. All estimates displayed are statistically significant at the .05 level.

that prior skills explains a greater proportion of the black-white achievement gap in reading (19 percent) than schooling behaviors even when prior skills are measured as previous grades. In sum, whereas schooling behaviors account for 13 percent of the black-white achievement gap in reading, prior test scores and grades explain 72 percent and 19 percent of the gap, respectively. Bars are not displayed for Asian Americans because they do not differ from whites in reading achievement.

The second panel in Figure 7.4 shows the same analysis for math achievement. The findings with regard to the black-white gap in math are nearly identical to those discussed above for reading achievement. The findings suggest that Asian Americans hold an advantage in math achievement relative to whites; analysis of this gap yields a different pattern than the one observed for the black-white gap. Specifically, whereas nearly half of Asian Americans' advantage in math (44 percent) can be attributed to their schooling behaviors, prior math skills account for only nine percent of the Asian American–white gap in math achievement. However, prior grades explain 47 percent of this gap. Thus, whereas prior test scores are more important for blacks' reading and math achievement, test scores are less important in accounting for Asian Americans' advantage in math than behaviors and prior grades; prior grades explain the greatest proportion of Asian Americans' advantage in math relative to whites, followed by high school behaviors. The findings in the bottom panel show that these patterns are similar even when grades serve as the outcome for achievement.

Are the Implications of Schooling Behaviors Overestimated?

A longstanding assumption held by many educators and parents alike is that youths' schooling behaviors are a major determinant of academic achievement during adolescence. Although this assumption seems reasonable, the findings in Figure 7.4 suggest that schooling behaviors might not be as important for achievement as many people might believe. As I mentioned above, it is difficult to cognitively adjust for factors when one is making mental calculations about the link between two indicators—which in this case are schooling behaviors and achievement. Thus, the implications that youths' schooling behaviors have for their achievement might be spurious and should be assessed only after accounting for students' prior skills.

The extent to which behavioral "effects" decline once prior skills are taken into account should reflect their overestimation in determining high school achievement. A large decline in behavioral effects would have two major implications for the resistance model. First, it would highlight the need to deemphasize oppositional behaviors as a mechanism for poor achievement during high school. Second, it would suggest that students' pre–high school skills should be incorporated into explanations of racial achievement differences observed at the end of K-12 schooling.

In Figure 7.5, I show how the implications that schooling behaviors during high school have for achievement change when prior skills are taken into account. The indicators are labeled on the side of their expected effects. For example, the first three indicators—disruptive, in trouble, and troublemaker—are labeled on the negative side of the figure, as increases in these factors should lead to declines in achievement. The findings show a predictable association between behavioral measures and reading achievement. Prior to accounting for prior skills, increases in being disruptive, in trouble, and a troublemaker lead to declines in reading scores ($b = -1.362$, $-.132$, and $-.805$, respectively), and reading scores increase as students spend more time on homework ($b = .994$), exert more effort ($b = 1.189$), and are more attentive in class ($b = 1.567$).

The estimates for both sets of schooling behaviors decline substantially after adjusting for prior skills. Specifically, the decline in reading achievement associated with a one-unit increase on the scale that measures disruptiveness changes from nearly -1.40 to -0.45 points after adjusting for prior skills, a decline of 67 percent. Thus, whereas the unadjusted estimate suggests that a student who scores a zero on the disruptiveness scale has a 5.4 point advantage in reading over one who scores a 4 on disruptiveness (1.36×4 on the scale), accounting for prior skills yields a 1.8 point separation between the least and most disruptive students (0.45×4 on the scale). Although these estimates seem small, recall that the black-white gap on the NELS measure for reading achievement is 4.8 after accounting for social class (it is 6.5 points prior to accounting for social class). With regard to the other schooling behaviors, adjusting for prior skills lead to declines in behavioral effects that range from 50 percent to 94 percent (the estimate for *in trouble* becomes nonsignificant).

The analysis in Figure 7.5 was also conducted for math achievement and grades (Harris and Robinson 2007). Accounting for prior skills led to declines in behavioral effects that range from 54 percent to 72 percent for math achievement. Specifically, whereas all behavioral effects were significantly associated with math achievement, once students' prior skills were taken into account, the negative effects for being disruptive, in trouble, and

Figure 7.5: Portion of Behavioral "Effects" on Reading Attributable to Prior Skills: NELS

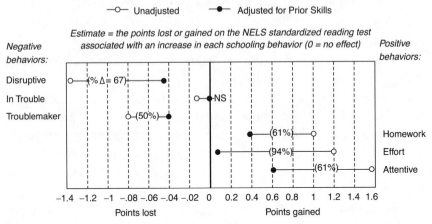

Notes: Values in parentheses represent the percent decline in the estimates after accounting for prior skills (reading, math, and grades). The unadjusted estimate only refers to prior skills; all estimates account for parents' education, family income, family structure, and youths' sex. Estimates were obtained from regression models (OLS) using robust standard errors. With the exception of NS (not significant), all estimates are significant at the .05 level.

a troublemaker declined by 63 percent, 54 percent, and 58 percent, respectively, and the positive effects of homework, effort, and attentiveness declined by 72 percent, 71 percent, and 71 percent, respectively. This pattern was also observed for students' overall grades, for which the declines in behavioral effects net of prior skills ranged from one-third to nearly three-quarters. The percent decline in behavioral effects after controlling for students' prior skills can be interpreted as the portion of the behavioral effects attributable to students' lack of skills before entering high school.

I also examined whether schooling behaviors are determined by the skills students acquire prior to high school (Harris and Robinson 2007) and found that increases in test scores and grades prior to high school were significantly associated with declines in the negative schooling behaviors and an increase in the positive schooling behaviors during high school. Specifically, increases in prior skills are associated with declines in the frequency of disruptive behaviors, being in trouble, and being recognized as a troublemaker, and increases in the time students spend on homework, their effort level, and in-class attentiveness. The implications of these results are best understood if coupled with results from Figure 7.5. Taken together, they suggest behaviors during high school are determined by the skills students have prior to entering high school.

Does This Pattern Exist at Earlier Stages of Development?

Thus far my focus in this chapter has been on testing an important assumption of the oppositional culture theory on middle and high school students, since the framework is usually applied to adolescents. The aforementioned findings could be critiqued for excluding students' academic experiences prior to this stage of their lives. Although this omission is partially addressed by estimating the implication of eighth-grade achievement for tenth-grade schooling behaviors, it is unclear whether the pattern described above also applies to earlier stages of students' academic careers.

I examine whether the patterns presented in this chapter among adolescents hold during preadolescence using time diary data from the Child Development Supplement (CDS) to the Panel Study of Income Dynamics (PSID). Specifically, I assess whether the achievement of middle school students is determined more by their skills acquired prior to middle school than their schooling behaviors during middle school. These results are presented in Figures 7.6 and 7.7. I first display findings for the amount of time youth spend on academic activities in middle school, followed by their reading and math achievement in middle school and their reading and math skills prior to middle school.[7] Achievement is measured as students' scores on the Woodcock-Johnson achievement test. As noted earlier, these results are presented without accounting for socioeconomic background factors.

The findings in the top panel of Figure 7.6 show that racial differences exist between the schooling behaviors of black and white students. Specifically, black youth spend slightly less time on homework, educational activities, and leisure reading per day than whites. Since the results represent averages, the values for the time youth spend on academic activities will appear relatively small. It is important to remember that 1) the averages are not conditional upon each individual student having engaged in the activity and 2) the averages assume a consistent pattern of behavior. Any particular daily average of time spent on an activity could reflect numerous behavioral patterns. For example, a daily average of 10 minutes could reflect the behavior of a student that engages in an activity twice a week for 35 minutes or once a week for 70 minutes.

Nevertheless, black youth spend less time — on average — than their white counterparts on academic activities during middle school, which might explain black children's lower achievement in both reading and math than whites displayed in the bottom panel of Figure 7.6. However, black children also have lower skills in both reading and math prior to entering middle school than whites. Therefore, it is possible that the racial achievement gap in middle school reflects a lack of early skill development among blacks rather than their lower levels of engagement in academic activities.

Figure 7.7 shows the proportion of the racial achievement gap during middle school that can be attributed to racial differences in schooling behaviors and academic skill levels prior to middle school. The analyses account for socioeconomic factors such as parents' income, education, and marital status. The findings suggest that schooling behaviors—measured as

Figure 7.6:   Academic Activities, Achievement, and Prior Skills among Middle School Youth: CDS

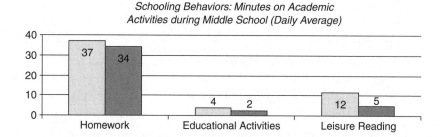

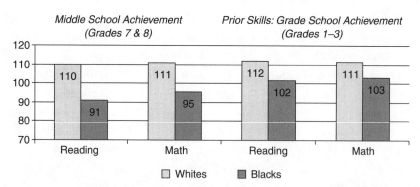

☐ Whites   ■ Blacks

Notes: Estimates are unadjusted. The academic activities were obtained from time diaries, which I discussed in Chapter 5. Reading and math scores are from the Woodcock-Johnson standardized achievement test. Reading achievement is a summation of the letter-word and passage comprehension scores. The math scores are based on a summation of the calculation and applied problems tests. All racial differences displayed are statistically significant at the .05 level.

time on homework, educational activities, and leisure reading—account for less than 1 percent of the black-white gap in both reading and math achievement. However, a deficiency in prior skills explains nearly one-third of the gap in reading and one-fifth of the gap in math achievement. These findings suggest that the pattern I described earlier among high school students also applies to students earlier in the academic life cycle.

It is important to mention that the focus here should be on the consistency of the pattern—that prior skills appear to be more consequential for

Figure 7.7: Percent of Middle School Black-Whites Gap Due to Schooling Behaviors and Prior Skills: CDS

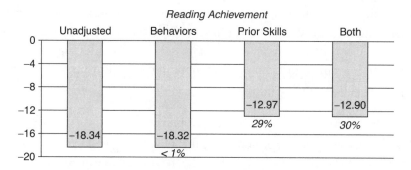

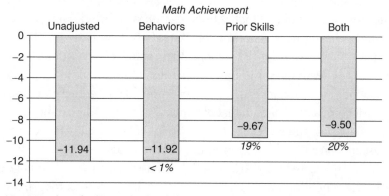

Notes: Unadjusted refers to schooling behaviors and prior skills; all bars show estimates after accounting for parents' education, family income, family structure, and youths' sex. Prior skills refer to reading and math in elementary school. Values were obtained from regression models (OLS). Whereas behaviors refer to the measures in the top panel of Figure 7.6, all measures of achievement (reading and math, and prior skills) are those displayed in the bottom panel of Figure 7.6. All racial differences displayed are statistically significant at the .05 level.

achievement than schooling behaviors throughout the academic life cycle—rather than on comparing the estimates for the high school sample based on the NELS to the middle school sample taken from the CDS. The two datasets utilize different measures for achievement that are assessed along different scales. Therefore, the scores are not directly comparable. Nevertheless, they both will still (and do) show a black-white achievement gap. Schooling behaviors are also measured differently across the datasets and along different units—4- or 5-point scales in the NELS and minutes on academic activities in the CDS. Thus, the percent change in the achievement gap associated with racial differences in schooling behaviors or prior skills cannot be directly compared across the datasets. The usefulness in comparing the results from Figures 7.4 and 7.7 is that it allows us to determine whether the relative importance of schooling behaviors and prior skills for the racial achievement gap is similar for youth at two different stages in the academic cycle. The consistency in the pattern across the two samples suggests that it might be inaccurate to promulgate an oppositional culture as the source of the racial achievement gap.

Chapter Summary

The empirical evidence presented in this chapter suggests that a new discussion on the centrality of oppositional behaviors as an explanation for the racial achievement gap is warranted. The current findings suggest students with low skill levels prior to high school are likely to have poor school achievement at the end of high school regardless of the schooling behaviors they have during high school. If blacks behaved similarly to whites and Asian Americans during high school, their achievement would be about 13 percent closer to the achievement of whites. However, if students entered high school with similar academic preparation, blacks' achievement would be about 70 percent closer to that of whites. Lack of academic success early in the schooling process seems to lead to poor educational practices prior to adolescence in a way that compromises children's achievement throughout their academic careers. I also assessed the consistency of these findings earlier in the schooling process and found that this pattern is robust; a deficiency in skills prior to middle school explains a greater proportion of the black-white gap among middle school students than schooling behaviors exhibited during middle school.

Learning is a cumulative process. Students begin to sort into cognitive trajectories as early as first grade. It seems unlikely that an oppositional culture stemming from beliefs about future educational returns plays a role in early school achievement. It is difficult to fathom children in kindergarten or elementary school—particularly poorly achieving blacks—resisting school because they project that they will encounter an unfair opportunity structure as adults. Previous research suggests that when younger children have deep ambivalence about their relationship to school, these feelings are independent from beliefs about the opportunity structure. For example, in a study of two all-black elementary schools, Tyson (2002:1184) finds that "children who were experiencing academic failure were more likely to express negative school-related attitudes than children who were not . . . children's negative statements about school reflected a desire to avoid further experiences of failure."

It is more reasonable to expect that racial differences in early academic preparation lead to racial differences in effective educational behaviors and achievement during elementary and middle school. Congressional testimony by Braddock (1990) warned that children who "suffer a crisis in their academic abilities . . . will begin adopting counterproductive, effort-avoidant strategies." The narratives of some children in Tyson's study provide evidence of the onset of this process. Archer and Hutchings (2000) show that a deficiency in prior skills for both working-class and ethnic minorities in the United Kingdom deters enrollment in higher-level high school courses and even deters enrollment in college altogether. Students in their sample construct the possibility of failure as a real risk with economic, personal, family, and social consequences. Therefore, poor performance early in the schooling process seems to produce the counterproductive schooling behavior observed among *some* blacks during adolescence, an order of causation that is the reverse of that suggested by the resistance model.

Numerous studies show that despite having poor school performance and ineffective schooling behaviors, many black youth desire to learn and become upwardly mobile (see, for example, Carter 2005; MacLeod 2009; Tyson 2002; Tyson, Darity, and Castellino 2005). Unfortunately, skills and quality of training are part of the equation, which if not acquired early in the schooling process can compromise one's potential for success (Harris and Robinson 2007). Farkas and colleagues find that reading below grade level by the end of the third grade can compromise learning through high school because students cannot maintain pace with the curriculum (Farkas 1993, 1996; Farkas et al. 1990). Thus, students who experience academic difficulty early in the schooling process are likely to continue performing poorly in school as they matriculate through the school system. It seems unreasonable to expect that proschool beliefs and attitudes alone can halt and/or reverse these trends by adolescence. Proponents of the resistance model do not take this into account when interpreting their observations, and therefore mislabel poor "student skills" as purposeful resistance to schooling.

While schooling behaviors are important to some degree (and as the findings in Figure 7.5 indicate, to a lesser degree than people might think), rather than attributing the racial achievement gap to black youths' schooling behaviors, it seems that educators should focus greater attention on children's academic skill development prior to high school. More specifically, a discourse on curtailing the uneven skill development between racial groups that occurs during the primary years of schooling seems more fruitful than a narrative about oppositional culture. This is difficult because the schooling behaviors of students in middle and high school observed by many educators are more salient to them than students' skills in elementary school. Furthermore, by the time students reach high school, they are viewed as fairly autonomous actors who are largely responsible for their academic inputs and outputs. However, given the uneven skill development between blacks and whites in elementary school, is it reasonable to expect that they would have similar schooling behaviors during middle and high school?

The current findings do highlight the usefulness of schooling behaviors for understanding differences in achievement between members from different minority groups. For example, schooling behaviors are better for explaining why Asian Americans perform well than explaining why blacks perform poorly relative to whites. Whereas the resistance model seems more capable of explaining the academic success of voluntary minorities, the current findings suggest that any theory for understanding achievement disadvantages of involuntary minorities should include students' early academic preparation. Resistance model theorists should deemphasize an oppositional ethos as a mechanism for blacks' poor achievement relative to whites. To be clear, my claim here is not that the achievement gap in high school stems from an achievement gap prior to high school or that blacks lack skills now because they lacked skills earlier. My major claim is that the skill deficiency prior to the stage of development during which the resistance model is applicable renders the current version of the oppositional culture theory less plausible.

8

DOES MARGINALIZATION EQUAL
RESISTANCE TO SCHOOLING?
A CLASS-BASED ANALYSIS

After testing and finding a lack of support for numerous tenets of the oppositional culture theory, I now shift the focus away from a *test* of the
theory to a *search* for evidence of the primary assumption underlying the
theory—that marginalized groups resist schooling (henceforward, the marginalization hypothesis). In order to capture the more general aspects of
being marginalized, I examined the marginalization hypothesis in a context
in which race is not the major dimension of stratification along which
groups are marginalized. In this chapter, I present results from my analysis
of marginalization in the United Kingdom, where it has historically occurred even more strongly along lines of social class than it has of race. That
is, focusing on the United Kingdom enables me to substitute social class for
race and thereby to capture another major dimension of marginalization.
Examining the implications that marginalization has for academic investment in general is an important step in developing a more comprehensive
sociology of stratification and education. Findings that fail to show a culture
of purposeful resistance to schooling among lower class youth would go far
toward confirming the title of this book and should lead educators to understand that even the most marginalized kids do not want to fail.

Although Ogbu's framework was specifically about race, testing components of the framework on other modes of stratification is appropriate and
important for refining our understanding of social stratification. The notion
that marginalized groups resist schooling is a general proposition that might
apply to dimensions of marginalization other than race. Extracting this
component of the framework moves the discourse in a direction Ogbu
never intended. Therefore, the analysis in this chapter is not a reformula-
tion of the resistance model, as any such modifications would require race
to be the focal point of a theory about racial disparities; testing the margin-

alization hypothesis is not equivalent to testing the oppositional culture theory. However, the consistent lack of support for the resistance model I have noted within my research is no reason to throw the baby out with the bath water; some of the theory's tenets might be supported more by a class-based rather than a race-based analysis. A class-based analysis is important because it is possible that proponents of the oppositional culture theory also attribute a class-based phenomenon to black youth.

The United Kingdom is an ideal setting in which to examine whether marginalized youth disinvest from schooling. The British education system is more stratified than the U.S. system, despite the introduction of state-sponsored comprehensive schools in the late 1960's to allow all students access to postsecondary education (Kerckhoff 2000, 2003). Though the vast majority of British youth today attend comprehensive schools, grammar schools (with courses aimed at passing college-entrance "A-level" examinations) and secondary modern schools (with more general curricula) still exist. As such, Britain was one of the six countries highlighted by Ogbu (1978) in his early work to underscore the cross-cultural applicability of his framework. Furthermore, similar to the United States, Britain is an industrially advanced society that is rapidly diversifying. The percentage of its foreign-born population has increased over the last two decades; the majority of immigrants to the United Kingdom are nonwhite Pakistanis, West Indians, Indians, Bangladeshis, and Black Africans (for a review, see Tienda 2005). Thus, the advantage of using the United Kingdom is that it has many similarities to the United States but provides a sufficiently different context that may yield patterns hidden within the United States and help distinguish between processes that are general and those that are more specific.

The gold standard for scientific study is to search for universals; that is, to move beyond culture-bound validity to the level of universality. This often involves turning toward a cross-cultural approach to extend the range of variation of the phenomenon of interest, which in this case is resistance to schooling by children from marginalized groups, or to clarify the relationship between variables. For example, whereas race is a prominent feature of American life, any legitimate discussion of marginalization within the United Kingdom must include social class. Thus, shifting the focus to an alternative setting in which race is not the primary dimension along which marginalization occurs allows for a more general assessment of the effects of being marginalized. The rationale for cross-cultural research is that transporting and testing ideas within other contexts allows us to determine whether the patterns we observe in our research apply in alternative settings, a process which can sometimes lead to the discovery of new insights that might otherwise remain undiscovered in the original setting (Berry et al. 2002).

Below I discuss how the marginalization hypothesis applies to lower-class groups within the United Kingdom. I then provide the findings from my analysis of the marginalization hypothesis by social class within the United Kingdom. To determine whether the patterns that emerge from this analysis are similar for the United States, I also provide results from this assessment using the Maryland Adolescent Development in Context Study (MADICS). I conclude this chapter by discussing the implications of the findings for our understanding of whether the experience of being marginalized should be linked to the notion of academic resistance.

The Primacy of Class-Based Marginalization within the United Kingdom

Groups have historically been marginalized along the dimension of social class within the United Kingdom. In contrast to characterizations of the United States, it has been commonplace for more than a century—since the publication of Tocqueville's *Democracy in America*—to characterize Great Britain as "classbound and inegalitarian" (Bell and Robinson 1980). While historically the United States has been described as emphasizing achievement, equalitarianism, universalism, and specificity, Great Britain has been regarded as emphasizing ascription, elitism, particularism, and diffuseness (Lipset 1963). This becomes particularly salient when one considers the historical development of the British education system.[1] England had separate systems of education for youth based on social class through the early part of the twentieth century. Whereas working- or lower-class youth attended only elementary school, middle- and upper-class youth attended secondary schools. Only a select few working-class children with exceptional ability and promise for successful assimilation into the middle class were granted access to secondary schools (Banks 1968:46). The rest were relegated to post-elementary schools lacking the prestige of secondary schools and the resources to prepare them to qualify for higher education. Reforms during World War II provided working-class youth with greater access to secondary schools.

In an attempt to address the imbalance in opportunities between marginalized and nonmarginalized groups, the United Kingdom has been transitioning from an elitist to a mass system of higher education over the past few decades (Williams 1997). The expansion of higher education has been rapid; findings by the Organization for Economic Cooperation and Development (OECD) show that the number of students pursuing higher education in Britain increased by 76 percent between 1990 and 1996 (OECD 2000). This growth rate is faster than observed in 27 of 28 OECD countries, which are mainly from Europe and the Americas. (Portugal had the highest growth rate.)

Despite the recent increase in the opportunity to use formal education as a mechanism for social mobility, research suggests that present-day Great Britain is far from being a meritocratic society. Ball et al. (2002) note that social class continues to be the main predictor of what schools students will attend and attainment of the General Certificate of Secondary Education (GCSE), both of which greatly determine admission to high-status universities. In addition, although broad differences in achievement during primary and secondary schools are attached to social class (Ashcroft, Bigger, and Coates 1996; Van De Werfhorst, Sullivan, and Cheung 2003), working-class youth are less likely than middle-class youth with similar qualifications to obtain any form of higher education, even when achievement is taken into account (Hatcher 1998; Metcalf 1997). Similarly, Breen and Goldthorpe (1999) find that merit—in terms of individual ability and effort—plays a limited role in the process of intergenerational mobility and does not annul effects of class origin. They conclude that less-advantaged youth need to display substantially more merit than more highly advantaged youth to enter similarly desirable class positions as adults.

Some scholars note that Britain's rigid class lines show few signs of changing and that its educational system continues to have a limited ability to function as a mechanism for upward mobility. For example, Marshall, Swift, and Robert (1997) showed that the importance of education for employment prospects and upward mobility was weaker at the close of the twentieth century than during the 1960s and 1970s. Regarding the long-term trend in the permeability of class lines in Great Britain, Goldthorpe (1987:327) notes that "the net association between the class position of individuals in the present-day population and their class origins remains essentially the same in its extent and pattern as that which existed in the inter-war period and even, it seems likely, as that which would have been found at the start of the [twentieth] century." In a longitudinal assessment of two British cohorts, Breen and Goldthorpe (2001) find minimal support for the notion that Britain is becoming more meritocratic; the extent to which merit affects social mobility has remained relatively unchanged over time.

Class-Based Marginalization and Academic Orientation

Despite the lack of support for the marginalization hypothesis in the United Kingdom when assessed along the dimension of race, it is reasonable to expect that being marginalized based on social class leads members of marginalized groups in the United Kingdom to define certain behaviors—particularly achievement—as inappropriate for them. Archer and Hutchings (2000) find that working-class youth in the United Kingdom position themselves outside the realm of higher education and view education as white or middle-class. They also show that working-class youth enrolled in higher education report experiencing a social cost for being different within networks in which members of their group have little history of participation. Other studies suggest working-class youth have a strong attachment to a working-class identity and therefore resist the middle-class education because it is incompatible with their class identity (Cohen 1988; Reay 1996); in this sense, academic engagement is viewed as betraying one's working-class origins (hooks 1994).

In a classic ethnographic study of English youth, Willis (1977) observed a counter–school culture among working-class boys (the "lads") that centered on opposing school authority and rejecting those youths who conformed to school rules and performed well academically. Willis (1977:108) noted that the "lads' experience in the counter-school culture most certainly smoothes their transition into work and produces appetites which manual work satisfies quite well." However, Willis's study suggests that the working-class youths' disidentification with school was in large measure a consequence of what they and their parents experienced in school. Students in his study were also subjected to tracking in school, although on the basis of class rather than on race. It seems that examining tenets of the resistance model by social class, then, does not shift the terrain: the key components remain prior skills, school practices, and treatment of students and parents. It is important to note, however, that marginalization on the basis of social class might not have a uniform effect by race (MacLeod 2009).

The marginalized status of lower-class youth is apparent within education, as the academic achievement gap by social class is similar to or greater than the racial achievement gap. This is illustrated in Figure 8.1, which shows differences in academic achievement by social class and race. The figure shows that achievement differences between youth from different social class backgrounds are even more substantial than achievement gaps by race in both the United Kingdom and the United States. Since multiple datasets are used, each finding is labeled by the dataset from which the indicator for achievement was obtained and the year during which achievement was measured. The top panel in Figure 8.1 shows the gaps by social class for British youth. The social class standing was established by stratifying the samples into four groups based on parents' occupation: those whose parent(s) hold 1) a professional or managerial occupation (upper class), 2) skilled nonmanual jobs (upper middle class), 3) skilled manual or semi-skilled jobs (lower middle class), and 4) unskilled laborers (lower class). To allow for comparisons across outcomes, I present standardized gaps relative to upper-class youth.

Among sixteen-year-old youth from the British Cohort Study (BCS70), vocabulary achievement and teacher evaluations are lower for non-upper-class youth than their counterparts with upper-class family backgrounds. The same pattern is observed for both English and math achievement using data from the LSYPE. Upper-class youth have the highest achievement followed by youth from upper-middle-, lower-, and lower-middle-class backgrounds. Comparisons across the datasets show that the achievement gap by social class has remained virtually unchanged during a span of nearly two decades and is similar across different achievement outcomes. The second panel of Figure 8.1 shows that an achievement gap along social class lines also exists within the United States. Children whose parents have completed a four-year degree have the highest achievement, followed by those whose parents attained some college schooling, were high school graduates, and did not finish high school.[2] Social class appears to be an important determinant for achievement in both the United Kingdom and the United States.

The bottom panel shows the racial achievement gaps in both countries. The findings for the United Kingdom show that indeed the story of inequality and marginalization with regard to schooling has more to do with social class than race: the achievement differences are larger for youth from different social class backgrounds than those from different racial groups. For the United States, the achievement differences by social class appear to be as substantial as those based on race. The finding that achievement is lower for youth from lower-class backgrounds should come as no surprise. In the

Figure 8.1:   Standardized Achievement Gap by Social Class and Race in the United Kingdom and the United States

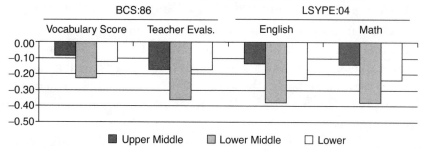

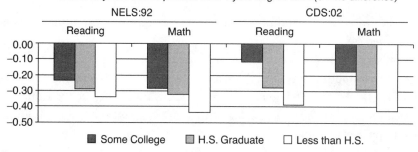

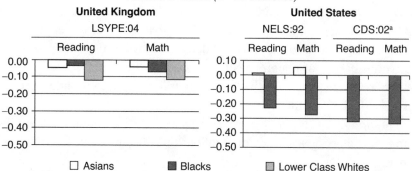

Notes: All scores are standardized and unadjusted. Scores from the British data are for youth ages 16 and 14 for the BCS70 and LSYPE, respectively. Scores from the NELS are for students in grade 12, and scores from the CDS are for youth in grades 7 through 12. See Appendix C for a description of the analytic plan. Scores for mixed-race youth in the United Kingdom do not differ from those of whites; their estimates are virtually identical to those of whites and thus would not appear on the graph.

[a] The CDS does not contain a sufficient nationally representative sample of Asian Americans for meaningful analysis.

next section, I determine whether marginalization along social class lines is associated with purposeful resistance to schooling.

Do Marginalized Groups in the United Kingdom Resist Schooling?

I begin my analysis by assessing the marginalization hypothesis within the United Kingdom. I compare youth from each of the social class groups on numerous indicators of academic orientation. I also assess whether marginalized groups resist schooling because they perceive that they are marginalized within society. In order for the findings to be fully consistent with the hypothesis, youths in the lower-class groups would have to show lower academic engagement than upper-class youth *and* these differences would have to be explained by their sense of marginalization. Since the findings in the previous chapters were overwhelmingly inconsistent with the resistance model, the latter condition was not necessary. However, the findings in this chapter show that differences in academic orientation by social class are more varied and pronounced. As such, a more careful analysis is warranted.

I present the first set of results of this analysis in Figure 8.2, which shows how upper-middle-, lower-middle-, and lower-class youth fare on the number of school-based activities youth engage in, the value they attribute to education, and their level of academic disengagement relative to children from upper-class backgrounds. Two estimates are displayed for each group. The first shows how each of the lower-class groups differs on the outcome from youth in the upper-class group. The second shows these differences after accounting for youths' sex and perceptions of discrimination—whether s/he has been treated unfairly/unjustly in the last twelve months due to any of the following: sex, skin color, dress, family background, speech, religion, or other reason (yes/no). The level of decline in the estimates after adjusting for youths' sense of marginalization represents the portion of social class variation on the outcome that can be attributed to group differences in perceived discrimination.

The findings in Figure 8.2 show that social class variation exists on the three indicators of academic orientation. Specifically, children from non-upper-class backgrounds participate in fewer school activities, attribute less value to schooling, and are more academically disengaged than their upper-class counterparts (recall that indicators are labeled on the side of the graph—positive or negative—that one would expect for the estimate if marginalized groups resisted schooling). The adjusted estimates show that per-

Figure 8.2: Academic Orientation by Social Class Relative to British Youths from the Upper Class: BCS70

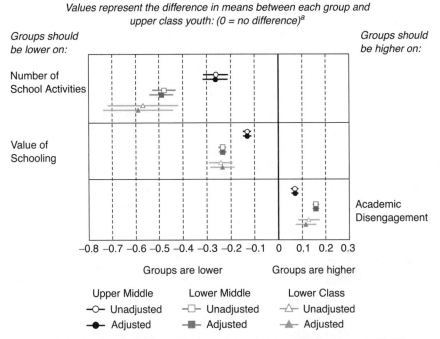

Values represent the difference in means between each group and upper class youth: (0 = no difference)[a]

[a] The graph displays the OLS estimates (circle, square, triangle) and standard errors (tails). The means for the upper class group (unadjusted) are 2.15, 2.58, and 1.59 for *number of school activities, value of schooling,* and *academic disengagement,* respectively. Changes in these means are negligible after adjusting for discrimination and sex. Adjusted estimates illustrate the group differences after accounting for youths' sex and perceptions of discrimination. All estimates are significant at the .05 level. See Appendices C and D for the analytic plan and the description of measures, respectively.

ceptions of discrimination have minimal implication for social class variation in academic orientation.

The pattern is similar for nonexcused absence from school. Figure 8.3 shows that the proportion of youth who have had an unexcused absence from school increases as social class declines. The proportions remain similar for each group after accounting for perceptions of discrimination. In general, it appears that within the United Kingdom a decline in social class is accompanied by a decline in academic orientation. In additional analyses, I find that the BCS70 and the Longitudinal Study of Young People in England (LSYPE) produce similar results for every indicator of academic orientation that I tested from both datasets, which suggests that the patterns described here are robust and have not changed over the past twenty years. Analysis of data from the LSYPE revealed that as social class declines, youth read less frequently for pleasure, are less happy at school, attribute less value to school, are more detached from academics, experience more behavioral problems in school, and have a decreased desire to attain education, but these differences cannot be attributed to youths' perceptions of discrimination by teachers because of skin color, ethnicity, race, or religion.

The findings in this chapter are consistent with years of research within the United Kingdom and suggest that youth in the lower-class groups have lower academic achievement and are less engaged in school-related activities than are students from higher social class backgrounds. If these findings showed that no variation exists on the measures of academic orientation, similar to many of the findings in the previous chapters, I would conclude that there is no support for the marginalization hypothesis. Although the results in Figures 8.2 and 8.3 seem consistent with the hypothesis, the lack of change in the differences on the outcomes between youth across class groups after controlling for perceived discrimination suggests that while youth from lower-class groups are less engaged than their upper-class counterparts, this disengagement does *not* result from their sense of marginalization. These findings illustrate what economists refer to as an "identification problem." Specifically, there is no way in this study to distinguish among multiple plausible explanations for the observed associations between social

Figure 8.3: Proportion of British Students Who Have Had an Unexcused Absence from School: BCS70

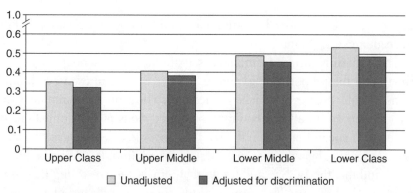

Note: Adjusted estimates illustrate the group proportions after accounting for youths' sex and perceptions of discrimination.

class and academic engagement. It could be, for example, that students from lower social classes simply have access to fewer of the social and material resources that provide the skills and incentives associated with academic engagement. We can, however, eliminate a sense of marginalization as a factor in class differences in academic orientation.

Do Marginalized Groups in the United States Resist Schooling?

The results are more conclusive when this analysis is replicated with a U.S.-based sample. Given the richness of the MADICS, I assessed the marginalization hypothesis by repeating the analysis presented in Chapter 5 with the sample stratified by social class rather than race. Although all of the outcomes capture aspects of academic orientation, some are more closely aligned with youths' academic approach while others are more indicative of their academic intent. Therefore, support for the marginalization hypothesis is contingent upon which outcomes show social class variation in the proper direction. The differences for the analysis based on the U.S. students are such that observing the direction of group disparities on the outcomes is enough to conclude that groups marginalized along the dimension of social class do not purposefully resist schooling.

These results are displayed in Table 8.1, which shows social class differences in students' perceptions about the value of school, schooling attitudes and behaviors, and the academic orientation of their peers. The first column shows the average on the outcomes for youth whose parents hold a four-year degree or greater. The next three columns show the differences on the outcomes for youth in each social class group relative to those from the four-year degree group. I italicize the outcomes for which the findings are consistent with the marginalization hypothesis. The findings show that educational aspirations and expectations decrease with each decline in social class. Similarly, the difference between students' aspired and expected educational attainment increases as youths' social class declines. Accounting for household income and family structure results in minimal changes in the estimates. However, the findings for youths' perceptions of educational returns, affect toward schooling, and their ratings with regards to whether they attend school because they enjoy it or because it is mandatory are *not* consistent with the marginalization hypothesis; social class is either unrelated to these outcomes or the difference is opposite to the marginalization hypothesis. Thus, while these results suggest that youth from lower social class backgrounds aspire and expect to receive lower levels of education

Table 8.1: Academic Orientation by Social Class in the United States

	Unadjusted Differences from 4-Yr Degree Group				Adjusted Differences from 4-Yr Degree Group			
	Avg. for 4-yrDeg.	<H.S.	H.S.	SmCol.	Avg. for 4-yrDeg.	<H.S.	H.S.	SmCol
Perceptions and Attitudes								
Returns to educ.	4.22	NS	NS	NS	4.06	NS	NS	-0.08
Educational Aspirations	8.02	-0.90	-0.57	-0.31	7.30	-0.82	-0.52	-0.32
Educational Aspirations	7.43	-1.44	-0.90	-0.54	6.39	-1.16	-0.73	-0.47
Affect toward Schooling	3.67	NS	NS	NS	3.62	NS	NS	NS
Attend School b/c Enjoy	4.28	NS	NS	NS	4.13	NS	NS	NS
Educ. Aspir. – Expect.	0.58	0.56	0.33	0.24	0.92	0.36	0.22	0.15
Attend School b/c have to	5.13	NS	-0.34	NS	4.94	NS	-0.28	NS
Schooling Behaviors								
Seek Help	2.89	NS	0.11	0.08	2.90	NS	NS	NS
Time on School Clubs	2.11	-0.90	-0.64	-0.53	1.44	-0.82	-0.53	-0.56
Time on Homework	4.81	-0.29	NS	-0.27	4.78	-0.34	-0.26	-0.28
Time on Educ. Activities	3.21	-0.24	-0.30	-0.23	3.11	-0.24	-0.25	-0.25
Importance of Academics	5.18	NS	0.13	NS	5.26	NS	NS	NS
Skip School / Cut Classes	1.54	NS	NS	NS	1.28	NS	NS	NS

Table 8.1. (continued)

	Unadjusted Differences from 4-Yr Degree Group				Adjusted Differences from 4-Yr Degree Group			
	Avg. for 4-yrDeg.	<H.S.	H.S.	SmCol.	Avg. for 4-yrDeg.	<H.S.	H.S.	SmCol.
Suspended	0.35	0.99	0.35	0.25	0.61	0.87	0.29	0.19
Importance of Non-Acad.	4.46	NS	NS	−0.27	5.07	NS	NS	−0.18
Peer Orientation								
Positive Acad. Orientation	3.52	−0.18	−0.14	−0.14	3.32	−0.21	−0.16	−0.18
Negative Acad. Orientation	2.23	NS	NS	NS	3.33	NS	NS	NS

Note: *Avg. for 4-yr Deg.* represents the average or mean on the outcome for youth whose parents hold a 4-year degree or greater. Adjusted estimates illustrate the group differences after accounting for family income, family structure, race, sex, and grade level. NS denotes that the group does not differ significantly from the youth whose parents hold a 4-year college degree or greater (*p is not* < .05). Outcomes for which the findings are not consistent with the marginalization hypothesis are in grey. See Appendix C and D for the analytic plan and the description of measures, respectively.

than their upper-class counterparts, the results from the other outcomes in the top panel of Table 8.1 do not suggest that they purposefully resist schooling.

The second panel contains group comparisons on eight indicators of schooling behaviors. Youth from lower class groups spend less time on school clubs, homework, and educational activities (for example, reading or watching educational programming), and are suspended more often than children whose parents hold a four-year degree or greater. However, the groups are similar on the extent to which they seek help with difficulties at school, the importance they place on academics, the frequency with which they skip school, and the importance they attribute to nonacademic activities. Furthermore, the group comparisons of peer academic orientation displayed in the bottom panel of Table 8.1 suggest that although youth from lower social class groups have peers with less positive academic orientation than those whose parents hold a four-year degree or greater, their peers are not more negative toward schooling. The variation between the groups whose parents do *not* have a four-year degree is minimal, indicating that youth with college-educated parents have an added advantage, because they tend to have peers who are more academically oriented. These findings do not show a clear culture of resistance to schooling among youth with lower-class backgrounds.

Do Lower-Class Youth Experience a Greater Social Cost for Good Academic Performance?

The notion that marginalized minorities experience a greater social cost for positive academic performance has received the most attention in the resistance model literature. This claim is commonly referred to as the "acting white" hypothesis within the United States. In Figure 8.4, I display a portion of the findings for an analysis that assesses whether negative sanctioning for high academic orientation is a mechanism by which youth from lower social class backgrounds resist educational goals. If these students perceive academics to be within the domain of individuals from dominant or nonmarginalized groups, such as those from more advantaged backgrounds, increases in academic orientation should be associated with declines in social standing and peer approval.

The top panel shows that there is no connection between academic orientation and social status within the United Kingdom. Attributing greater value to schooling does not result in having fewer friends or increases in feelings of loneliness at school. More importantly, the patterns are identical regardless of social class. The results are the same when 1) academic orientation is measured using vocabulary scores and teacher assessments, 2) youths' self-reported popularity serves as the outcome, and 3) measures of social standing and academic orientation are assessed using data from the LSYPE. The bottom panel of Figure 8.4 shows the same pattern within the United States. Increases in academic achievement do not compromise

Figure 8.4: Negative Peer Sanctioning by Social Class in the United Kingdom and the United States: BCS70 and MADICS

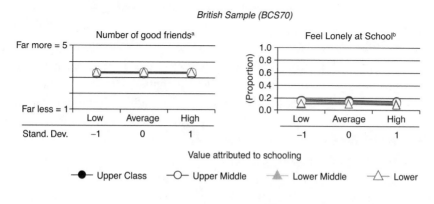

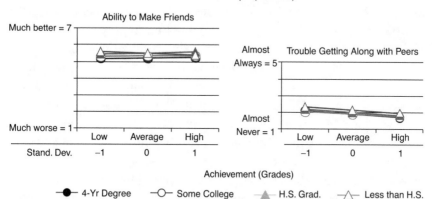

Note: Results for the British sample account for achievement (vocabulary test scores and teacher assessment displayed in Figure 8.1) and sex. Results for the U.S. sample account for race, sex, and family structure. Slopes for each outcome do not differ significantly at the .05 level.

[a] Compared with an average teenager of my same age and sex, the number of good friends I have is (far less to far more).

[b] Proportion of youth who respond "yes" to the following question: "Do you often feel lonely at school?"

youths' ability to make friends. In fact, youth with higher academic achievement report having slightly less trouble getting along with peers than those with lower academic achievement. Similar to the United Kingdom, youth from lower social class groups do *not* experience greater negative sanctioning for good academic performance than those in the higher-class groups. The relationship between achievement and social standing is identical across social class.

Chapter Summary

The purpose of this chapter was to examine the general link between marginalization and resistance to schooling by assessing whether youth who are marginalized on a dimension of stratification other than race are resistant toward education. The findings within the United Kingdom suggest that relative to youth from upper class-backgrounds, children from lower-class backgrounds participate in fewer school activities, attribute less value to schooling, are more academically disengaged, read less frequently for pleasure, are less happy at school, attribute less value to school, are more detached from academics, experience more behavioral problems in school, and desire to attain less education. Within the United States, youth from lower-class backgrounds have lower educational aspirations and expectations, spend less time on school clubs, homework, and educational activities, and are suspended more often than children whose parents hold a four-year degree or greater. All of these outcomes concern patterns of achievement, time use, and behavior, but not necessarily active resistance to education or schooling. They confirm what many readers might already expect: youth from lower-class backgrounds are more counterproductive and less efficient when it comes to schooling, factors related to low academic achievement. However, these factors alone are not enough to determine whether a group of students are purposefully resisting schooling.

In the case of the United Kingdom, class differences in academic orientation are unrelated to youths' perceptions of discrimination. If the differences in disengagement were attributable to perceptions of discrimination, one could interpret the disengagement of lower-class youth as a response to their marginalized status. However, the findings for the United Kingdom challenge the notion that marginalized groups resist schooling *because* they perceive a lack of acceptance by society (or the dominant group) for members of their group. This finding is consistent with the role of perceived barriers among adolescents within the United States—specifically, that they are inconsequential for group difference in academic orientation—and suggests that the lower school orientation of youth from lower-class backgrounds is open to alternative explanations.

Within the United States, despite having lower educational aspirations and expectations than youth whose parents hold more than a four-year degree, children from less advantaged backgrounds *do not* 1) perceive fewer educational returns, 2) express lower favorable affect toward schooling, 3) seek less help with school, 4) attribute less importance to school, 5) skip school more often, or 6) navigate more negative peer groups with regard to schooling. Furthermore, in neither the United Kingdom nor the United States do youth experience a greater social cost for high achievement. All of these factors concern phenomena for which the logical relationships to a culture of resistance seem more apparent or intuitive—affect (emotions regarding schooling), perceptions (beliefs about discrimination), peer supports (reinforcements for achievement)—and yet none of these factors suggests that lower-class youth resist schooling.

In sum, the evidence in this chapter does not support the notion that a pervasive culture of purposeful resistance to schooling exists among youth marginalized by social class. The findings do suggest that students from lower social class backgrounds perform less well in school and are less engaged in school-related activities than are students from higher social class backgrounds, which is not a novel finding. However, disengagement alone does not equal resistance; the disengagement must be accompanied by perceptions and attitudes that suggest intent to fail. The findings for the affective and peer culture measures lead me to conclude that the lower engagement for youth with lower social class backgrounds does not stem from a culture of resistance to academics.

9

REFOCUSING UNDERSTANDING OF RACIAL DIFFERENCES IN ACADEMIC OUTCOMES

The oppositional culture theory offers a popular theory for explaining racial differences in academic outcomes. Despite work by numerous scholars challenging the notion that an oppositional culture is prevalent among blacks (Ainsworth-Darnell and Downey 1998; Akom 2003; Carter 2005; Cook and Ludwig 1998; O'Connor 1997; Tyson 2002; Tyson, Darity and Castellino 2005), the theory remains popular among researchers, educational practitioners, and the general public. For example, in *The Content of our Character* (1990:51) Shelby Steele sternly asserts that even in the very worst schools "there are accredited teachers who teach the basics, but too often to students who shun those among them who do well, who see studying as a sucker's game and school itself as a waste of time." Steele further claims that "one sees in many of these children almost a determination not to learn, a suppression of the natural impulse to understand, which cannot be entirely explained by the determinism of poverty." John McWhorter (2000:28) argued that blacks suffer from a culture of "self sabotage" that "condones weakness and failure." However, treating the theory as an overriding explanation for racial differences in achievement might lead policy makers to narrowly conceive of the gap's causes and to assume convergence is unlikely, based on the supposition that blacks refuse to learn.

The resistance model makes a compelling link between societal conditions—such as intergroup relations, discrimination—and youths' academic investment in order to explain racial differences in school outcomes. Ogbu (1978) notes Americans are motivated to maximize school achievement because of the belief that more education leads to better jobs, higher wages, and social status. He argues that for quite rational reasons, not everyone is inclined to believe in this achievement ideology. For example, Ogbu (1990:50) writes that "by denying minorities an opportunity to enter the labor market and to advance according to their educational qualifications and abilities and by denying them adequate wage rewards for their educational efforts, American society has probably discouraged minorities from investing their time and effort into the pursuit of education and the maximization of educational accomplishments." Although the notion that marginalized groups place little value on schooling as a mechanism for upward mobility appears reasonable, the findings presented in this study paint a different picture. Below I answer several questions addressed by this study that are important to our understanding of the implications that membership in a traditionally marginalized group has for how one situates oneself with regard to education.

Are Black Youth (Socialized to Be) Pessimistic about School as a Means for Upward Mobility?

In Chapter 3, I find that although black parents—youths' primary socializing agents—report experiencing more discrimination than their white counterparts and have a greater belief than whites that their children will experience barriers to upward socioeconomic mobility, these beliefs do not compromise youths' academic investment. Rather, it is parents' beliefs and messages about the value of schooling that are positively related to youths' academic orientation. Furthermore, the findings in Chapter 4 show black youth attribute greater value to schooling despite also perceiving more barriers to upward mobility than whites. More importantly, whereas an increase in beliefs about the value of school is associated with increases in academic outcomes, merely believing in barriers is inconsequential for both achievement and college enrollment. The findings are similar even when perceptions of barriers are assessed with regard to gender and race. Specifically, adolescent girls anticipate that their sex will serve as an obstacle for attaining their desired level of education and occupation, yet they attribute more importance to schooling than their male counterparts. These findings demonstrate that belief in barriers based on both sex and race within education, the labor force, and life in general are not related to academic investment.

The findings in Chapter 4 provide a better understanding of how beliefs about the system of social mobility affect students' schooling behaviors. While the findings support a link between perceptions about the system of social mobility and students' behaviors, the multidimensionality of beliefs suggests the connection is complex; it is belief in the value of schooling and *not* belief in barriers that matter for academic investment. The conceptual and analytic distinction between belief in the value of schooling and barriers to upward mobility helps to reconcile the findings from some studies that show blacks perceive more racial barriers than whites (Fordham and Ogbu 1986; Mickelson 1990; Ogbu 2003) and others that find blacks believe in the achievement ideology (for example, Ainsworth-Darnell and Downey 1998; Harris 2006; MacLeod 2009; O'Connor 1999). Adolescents from groups in weaker positions within society with regard to race and gender make nuanced distinctions about what schooling can do for them (improve their life chances) and what it cannot do for them (lead to sex/racial equality in wages and other life-chance outcomes).

Do Black Youth Really Resist Schooling?

When I moved away from perceptions about the opportunity structure, an extensive test of the affective and behavioral components of the resistance model produced results that challenge the existence of a pervasive oppositional culture among blacks. The major tenets of the theory were not supported (see Chapter 5). It seems the resistance model fails to account for the high degree of variability within the black student population. This finding even extends to ethnic minorities within the United Kingdom (Asians and blacks), who score either the same or greater on proschool measures, are less academically disengaged, and are *less* likely to *not* desire post–compulsory education than their white counterparts. These findings are consistent with others that show that blacks in the United Kingdom are more likely to persist in school beyond compulsory level than whites (for a review, see Tomlinson 1991) and are overrepresented in higher education (Bird, Shebani, and Francombe 1992). It appears that marginalized racial groups do not necessarily respond to their marginalization by resisting school goals.

Even if the focus is shifted toward a social class-based analysis, results do not support the notion that marginalization results in resistance to schooling. I examined this marginalization hypothesis in the United Kingdom, a setting that is arguably more stratified and has fewer opportunities for upward mobility than the United States. Even within this context, in which the structural inequalities that drive the culture of school resistance are more pronounced, there is not strong support for the notion that lower social class youth resist schooling because they perceive that they are marginalized. This contributes to our understanding of the implications that belonging to a marginalized group has for upward mobility; it appears that membership in a marginalized group (whether based on race, class, or gender) does not necessarily mean that one will resist schooling.

What to Make of the "Acting White" Hypothesis?

The findings from this study did not support the "acting white" hypothesis, perhaps the most widely known tenet associated with the oppositional culture theory. Youth from marginalized groups do not experience greater social cost for academic investment than those from nonmarginalized groups. Numerous studies show blacks do not experience greater social cost for high achievement than whites (e.g., Akom 2003; Carter 2005; Harris 2006; Horvat and Lewis 2003; O'Connor 1999; Tyson, Darity, and Castellino 2005). However, the findings from this book also show that racial minorities within the United Kingdom, who average lower school achievement than their white counterparts, do not experience a greater social cost for good academic performance. In fact, even when marginalization was assessed along the lines of social class in Chapter 8, the findings were not consistent with the notion that high achievement comes with a greater social cost for marginalized groups. It appears that adolescent peer groups are not monolithic and allow space to affirm academic identity in both the United States and the United Kingdom.

This study produces further evidence that contradicts the "acting white" hypothesis in Chapter 6, which provides an examination of whether adopting a raceless identity to circumvent the negative sanctioning for good performance attributed to the black community is an effective strategy for academic success among black youth. Black adolescents who feel no connection to other blacks are among the least academically invested. Academic investment is greater among blacks with favorable affective feelings toward their race and lower among those who express regret about being black. Thus, rather than distancing themselves from the black community, black youth should be encouraged to have a strong connection to their race and a positive racial identity.[1]

While some dimensions of the oppositional culture theory may apply to individual members of marginalized racial groups, the extent to which the theory can explain racial differences in achievement is limited. As mentioned above, the results from Chapters 4 and 5 suggest that oppositional culture observed among *some* blacks does not stem from students' perceptions of their prospects within the opportunity structure or from their resentment of the dominant group. In fact, the findings showed that blacks have a more favorable academic orientation than whites, a result that yields a paradox among blacks similar to that addressed by Mickelson in 1990. The limited support for the resistance model raises two important questions. First, if blacks attribute more value to schooling than whites, then why do they perform worse in school? Second, is there an alternative interpretation for the counterproductive schooling behaviors displayed by some blacks, documented by proponents of the resistance model and observed by many educators?[1]

Can Blacks Value School Yet Have Poor Academic Achievement?

The answer is yes. The findings in Chapters 4 and 5 show that despite having lower school achievement than whites, blacks attribute more value to schooling and have a more positive orientation toward education than whites. In a strict sense, these findings would be paradoxical only if the value of schooling and academic orientation represented the universe of factors that affect achievement and its observed effect contravened expectations. However, this is not the case. Achievement is essentially a summary measure representing a collection of contributing effects from various factors, some based on personal, home, school, and neighborhood characteristics. We might take the sport of golf as an example: an affinity for the sport of golf does not necessarily translate into an ability to perform like Tiger Woods, regardless of how much importance one places on golf. Indeed, many spectator events (sporting events, operas, and so forth) are comprised of audience members and fans who may lack the necessary talent to be participants. It is important to separate intended or desired behavior from actual behavior. The outcome of any given effort should not be taken as synonymous with the intent behind the effort. Blacks' greater academic orientation and lower achievement than whites does not seem paradoxical when thought of in this context.

Why Do Proponents of the Resistance Model Continue to Find Support for the Theory?

Ogbu's work tended to involve qualitative methods, which perhaps allowed him to solicit experiences and processes current quantitative data cannot. The research presented in this study however, failed to identify strong support for Ogbu's theory, suggesting that his theory might be better served by more dynamic quantitative techniques. It could be that qualitative researchers, by using more open-ended questions or obtaining respondents' reactions to descriptions of real-life scenarios, can better capture how adolescents process ordinary daily experiences. However, numerous qualitative studies also do not find support for the theory (Akom 2003; Carter 2005, O'Connor 1997; Tyson, Darity, and Castellino 2005). If an oppositional culture were prevalent among black youth, the theory would not require explanations about why some methods yield support while others do not.

The findings in Chapter 7 might provide some clarity for the differences between studies that find support for the framework and those that do not. Proponents of the resistance model consistently point to an oppositional culture among black adolescents characterized by counterproductive schooling behaviors as the primary reason for their lower school achievement relative to other groups. However, I cautioned that proponents overestimate the effects of schooling behaviors by failing to consider students' skill levels prior to adolescence. I found that whereas schooling behaviors are more useful for explaining Asian Americans' achievement advantage relative to whites, schooling behaviors account for a little more than one-tenth of the black-white achievement gap. In contrast, academic skills prior to adolescence explain nearly three-fourths of the black-white gap. Additionally, the implications of schooling behaviors for achievement during high school decline substantially once prior academic skills are taken into account. This suggests that schooling behaviors matter in high school to a much lesser degree than proposed by the oppositional culture theory. The skills students acquire before entering high school are an important factor in determining what schooling behaviors they employ during high school.

This book represents my attempt to provide an extensive assessment of the theory as a complete entity, by testing most of the assumptions within the framework. My aim has been to move the discourse past the cultural deficiency narrative toward a more fruitful discussion about how the gap should be addressed. If educators remain resolute in their belief in a theory for which research yields minimal empirical support, they will conclude that effective strategies for closing the achievement gap must involve cultural change among blacks, an approach that could compromise the implementation of strategies that might actually be effective for reducing the gap. Although providing concrete remedies to close the racial achievement gap is beyond the scope of this book, below I discuss the direction in which a new discourse should emerge to help uproot the black cultural deficiency narrative.

Where Should Educators Focus Their Attention?
Teachers' Perceptions of Black Youth

An important step toward addressing the educational disadvantage of black youth is to deal with the reality that some teachers do not believe in black students; they stereotype and attempt to avoid them. Several studies suggest that students' race remains a significant factor among teachers and can compromise the quality of schooling black children receive. For example, Hanushek, Kain, and Rivkin (2004) provide strong evidence that a higher rate of minority enrollment increases the probability that white teachers will exit a school, even more so than wages. They find that a 10 percent increase in black enrollment would require about a 10 percent increase in salaries in order to neutralize the elevated probability that white teachers would leave the school. Furthermore, they find that the racial composition of schools is an important determinant of the probability that white teachers—particularly newer teachers—will leave public schools entirely and switch school districts. In contrast, black teachers tend to move to schools with a higher proportion of black students than the schools they left, regardless of whether they change districts. Freeman, Scafidi, and Sjoquist (2005) also find that white teachers are much more likely to leave schools that serve higher proportions of black students in favor of schools that serve lower proportions of black and low-income students and that have students who scored higher on achievement exams.

Jackson (2009) finds that the implications of schools' racial composition extend to teacher quality. Jackson's research investigated the impact of a policy change that ended a busing program in 2002 in the Charlotte-Mecklenburg school district in North Carolina. The busing program entailed busing students across neighborhoods to maintain racial balance of the student bodies across schools within the district. The repeal of the program led to a sudden convergence between the demographic makeup of schools and their surrounding neighborhoods while other school and neighborhood characteristics remained largely unchanged. Jackson's findings revealed that schools with an inflow of black students experienced an exodus of high-quality teachers. Specifically, he found that in schools where the share of black student enrollment increased there was a decrease in the proportion of experienced teachers, in teachers with high licensure exam scores, and in teachers who had previously demonstrated an ability to improve student test scores. Jackson's study design supports the conclusion that the absence of high-quality teachers in schools with high proportions of black students is due to the racial composition of the schools rather than to neighborhood characteristics. Jackson further determined that the change in school quality immediately following the repeal of the busing program indicated that teachers exited in anticipation of the arrival of more black students. Jackson contends that the avoidance of black students by high-quality teachers may substantially contribute to the black-white achievement gap, as black students consequently receive lower-quality instruction.

Early Skill Development

The findings presented in this study suggest that educators should shift their attention away from explanations that point to a culture of academic resistance among black children as the driving force behind the racial achievement gap. This explanation is usually associated with adolescence, which seems logical given the racial differences in schooling behaviors observed by many educators and the fact that many people perceive adolescence as a stage during which children can assume some accountability for their academic orientation. However, the findings from Chapter 7 suggest that discussions regarding the source of the achievement gap should not focus on adolescence but should consider preadolescence as the important stage in the gap's development.

I argue that the discourse on the racial achievement gap will be better served by focusing on the early portion of the schooling cycle, when children are less accountable for their academic orientation. There is a growing body of literature that suggests early experiences, from birth to age 5 or 6, are critical to skill development and school readiness. In fact, there is evidence that roughly half of the black-white achievement gap observed in high school is apparent when children enter school (Brooks-Gunn et al. 2003; Fryer and Levitt 2006; Phillips, Crouse, and Ralph 1998). These studies find that the average black child enters school with substantially lower skills in reading, math, and vocabulary than the average white child. I illustrate this in Figure 9.1, which shows the black-white gap across various dimensions of academic skill for children prior to the first grade, as reflected in standardized tests.

Since the exams displayed in Figure 9.1 differ in the content that they assess and the sample from which the scores were collected, the black-white gaps are displayed in standard deviation units. Therefore, a brief discussion of standardized scores will be useful at this point. Standard deviation is a statistical term that represents the average distance of each unit—in this case individual students—from the mean for the entire sample.[2] Standard deviation is a valuable measure, because it illustrates the width of a distribution of scores around an average score. Most students will score below or above the group average, and the standard deviation formula calculates the *average distance* between each student's score and the group average. If the standard deviation for a particular test with an average of 100 is 10, then a score of 115 is 1.5 standard deviations from the mean. Likewise, a score of 66 on an exam with an average of 60 and a standard deviation of 4 is also 1.5 standard deviations above the mean. Thus, standard deviations are useful because they are "scale free"; expressing scores in standard deviations allows for comparisons to be made across exams that measure achievement along different metrics, samples, and time.

While each exam in Figure 9.1 measures a different aspect of skill level, what is important here is that the patterns are relatively similar. Specifically, the scores from the first three exams show that the black-white achievement gap in vocabulary and IQ is over one standard deviation. However, the darker bar for each exam suggests that a substantial portion of these gaps can be attributed to blacks' lower social class compared to whites. Nevertheless, sizable gaps remain after accounting for social class.

The final set of bars shows the black-white gap in reading and math among kindergarteners within the Early Childhood Longitudinal Study kindergarten cohort (ECLS-K)—a nationally representative sample of over twenty thousand students entering kindergarten in 1998. Though these exams provide a substantially smaller gap than the previous three exams, they also show a black skill disadvantage. However, accounting for social class reverses the achievement gap in reading and virtually eliminates the gap in math. The ECLS-K was designed more recently, contains a larger and more current database, and measures a more expansive set of skills (reading and math rather than vocabulary and IQ), which might account for the differences between these findings and those from the first set of bars in Figure 9.1. Nevertheless, these exams show a black disadvantage in skills critical for academic success *before* children enter the first grade.

Numerous studies show that experiences early in life are consequential for skill development. Chief among the reasons often given for racial differences in school readiness is the lower socioeconomic background of blacks and other racial minorities. Socioeconomic status is an umbrella term often used to refer to a variety of factors, such as parents' level of education,

Figure 9.1: Standardized Black-White Skills Gap in Early Childhood

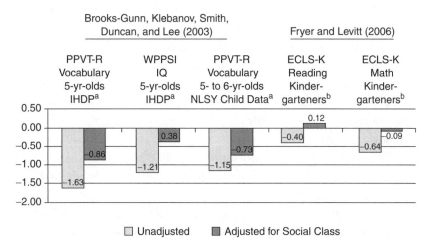

Source: Brooks-Gunn et al. 2003; Fryer and Levitt 2006.
Notes: PPVT-R is the Peabody Picture Vocabulary Test-Revised; IHDP is the Infant Health and Development Program; WPPSI is the Wechsler Preschool and Primary Scale of Intelligence-Revised; NLSY is the National Longitudinal Survey of Youth Child Supplement; ECLS-K is the Early Childhood Longitudinal Study kindergarten cohort.
 [a] Adjusted estimate accounts for family income, female hardship, mother's education, mother's age at birth, and home environment.
 [b] Adjusted estimate accounts for 1) family socioeconomic status (parental education, occupation and income), 2) number of children's books in the home, 3) child's sex, 4) child's age, 5) child's birth weight, 6) mother's age at the time of her first birth, and 7) whether the family receives assistance from the Women, Infants, and Children supplemental food program (WIC).

occupation, and family earnings, that determine one's access to economic and social resources. Just about any study within the United States will find that most black children live in households with fewer socioeconomic resources than white children. For example, relative to whites, black children are more likely to live in single-parent households, households with lower total earnings, or segregated communities with fewer resources; they are also more likely to have parents with lower levels of education and to have fewer books in the home. All these factors are often used as indicators of social class and shown to compromise achievement because they provide children in these conditions with fewer opportunities to learn (Duncan and Brooks-Gunn 1997; Massey and Denton 1993; Wilson 1987, 1996). In general, research suggests that socioeconomic background accounts for roughly half of the black-white gap in school readiness (Brooks-Gunn et al. 2003; Duncan and Magnuson 2005).

Other factors used to explain the black-white difference in early skills are racial differences in the occurrence of low birth weight and overall physical health. Black women within the United States are twice as likely to have low birth weight babies as their white counterparts (Martin et al. 2006), even when the comparison is made among college-educated women (Schoendorf et al. 1992). Low birth weight is associated with compromised social and cognitive development (for a review, see Reichman 2005). While some studies find that low birth weight accounts for less than 2 percent of the black-white gap on measures of school readiness (Brooks-Gunn et al. 2003; Padilla et al. 2002), others estimate that low birth weight can account for up to 4 percent of the black-white gap in academic skill prior to the first grade (Reichman 2005). Furthermore, Currie (2005) estimates that while numerous health conditions that impair cognitive skills and behavior in children (for example, attention deficit hyperactivity disorder, asthma, lead poisoning, iron deficiency, and maternal health) taken individually explain only a small proportion of the racial gap in school readiness, when taken together these conditions could explain up to a quarter of the black-white gap in skills.

Black children's greater exposure to socioeconomic and health disadvantages can also inhibit skill development because early childhood experiences influence neurocognitive development and lead to functional and anatomical changes in the brain. For example, exposure to chronic stress and/or abuse leads to increased production of stress hormone, which compromises the development of the hippocampus, the portion of the brain critical for learning and memory (Noble, Tottenham, and Casey 2005). Developmental studies typically find that children who live in situations characterized by prolonged and acute stress have abnormally developed frontal lobes and reduced hippocampal volume, which has been linked to poor performance on learning and memory tasks and difficulty in replacing old stimulus-response associations with newer ones (Noble, Tottenham, and Casey 2005). Given the connection between stress and socioeconomic and health disadvantages (McCloyd 1990), and that blacks are more likely to be exposed to these conditions than whites, the racial gap in skill also stems from physiological differences strongly governed by children's environments.

Perhaps the most prominent scholar in this area of research is Nobel laureate in Economics James Heckman, who notes that early experiences shape temperament, social development, perceptual and cognitive abilities, and even brain architecture, gene expression, and neurochemistry (Heckman 2006; Heckman and Krueger 2004; Knudsen et al. 2006). In his work regarding the implication of early skill development for economic success in adulthood, Heckman identifies four core concepts relevant for understanding the general process of skill acquisition. First, the process of skill formation is influenced by environmental experiences, which trigger the expression of certain genes. Second, the mastery of skills and the development of their underlying neural pathways follow hierarchical rules in a bottom-up sequence resulting in later attainments that stem from the foundations laid down earlier. In short, learning is cumulative, and the developments of the physical components critical to learning build upon earlier development. Third, early experiences shape cognitive, linguistic, social, and emotional competencies. Finally, although learning and adaptation occurs throughout the life course, abilities are formed in a predictable sequence of sensitive periods, during which the development of neural circuits and the behaviors they mediate are most malleable and receptive to environmental factors. Heckman's work underscores the importance of normative early experiences for the development of neural circuits that are crucial for the acquisition of skills important for academic success. Heckman notes that an impoverished early environment produces a reduced capacity that is virtually impossible to remediate later in life.[3]

The Growth in the Black-White Skills Gap

Not only is there a black-white skill (or achievement) gap prior to students entering grade school, but that gap widens over time as children matriculate through the early schooling process. Among the best supporting evidence for this is provided by Roland Fryer and Steven Levitt (Fryer and Levitt 2004, 2006).[4] Using data from the ECLS-K (the same data displayed in Figure 9.1), Fryer and Levitt show that black children lose substantial ground in academic achievement relative to whites over the first four years of school. Their findings are presented in Figure 9.2. Since the focus here is on racial differences relative to whites, the achievement for white students is represented by the bold line along the "zero" value on the Y-axis.

The figure shows that a racial disparity in academic skills exists at the entry point of the academic cycle. Specifically, whereas Asian Americans enter kindergarten with more skills in both reading and math than whites, blacks enter school with a substantially lower set of skills. The top panel of Figure 9.2 shows that when the comparison is made after accounting for

Figure 9.2: Standardized Racial Differences in Achievement during Early Schooling: ECLS-K

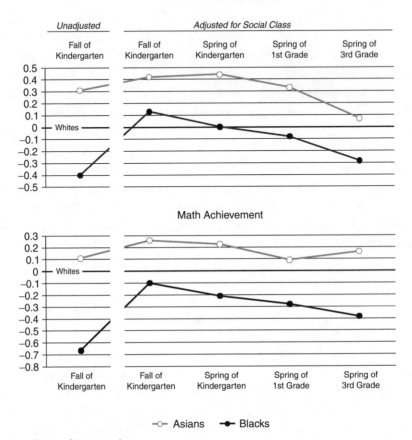

Reading Achievement

Math Achievement

Source: Fryer and Levitt 2006.

[a] Social Class consists of 1) family socioeconomic status (i.e., parental education, occupation and income), 2) number of children's books in the home, 3) child's sex, 4) child's age, 5) child's birth weight, 6) mother's age at the time of her first birth, and 7) whether the family receives assistance from the Women, Infants, and Children supplemental food program (WIC).

social class, black children actually have an advantage in reading achievement relative to whites. This suggests that on average, black children who are similar to whites with regard to social class enter kindergarten with higher reading skills than their white counterparts. However, they lose this advantage as they matriculate through school; their achievement is similar to whites during the spring of kindergarten, but progressively declines below the achievement level of whites by the spring of the third grade. Despite experiencing some decline in reading after the spring of kindergarten relative to whites, Asian Americans retain their advantage over whites throughout this period. The bottom panel shows that the patterns for math achievement are similar to those observed for reading with one exception: differences in social class do not entirely account for blacks' initial disadvantage in math achievement. Social class, however, does account for 85 percent of the black-white gap in math.

Fryer and Levitt were able to track the development of the gap only through the spring term of the third grade because this was the latest wave of data available in the ECLS-K at the time of their study. Therefore, I examined data from the Child Development Supplement (CDS) to the Panel Study of Income Dynamics (PSID) to determine whether this divergence occurs throughout the schooling cycle prior to high school. Since that assessment was not based on panel data—it offers a snapshot of children in grades 1 through 8 during 2002—the pattern it reveals is suggestive of how the black-white gap changes during every year of the schooling cycle prior to high school. In general, blacks seem to lose ground relative to whites from grades 1 through 5. During this period, black children in each grade had lower academic skills in both reading and math relative to whites than their counterparts in the previous grade level. The black disadvantage remained relatively constant across the middle school cohorts. This suggests that if an oppositional culture exists, it exacerbates the gap during grades 1 through 5 and is inconsequential for the gap during middle school. This also assumes that six-year-old black children are deliberately cultivating a culture of resistance to schooling because they perceive fewer benefits of education in adulthood than whites or they simply decided at this point that they want to lead unproductive lives.

The findings by Fryer and Levitt highlight the point that racial disparities in academic skills exist early in the schooling process. They also show that despite the relative skill similarity between blacks and whites with *similar* social class backgrounds, the divergence in reading skills between these groups begins *after* they enter the K-12 school system, and the black disadvantage in both reading and math *increases* (rather than remain constant) as they matriculate through the early stages of schooling. Thus, despite the black achievement disadvantage in unadjusted racial comparisons, blacks are most similar to whites in academic skills prior to entering school. Pairing this with the findings I presented in Chapters 3 through 6 yields an interesting scenario. If an oppositional culture is to blame for the achievement gap, this culture must arise (or intensify) during kindergarten and disappear (or fail to become detectable when under systematic scientific scrutiny) during adolescence.

Final Thoughts

Many of the resistance model's tenets seem quite reasonable, which has likely contributed to the pervasiveness of the black cultural deficiency narrative among many teachers and casual observers. It is a rich and complex framework composed of numerous components such as incorporation into societal systems, group classification, discrimination, racial identity, and inter- and intragroup conflict (for example, the "acting white" hypothesis), which are configured in an elegant manner. Each component of the theory triggers the next, giving the framework a sound internal structure that would be considered sophisticated even by the purest logicians. However, it is amenable to being reduced to one or two elements, usually the "acting white" hypothesis and a nebulous conception of "bad" culture among blacks. The persistence of this narrative suggests that proponents of the resistance model continue to observe blacks' academic disengagement within schools. However, the findings from this study suggest that proponents of the resistance model, having observed behaviors among black youth typically displayed by students with poor academic preparation, are mislabeling these behaviors as oppositional.

What accounts for this continued mislabeling? The layman's application of the theory is in part to blame for the false positive identification of resistance to schooling, and subsequently, its popularity. The primary example of this is the "acting white" hypothesis. Being teased for "acting white" is often attached to high achievement in common parlance, when in actuality high academic achievement is not the reason that some black youth experience this perceived insult. It might simply be that they are "acting white"—independent of achievement—in the manner often described in the routines of most black comedians (for a thorough discussion of this issue, see Carter 2005).[5] Of course, blacks who are perceived in this manner often do not have this perception of themselves and thus attribute the insult to their high academic achievement. "Acting white" is detached from the notion that blacks refuse to embrace education because academic failure is a marker of black identity, a proposition that would not find much support within the larger black community. When considered in this light, the consistent lack of widespread *empirical* support for this hypothesis—that high achievement for blacks comes with a social cost—is not surprising. To be clear, being accused of "acting white" is not enough to confirm the hypothesis; one must establish that the accusation is directly tied to achievement.

Another example of why the theory is incorrectly perceived is the nebulous conception of "bad" culture attributed to blacks, the characterization of which includes lack of effort, aspirations, and work ethic, and a disregard for authority. Ebonics and sagging jeans are taken as markers of academic orientation. However, most black youth to whom this culture is attributed understand the importance of work ethic or "hustle" (working hard to achieve some goal as efficiently as possible), which they exhibit on tasks for which their skill sets permit. Unfortunately, the achievement gap is an indication that those skill sets do not lie within the academic domain. This cultural narrative takes on a life of its own and is detached from the notion that blacks *try* to fail in school. Ironically, rap music, often cited as a source for this culture, often promotes unattainably high aspirations and messages of success; much of this music glorifies bling (shiny accessories), ice (diamonds), big cribs (houses or mansions), expensive whips (cars), and ballin or stunting (having and displaying markers of obscene wealth). My point here is that when one considers that black youth have developed an entire vernacular around the importance of success, the notion that blacks would purposefully resist any mechanism for attaining upward social mobility seems out of touch. An investment in mechanisms for upward mobility other than schooling does not imply resistance of schooling but rather an investment in a mechanism for which one is better equipped.

Given the findings presented in this book and the numerous studies that do not find support for the resistance model (for example, Akom 2003; Carter 2005; Cook and Ludwig 1998; Ainsworth-Darnell and Downey 1998; O'Connor 1997; Tyson 2002; Tyson, Darity, and Castellino 2005), educators and policy makers should reconsider the extent to which they attribute blacks' lower school achievement to lower levels of desire for success. The lack of support for many of the theory's major tenets suggests blacks' lower school performance should be open to alternative explanations. Blacks' pro-school beliefs and attitudes suggest that their lower school achievement might result from such things as racial variation in the quality of the schools students attend, and/or in social, economic, and cultural capital (Lareau and Horvat 1999; Lewis 2003, Noguera 2003).

It is also possible that young black children perceive and internalize teachers' and peers' lower expectations for their performance; if so, they might feel less capable of succeeding, and subsequently put forth less effort towards schooling. Many studies suggest that school personnel treat black children differently than they do white and Asian American children, perhaps stemming from their beliefs that black youth are resisting educational goals (for example, Delpit 1995; Ferguson 2000; Lewis 2003; Morris 2005; Tyson 2003). This has also been the case within the United Kingdom, where West Indian youth are subjected to discrimination by teachers (Ogbu 1978) and empirical evidence suggests that teachers have lower expectations for black youth (Newham Council 1989). In fact, the findings in Chapter 5 show that the black advantage on negative behaviors within the United Kingdom disappears when perceived discrimination is taken into account.

To support the oppositional culture theory, one must assume that black and white children have similar skills that blacks refuse to employ. I present evidence that suggests black youth want to learn; they simply are not acquiring the skills necessary for academic success. I show that academic preparation prior to high school is more important for blacks' achievement relative to whites than their schooling behaviors during high school. In order to have a more fruitful discussion about the racial achievement gap, educators must remain open to the notion that negative attitudes of some blacks might reflect their desire to avoid future experiences of failure. They must also accept that ineffective schooling behaviors might reflect deficiencies in skills necessary for academic success rather than a lack of desire to learn. The lack of support for the resistance model highlights the importance of separating students' academic behaviors and results from their academic intent. It is perhaps most important for educators, scholars, and policy makers to revisit and internalize the title of this book. Only then will we approach children's education with the presumption that kids truly do not want to fail.

APPENDIX A

APPENDIX B

APPENDIX C

APPENDIX D

NOTES

REFERENCES

ACKNOWLEDGEMENTS

INDEX

APPENDIX A:
NOTE OF CAUTION ABOUT TESTING

In a comprehensive account of the origin and growth of testing throughout the twentieth century, Sacks (1999) argues (and provides evidence) that standardized tests reward passive and superficial learning, drive instruction in ways that promote test-taking skills rather than exploration and discovery, and thwart meaningful educational reform. Evidence for these same arguments emerged from McNeil's (2000) ethnographic study of Houston Independent School District—the seventh-largest school district in the United States. McNeil's findings showed how schools respond to pressure to increase test scores by essentially becoming test-prep centers, in which the scope and quality of course content is reduced, the role of teachers diminished, and students are distanced from the process of active learning. Even more alarming is that both Sacks and McNeil show that the negative aspects of the testing movement have deleterious effects for disadvantage minority youth and youth who attend schools in low-income communities.

Standardized tests are intended to provide three primary objectives. First, they are designed to be an objective assessment of students' academic aptitude (or intelligence). Second, they provide an equal measuring stick by which to evaluate students (or job applicants). Third, tests often serve as a predictor of future performance on both proximal (for example, first-year GPA) and distal (for example, job performance and educational attainment) outcomes. These objectives directly deal with the lack of uniformity in standards (and curricula) across schools, an inconsistency that contributes some uncertainty to the use of GPAs as a measure of aptitude. However, the extent to which standardized tests accomplish these objectives has been strongly challenged.

Researchers have learned during the past several years that test scores are not the only indicator of future success and that so-called noncognitive skills are important predictors of future well-being. The culture of testing has relegated other forms of student assessments to a subordinate status, as policy makers seem to focus entirely on test scores. Even in the admissions departments of many top graduate programs, other measures of student assessments are considered only for students above some designated test score. Proponents of testing provide evidence that standardized tests are indeed valid and unbiased, and note that exams can account for up to 30 percent of the variation in first-year college GPA (see Sackett, Borneman, and Connelly 2008). However, there is a clear misalignment between the tasks admissions tests measure (and the testing conditions itself) and the tasks on which students are evaluated in college, graduate programs, and professional schools. In most cases, students (and professionals) are assessed by how well they perform in real-world situations, which often does not involve a "shot clock."[1] Indeed, offices are stacked with books, dictionaries, and computers that can be consulted when we are presented with questions for which we lack answers. The skill is in *finding* an appropriate answer (and sometimes in questioning the question), particularly in the sciences. I have never been asked to simplify $(6x^8 \, , \, x^2) + x^3$ or to determine which value of y can satisfy both $\frac{1}{2}6 - 16y\frac{1}{2} = 2$ and $\frac{1}{2}14 - 8y\frac{1}{2} = 10$ before my work can be published in peer-refereed journals.[2]

Perhaps the most popular critique levied against standardized tests is that they are not perfect measures of academic skills. In a critique of the Armed Forces Qualification Test (AFQT), a measure of achievement that is often used by researchers to highlight racial differences in skill levels, Rodgers and Spriggs (1996) show that AFQT scores do not measure the same set of skills across racial groups. If AFQT measures skills obtained from school quality, motivation, and family background, then these factors should contribute similarly to AFQT scores across racial groups, even if the means on these factors vary by race. Rodgers and Spriggs (1996) show that this is not the case; these factors predict higher scores for whites than blacks. Brooks-Gunn, Klebanov, and Duncan (1996:404) reach a similar conclusion—that socioeconomic factors explain a greater portion of the variation in scores among whites than blacks—using the Wechsler Preschool and Primary Scale of Intelligence (WPPSI). A prime illustration of the fact that testing misses a large component of the academic experience is that the proportion of college degrees earned by women in biology, business, computer science, engineering, math, and the physical sciences has been increasing despite the female disadvantage in test scores relative to males (Livingston and Wirt 2004).

With regard to the predictive validity of standardized tests, numerous studies suggest that admissions tests do not predict academic outcomes to a greater degree than GPA. In a study of over ten thousand students at eleven selective public and private institutions of higher education, Vars and Bowen (1998) found that a 100-point increase in SAT combined scores led to a one-tenth of a grade point gain for college GPA net of race, gender, and field of study. The increase in SAT score, then, offered no greater predictive value than the educational attainment of an applicant's parents. Furthermore, the ability of SAT scores to predict freshman grades, undergraduate class rank, college graduation rates, and attainment of a graduate degree is weaker for black students than for whites (Bowen and Bok 1998). In fact, the relationship between SAT scores and academic performance is generally weaker for blacks, Latinos, and women than for whites, Asians, and men (Mattern et al. 2008).

The relative predictive benefit of standardized tests for graduate school has also been studied. Kuncel, Hezlett, and Ones (2001) conducted a metaanalysis that synthesized the results from 1,753 independent samples that included over 82,000 students and 6,589 correlations across various areas of study (humanities, social sciences, life sciences, and math-physical sciences). They find that in general the GRE and undergraduate GPA have similar levels of validity in predicting graduate GPA, first-year graduate GPA, faculty ratings of students, and comprehensive exam results. The most ironic of these findings comes from a metaanalysis of 123 studies and 715 effect sizes conducted by D'Agostino and Powers (2009), which finds that teachers' test scores—mandated by state practices and federal laws for licensure purposes—are less related to teaching performance than teachers' success levels (GPAs) in the very teacher training programs that such tests were designed to hold accountable.

Even if we concede that admissions tests are statistically valid, Lucas (2008) shows that the procedures involved in the construction of some admission exams actually maintain the existing patterns of inequality. In general, tests created by the Educational Testing Service (ETS), such as the SAT and GRE—two of the most widely used admissions tests—are designed to correlate very strongly with one another, and questions selected for inclusion are expected to parallel the outcomes of the test overall. For example, questions for which a greater percentage of low scorers respond correctly relative to high scorers are regarded as flawed and excluded from official versions of the test. Although race is not explicitly considered, racially disparate scores drive question selection. Thus, racially disparate test results are maintained by an internally reinforcing cycle (Lucas 2008; Rosner 2003).

The limitations associated with standardized testing should not overshadow the real racial inequalities that exist in American schools, even if testing partially contributes to (rather than simply measures) these inequalities. However, standardized tests have become *the* achievement measure of consequence, as the culture of testing is an institution in our educational system and is deeply entrenched in the American notion of meritocracy. My point here has been to note that there are a vast number of critiques of standardization that must be considered in any discussion of the racial achievement gap. Given these limitations, test scores are not a major outcome in this study and account for less than 10 percent of the more than 150 outcomes I employ. As I will soon make clear, explaining the achievement gap is *not* the purpose of this study. My interest is in whether a culture of resistance to schooling is at the heart of the differences in achievement and general schooling outcomes between black and white youth, regardless of how achievement is measured.

APPENDIX B: SOURCES OF DATA

This study relied on six datasets. Four are based on samples of youth in the United States: 1) The Maryland Adolescent Development in Context Study (MADICS), 2) National Education Longitudinal Study of 1988 (NELS), 3) Education Longitudinal Study of 2002 (ELS), and 4) the Child Development Supplement (CDS) to the Panel Study of Income Dynamics (PSID). Although the bulk of the analyses in this study are based on the MADICS, the latter three datasets are based on nationally representative samples and are employed to supplement the MADICS. Additionally, in order to provide an assessment of various aspects of the oppositional culture theory, two British datasets are used: the British Cohort Study of 1970 (BCS) and the Longitudinal Study of Young People in England (LSYPE). Below I provide a description of each dataset used in this study.

Maryland Adolescent Development in Context Study (MADICS)

The MADICS contains a unique collection of measures on 1,407 black and white families (66 percent and 34 percent, respectively) from a county on the eastern seaboard of the United States. The sample was selected from approximately 5,000 adolescents in the county who entered middle school during 1991 via a stratified sampling procedure designed to get proportional representations of families from each of the county's twenty-three middle schools. As such, students' socioeconomic status (SES) is varied, as the sample includes families from neighborhoods in low-income urban areas, middle-class suburban areas, and rural farm-based areas. While the mean family income in the sample is normally distributed around $45,000–$49,000 (range $5,000–$75,000), white families report significantly higher incomes ($50,000–$54,999) than black families ($40,000–$44,999).

Data were collected from the time the target youth entered middle school in the fall of 1991 until they were three years removed from high school. Specifically, the MADICS consists of five waves of data collected when youth were in grade 7 (n = 1407), 8 (n = 1004), 11 (n = 954), one year post high school (n = 832), and three years post high school (n = 853). The first three waves of data also include surveys collected from youths' parents (or primary caregiver). In supplemental analyses not shown, blacks were *not* less likely to be retained than whites; the proportion of blacks and whites within the sample remains constant across waves. Also, most attrition occurs between grades 7 and 8; only 3 percent of the sample is lost between grades 8 and 11. Therefore, it is unlikely sample attrition results from students dropping out of high school (see Harris 2006 for an assessment of attrition bias).

Despite the limitation that the MADICS was not designed to draw inferences about the national population of students, it is well suited to the goals of this study. It has the necessary quality, and it has greater breadth than previous datasets used to assess the resistance model. The MADICS is primarily used by psychologists for understanding psychological determinants of behavior and developmental trajectories during adolescence. Therefore, its richness and longitudinal design provide a good opportunity to determine whether development from middle school to high school leads to greater opposition toward schooling among blacks than whites using a wide range of measures. Furthermore, as I discuss in Chapter 5, I am unaware of theoretical models positing that the underlying causal mechanisms of school resistance vary by social class or geographic area (for example, east/west, urban/suburban); the resistance model attributes an oppositional cultural frame of reference to the wider black community. Nevertheless, although the MADICS yields results similar to those obtained from national data (that is, Ainsworth-Darnell and Downey 1998; Cook and Ludwig 1998), I supplement this study with three national datasets, discussed below.

National Education Longitudinal Study of 1988 (NELS)

The NELS is a nationally representative longitudinal dataset collected by the National Center for Education Statistics (NCES). Sponsored by the U.S. Department of Education (USDOE), it was designed to provide trend data about critical transitions experienced by students as they leave middle or junior high school and progress through high school and into postsecondary institutions or the work force. The sample consists of nearly 25,000 students who were in the eighth grade during the first wave of data collection in 1988. The first and second follow-up surveys were conducted at two-year intervals, when respondents were in grades 10 (1990) and 12 (1992).

These waves featured surveys collected from students, parents, and teachers. The NELS also contains two post–high school waves collected in 1994 and 2000, eight years after the scheduled date of high school graduation. The sample was obtained using a two-stage stratified sampling design. In the first stage, 1,057 schools were selected from a national sampling frame stratified by region, school type (public or private), urbanicity, and minority concentration. In the second stage, over 24,000 students in these schools completed base-year surveys.

My analysis of the NELS is restricted to youth who responded to the 1988, 1990, and 1992 surveys. Attrition across survey waves reduces the sample size to 12,144 respondents. However, the NCES provides a weight that allows for the estimation of parameters that describe the population of eighth graders during the spring of 1988 (U.S. Department of Education 2002). Thus, all analyses are based on weighted data using the appropriate NELS panel weights to adjust for sampling design (that is, stratification, disproportionate sampling of certain strata, and clustered, multistage probability sampling), sample attrition, and nonresponse (Ingles et al. 1994), which allows for unbiased population estimates.

The NELS is part of a larger program established by the National Center for Education Statistics (NCES), which is the primary federal entity for collecting and analyzing data related to education within the United States. The National Education Longitudinal Studies program was created to study the educational, vocational, and personal development of young people beginning with their elementary or high school years and following them over time as they begin to take on adult roles and responsibilities. Thus far, the NCES longitudinal studies program consists of four major studies: the National Longitudinal Study of the High School Class of 1972 (NLS-72), High School and Beyond (HS&B), the National Education Longitudinal Study of 1988 (NELS), and the Education Longitudinal study of 2002 (ELS). For this study, I used data from the NELS and ELS (which I discuss further below).

Education Longitudinal Study of 2002 (ELS)

The ELS is a nationally representative longitudinal dataset that follows a cohort of students from the time they were high school sophomores in 2002 through the rest of their high school careers. It is the fourth in a series of school-based longitudinal studies conducted by the NCES. It contains a freshened sample to represent the high school class of 2004, which allows for trend comparisons against the high school classes of 1972 (NLS-72), 1980 (HS&B), and 1992 (NELS). Therefore, the ELS is an updated version of the NELS and has many of the same qualities of the NELS, with the primary difference being students' grade level at the base year of the study; ELS first sampled students in grade 10 rather than grade 8.

The sample consists of 15,362 students from 752 schools obtained in 2002 using the same two-stage stratified sampling design employed in the NELS. In 2004, the first follow-up year, the sample was augmented to make it representative of seniors as well. Thus, although the ELS began with a representative sample of high school sophomores in 2002, it contains a fully representative sample of high school seniors two years later. The base year cohort was freshened to include seniors who were not sophomores in the United States in 2002 (for example, students who were out of the country or who were in another grade sequence because of skipping or failing a grade). The ELS continued to follow these students into postsecondary education and/or the labor market. Students were surveyed again in 2006, when many sample members were in college for up to their second year of enrollment, while others were employed and may not have ever attended college. All sample members who were respondents in the base year and/or the first follow-up were included in this study.

As part of the NCES longitudinal studies program, the ELS closely reflects the research purposes and designs of its three predecessor studies (NLS-72, HS&B, and NELS:88). For example, the ELS collected data from students and their parents, teachers, and school administrators. Also, it contains measures of student achievement and information about students' attitudes and experiences. It is designed to monitor the transition of young people as they progress from tenth grade through high school and on to postsecondary education and/or the world of work. It allows researchers and policy makers to explore and better understand such issues as the importance of home background and parental aspirations for their child's success, as well as the general schooling experiences of adolescent youth. ELS is conducted on behalf of the NCES of the U.S. Department of Education by the Research Triangle Institute—a not-for-profit university-affiliated research organization with headquarters in North Carolina.

Child Development Supplement (CDS)

The Child Development Supplement (CDS) is a dataset collected to provide information about youth from the Panel Study for Income Dynamics

(PSID). Since 1968, the PSID has collected data from a nationally representative sample of 5,000 American families on family composition changes, housing and food expenditures, marriage and fertility histories, employment, income, time spent in housework, health, consumption, wealth, pensions and savings, and philanthropic giving. Families were interviewed every year until 1997, after which data collection occurred biannually. Data was collected from members of the original sample families as well as from families formed by children of the initial sample members. In 1997, the PSID added the CDS to address the lack of information on children. Thus, the objective of the CDS was to provide a nationally representative longitudinal database of children and their families to support studies on the dynamic process of early human capital development. It contains a broad array of developmental outcomes including physical health, emotional well-being, and intellectual and academic achievement. I use the CDS in this study because it includes time diary methodology on a national sample of youth.

The CDS contains three waves of data. The first wave (CDS-I) contains 3,563 children between the ages of 0 and 12 sampled from PSID families in 1997. The first follow-up wave (CDS-II) was conducted in 2002–2003 among 2,908 children whose families remained active in the PSID panel. The children were then between the ages of 5 and 18. A third wave of data was collected in 2007, when youth were approximately ages 9 to 22. Since the analysis of the CDS is based on time diaries for school-aged youth, the sample in this study is restricted to the roughly 2,000 youth that completed time diaries during CDS-II. For all analysis based on the CDS, I employ a weighting system devised by the PSID staff to account for the effects of the initial probability of being sampled and attrition over time—which is generally low—and incorporates a poststratification factor to ensure the data are nationally representative (see http://psidonline.isr.umich.edu/CDS/weightsdoc.html for a detailed description of the CDS weight construction).

British Cohort Study of 1970 (BCS70)

The British Cohort Study (BCS70) is a nationally representative longitudinal study on over 17,000 people born in Britain during April of 1970. The BCS70 began when data were collected about the births and families of babies born in England, Scotland, Wales, and Northern Ireland in one particular week in 1970. The first wave, called the British Births Survey, was carried out by the National Birthday Trust Fund in association with the

Royal College of Obstetricians and Gynaecologists. Its aims were to examine the social and biological characteristics of the mother in relation to neonatal morbidity and to compare the results with those of the National Child Development Study (NCDS), which commenced in 1958. Participants from Northern Ireland, who had been included in the birth survey, were dropped from the study in all subsequent waves, which only included respondents from Great Britain. Although the BCS70 began as a study of births in the United Kingdom, with each successive wave the scope was broadened from a strictly medical focus at birth to encompass physical and educational development at age 5, social development at ages 10 and 16, and economic development at age 26 and beyond.

The sample was followed up subsequently at ages 5, 10, 16, 26, 30, and 34 (2004–2005). In both 1975 and 1980 (the age 5 and 10 waves, respectively), the cohort was augmented by the addition of immigrants to Britain who were born in the target week in 1970. Given that my interest is on adolescent youth, I assess data from the surveys completed at age 16. There were 8,900 respondents who completed data on social class during age 16. However, attrition analysis reveals that the effects of attrition are generally negligible (see, for instance, Bynner and Parsons 2002); the demographic characteristics of the sample remain similar to the base-year survey (Bynner, Ferri, and Shepherd 1997).

Data has been collected using various methods and from various sources. For example, in the birth survey, information was collected by means of a questionnaire that was completed by the midwife present at the birth, and supplementary information was obtained from clinical records. The subsequent waves contained questionnaires from parents and head teachers, as well as information gathered from the school health service (which carried out medical examinations on each child). The maternal self-completion questionnaire contained questions on the behavior of the child at home, maternal depression, attitudes towards child rearing, maternal employment, television viewing, and hospital visiting. In the first two follow-up waves (1975 and 1980), parents were also interviewed by health visitors. Target youth completed educational assessments at each wave, and two four-day diaries (one for nutrition and one for general activity) and questionnaires (starting at age 10).

Data for the BCS70 was collected by various agencies. Whereas the base-year survey was conducted by the National Birthday Trust Fund, the five-year and ten-year surveys were conducted by the Department of Child

Health at Bristol University, and these surveys were referred to as the Child Health and Education Study (CHES). The 1986 survey was carried out by the International Centre for Child Studies and was named Youthscan. The most recent follow-ups, conducted in 1999–2000 and 2004, were managed by the Centre for Longitudinal Studies, and fieldwork was conducted by the National Centre for Social Research.

Longitudinal Study of Young People in England (LSYPE)

Since the BCS70 does not contain data on race, I also employ the LSYPE, which contains data on over 15,000 young people born in England between September 1989 and August 1990. The LSYPE is a major panel study of young people that brings together rich and detailed data from interviews with young people and their parents with test data from the National Pupil Database. It was developed to understand the factors affecting young people's transition from the later years of compulsory education, through any subsequent education or training, and into the labor market. Thus, it contains extensive information on family circumstances and pupil and parental aspirations, which offers researchers the potential to identify factors influencing attainment and progress in early secondary education. The diverse sample, which includes 13,529 whites, nearly 1000 Asians, and nearly 400 blacks, allows for the opportunity to greatly extend knowledge about the experience of minority ethnic pupils in British schools. The LSYPE is particularly useful for this study because it contains data on race as well as social class. Similar to the other datasets in this study, data collection was based on face-to-face interviews of target youth and both parents (where present).

Data for the LSYPE have been collected annually since the respondents were in year 9 (ages 13–14) or equivalent in schools in England on February 2004. The sample was selected using a two-stage sampling procedure. The 15,570 respondents, who were sampled in the first stage, were drawn from 647 schools in England. However, not all of these cases were eligible for inclusion in this analysis, as 354 respondents were not interviewed or refused to give their ethnicity. Several students also lacked information on measures of academic assessment and a smaller number (193) either refused the computer-assisted component or were lost because of interpreter problems. As such, the true eligible sample is nearer to 14,000 students.

The LSYPE contains an oversample of ethnic minorities from the following six groups: Black African; Black Caribbean; Bangladeshi; Indian; Pakistani;

and mixed heritage. In a conventional two-stage sample design, such boosts will deliver variation in either cluster size or within-subpopulation sampling fraction. In contrast, the method used in the LSYPE delivered both a constant sampling fraction for each subpopulation and a fixed cluster size. It therefore avoided precision losses through corrective (design) weighting and excessive variation in cluster sizes. These boosts are representative samples of the relevant subpopulations as a whole, rather than drawn disproportionately from areas or schools with high numbers of minority ethnic pupils.

Similar to the NELS and ELS, which also use two-stage sampling procedures, the LSYPE data have been weighted to compensate for differential selection chances in the sample design, clustering, and to remove nonresponse biases. Nonresponse weights were calculated through comparison of respondents to the Pupil Level Annual School Census (PLASC) data. These weights are the reciprocals of the selection probabilities. Clustering was accounted for by identifying the school (the primary sampling unit) as a cluster variable. The application of these features ensures the calculation of appropriate standard errors and allows for unbiased population estimates.

There are several advantages to using both the BCS70 and the LSYPE. First, using both datasets allows me to examine a greater breadth of measures of academic orientation. As such, this study consists of a series of group comparisons on twenty-two outcomes on British youth. Second, I examine the academic implications of marginalization along both social class and race. Third, I am able to examine differences in academic orientation between youths from marginalized groups (based on social class) and their nonmarginalized counterparts for cohorts born twenty years apart. In Appendix C, I discuss the analytic plan for all analyses conducted in this study.

APPENDIX C: METHODOLOGICAL APPENDIX

This appendix discusses the technical aspects of the data analysis for this study. The discussion is divided into two sections: general strategy and chapter-specific descriptions. The first section contains information that applies to all analyses throughout the study. Specifically, I discuss what is meant by socioeconomic status (SES), provide a brief description of the figures that appear most frequently to convey the findings, and describe the strategy employed to deal with missing data and sample weights. In the second section, I describe aspects of the analyses that are specific to each chapter. Only figures based on statistical analyses that require substantial information for the purposes of replication are discussed. I do not provide descriptions of figures that illustrate raw scores or percentages.

General Strategy

Four major points of clarification are central to the interpretation of the findings presented in this study. First, most of the analyses control for the SES backgrounds of youth's families. Since Ogbu posits that being an involuntary minority leads to oppositional culture independent of social class, it is important to assess racial differences net of SES factors associated with race and the outcomes. Thus, within the context of methodological discussions throughout this appendix (and book), the term *social class* (or SES) refers to a vector comprised of family income, parental education, family structure (single- or two-parent household), and youth's sex. Although these measures are far from perfect, they represent a reasonable set of factors that characterize the socioeconomic standing of youths' families.

Second, the goal of this study is to determine whether blacks have lower academic orientation than whites. Therefore, most of the analysis in this book is based on simple mean comparisons, which can be expressed as an equation:

$$Y = \alpha + \beta \, (\text{black}) + e \tag{1}$$

where Y is the outcome or measure for which the racial comparison is being made, α represents the constant, β represents the estimate for blacks, e represents the error term, and whites are the omitted category. Since this equation does not include any controls, I refer to it henceforward as the unadjusted equation. This means that α actually represents the mean score for whites on the outcome and β the mean score for blacks *relative to* whites. That is, the actual mean score for blacks can be obtained by adding α and β. One manner in which these estimates are displayed throughout the book is in a series of bar graphs, as shown below:

Figure A.1:   Perceptions of (outcome)

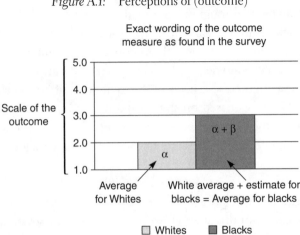

Notes: The notes at the bottom of the figures contain any information relevant to the interpretation of the figure. In this example, the average score for whites is 2 ($\alpha = 2$) and the estimate for blacks from the unadjusted equation is 1 ($\beta = 1$), which is the black score *relative to* the score for whites. Thus, the average score for blacks is $\alpha + \beta$ or $2 + 1$, which $= 3$.

Figure A.1 depicts the type of figure that appears most frequently in this book.

Since blacks have lower socioeconomic standing than whites, the comparison as specified in Equation 1 (which shows the raw *unadjusted* group means) is an "apples-to-oranges" comparison; it is unclear whether any observed black disadvantage relative to whites can be attributed to blacks' lower SES or an actual culture of oppositionality independent of SES.

Thus, before any claims of an oppositional culture can be attributed to black youth, it is important that the racial comparison be an "apples-to-apples" comparison. I do this by showing the racial comparison after adjusting for SES, as follows:

$$Y = \alpha + \beta_1 \text{ (black)} + X\beta_2 + e \tag{2}$$

where X represents the matrix of the aforementioned SES variables and observations specified in the model and β_2 represents its associated vector of coefficients. Thus, Equation 2 shows the estimated racial difference on the outcome after accounting for social class. That is, β_1 represents the estimate for blacks *relative to* whites if both groups had similar SES (for example, family income, parental education, and family structure) and $\alpha + \beta_1$ can be interpreted as the score for blacks, relative to whites, if blacks and whites were similarly situated with regards to social class.

Throughout the book, the unadjusted estimates obtained from Equation 1 and depicted in Figure A.1 (both α and $\alpha + \beta_1$) are always accompanied by the estimates obtained from Equation 2. The unadjusted estimates and the estimates that adjust for social class are depicted in bar graphs that contain two pairs of bars for each outcome; whereas the first pair displays estimates from Equation 1 (as shown in Figure A.1) and are labeled "unadjusted," the second pair of bars displays the estimates from Equation 2 and are located to the right of the first set of bars and labeled "social class" (see Figure 3.2, for example).

While the bar graphs are useful for displaying means on an outcome for both blacks and whites, in some cases I place the emphasis on the black-white difference (β_1). This is particularly the case for measures of academic orientation that will not serve as predictors of academic outcomes, such as in Chapters 5 and 8. In these chapters, I show black-white differences on academic orientation in estimate graphs, which is the second-most frequent graph to appear in this book, as follows:

Figure A.2:   Example of How Racial Differences on a Series of Academic
Orientation Measures Are Displayed

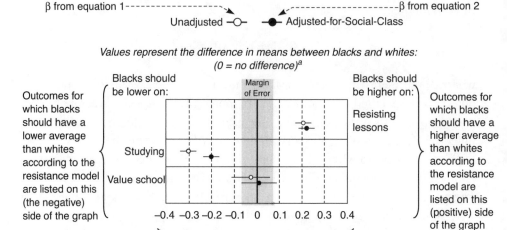

The notes at the bottom of the figures contain any information relevant to the interpretation of the figure.[a]

In these graphs, the average score for whites is represented by the "o"
($\alpha = o$), and the actual estimates (β_1) for blacks are displayed, not their averages on the outcomes ($\alpha + \beta_1$). The unadjusted estimates—represented
by the open circle—were obtained with Equation 1 and the class-adjusted
estimates—represented by the full circle—were obtained using Equation 2.
Thus, the emphasis in this type of figure is on the direction of the racial difference before and after adjusting for SES.

There are several points of clarification with regard to estimate graphs.
First, the names of the survey indicators of academic orientation are listed
on the side of the expected "effect"; indicators for which blacks should score
lower than whites according to the resistance model are labeled on the
negative side of the zero, while those indicators on which blacks should
score higher are labeled on the positive side of the zero. Second, since variation exists on the scale along which the indicators are measured, the estimated effect sizes (β_1) should not be interpreted across indicators. Rather,

the focus should be on the location of the estimates—whether they are on the negative or positive side of the graph. Recall that the focus is on whether blacks have a higher or lower academic orientation than whites. Third, the standard errors are represented by the tails on both sides of the estimates. Fourth, for ease of interpretation, I provided a shaded area that represents the margin of error. Estimates within the margin of error suggest that the racial difference on the outcome is not significant at the .05 level.

In the example provided above in Figure A.2, relative to white youth, black youth should have a higher score on the survey indicator which measures *resisting lessons* according to the oppositional culture theory. Therefore, it is listed on the positive side of the graph. In contrast, black youth should have a lower score than whites on the indicators that measure *studying* and *value school.* As such, these measures are listed on the negative side of the graph. In this example, the estimates indicate that blacks resist lessons more than whites (unadjusted $\beta_1 = 0.2$), even after accounting for their socioeconomic disadvantage (adjusted $\beta_1 = 0.22$). The estimates for the second measure indicate that black youth study less than whites (unadjusted $\beta_1 = -0.3$) and only one-third of this disadvantage can be explained by social class (adjusted $\beta_1 = -0.2$). For the final measure, black youth do not differ from their white counterparts in the value they attribute to school; both estimates are within the margin of error.

It is important to emphasize that the aim of this study is to determine whether blacks are more resistant to schooling than whites. Thus, to maintain the focus of this presentation, I only display estimates for the race "effect." This appendix does provide the equations from which these estimates were extracted, however. In most cases, I provide a citation for the published work in which the results for the full equation can be found. Furthermore, if a finding on a particular measure of academic orientation suggests that blacks have a positive advantage relative to whites (such as educational aspirations), then the question has been answered, and including controls is not necessary. Accounting for SES or other factors on which black youth are disadvantaged and that might affect academic orientation would only further widen the black advantage relative to whites. Alternatively, a black advantage on a particular measure of academic orientation means a white disadvantage. Explaining white disadvantage is beyond the scope of the oppositional culture theory and this study.

The third major methodological point regards missing data. Since an analysis using listwise deletion rapidly reduces sample size, particularly with an increase in covariates, I include missing values as dummy categories within each predictor variable. Thus, missing cases for the predictors were bottom coded and each predictor was entered into the models along with a flag or "missing information" measure—coded as 0 if not missing and 1 if missing. This has certain advantages since it 1) prevents the loss of explanatory power that would come from listwise deletion; 2) allows for the direct modeling of missing data rather than imputing values—for example, by mean substitution, which has its own interpretative problems; 3) ensures a consistent base in terms of the sample size across a range of regression models that include a large number of explanatory variables; 4) yields estimates identical to those attained via listwise deletion for the variable with the substituted values; and 5) allows all cases with values on the outcome to remain in the analysis. Therefore, the number of cases (n) in all analyses totals the n that responded to the outcome being assessed.

Finally, in order to obtain unbiased population estimates, I employ sample weights for analyses based on the National Education Longitudinal Study of 1988 (NELS), the Education Longitudinal Study of 2002 (ELS), and the Longitudinal Study of Young People in England (LSYPE), the three datasets that employ two-stage stratified sampling design. Specifically, the weights account for sampling design (stratification, disproportionate sampling of certain strata, and clustered, multistage probability sampling), sample attrition, and nonresponse (Ingles et al. 1994). Furthermore, the sum of the sample weights were adjusted to equal the size of the unweighted sample, which accounts for the extremely small standard errors and inflated likelihood of finding significance due to panel weights' adjustment of the sample size to the national population of high school youth (Hanson 1994; Moser and Kalton 1972; Muller, Stage, and Kinzie 2001). For analyses based on the Child Development Supplement (CDS), I also employ a weighting system devised by the Panel Study of Income Dynamics (PSID) staff to account for the effects of the initial probability of being sampled and of attrition over time—which is generally low; the PSID weighting system also incorporates a post-stratification factor to ensure the data are nationally representative.

Chapter-Specific Analytic Descriptions

Below I discuss the strategy I employed to obtain the findings reported in each figure in this book. Again, the following discussion applies to figures that summarize results based on statistical analysis and not those that illustrate raw scores or percentages. My discussion begins with Chapter 3, the first analytic chapter in this book. I focus on the statistical analysis and not the measures used in the analysis. A detailed description of all measures is contained in Appendix D (constructs comprised of multiple items are the weighted sum of the items within the scale).

Chapter 3

The purpose of this chapter is to examine the intergenerational transmission of beliefs about opportunities for upward mobility. I examine whether parents' beliefs of racial barriers and educational aspiration are associated with youths' own educational aspirations and academic outcomes. The Maryland Adolescent Development in Context Study (MADICS) was used for this analysis because of its longitudinal design, data on parents, and rich collection of measures on perceptions about the opportunity structure from both parents and youth. Whereas all parental measures are based on responses from wave 1 (grade 7) and 2 (grade 8), the youth outcomes are from wave 3 (grade 11).

I begin my analysis by determining whether a racial difference exists in the frequency with which 1) parents perceive that they have experienced discrimination because of their race and 2) believe that their child will experience discrimination because of race (see Appendix D for a description of all measures used in this study). The black-white comparisons on these beliefs were obtained using Equations 1 and 2 and are displayed in Figure 3.2 in the manner described in Figure A.1. The bottom panel of Figure 3.2 shows racial comparisons for whether parents 1) believe that their race has made it more difficult for them to get ahead in life and 2) whether their race will make it more difficult for their child to get ahead in life. I show the odds that parents will respond affirmatively to each belief for blacks relative to whites. Odds are calculated as follows:

$$\text{Odds} = P / 1 - P \tag{3}$$

where P refers to the probability that parents will respond yes to the latter two measures. Probability is the calculated chance that an event, in this case a response of yes, will occur. For example, if 75 out of 100 black parents respond yes, then the chance (or probability) that blacks will affirm the measure is .75 (or 75 percent). In contrast, the probability of responding no is .25. In this case, the odds of expecting that black parents will believe their race has made it difficult for them to get ahead in life is $.75/(1 - .75) = 3$. Thus, the odds that blacks will respond yes to the question are 3 to 1 (or three affirmative responses for every no). Note that if half of the black sample responded yes, then $P = .5$ (or 50–50 percent chance), and the odds of "yes" would be $.5/(1 - .5) = 1$; there would be one response of yes for every response of no.

Equation 3 yields unadjusted odds. Therefore, in order to show both the unadjusted and SES-adjusted odds for black and white parents, I estimate the log of the odds of responding yes to the aforementioned measures. Since it is difficult to model a dichotomous measure (in this case, yes/no), log odds are employed because they expand the range of the probability of a yes response beyond 0 (no) and 1 (yes) from negative infinity to positive infinity. The estimate from the log of the odds is known as the logit-transformed probability and is calculated as follows:

$$\text{Logit } P = \text{Log odds} = \frac{P}{1-P} = \alpha + \beta_1 \text{ (black)} + e \qquad (4)$$

where α and β represent the estimates for whites and blacks, respectively, and e represents the error term. The SES adjusted estimates are obtained as follows:

$$\text{Log odds} = \frac{P}{1-P} = \alpha + \beta_1 \text{ (black)} + X\beta_2 + e \qquad (5)$$

where X represents the matrix of SES variables and observations specified in the model and β_2 represents its associated vector of coefficients. Thus, logit-transformed probability allows for the estimation of linear relationships with the predictor variables (being black and the SES factors).

A final racial comparison is made on parental views about the importance of schooling. Specifically, I examine whether black parents differ from whites in 1) the educational aspirations they have for their child and 2) the belief that their child will not be successful in life if they are not successful in school. The comparisons on these measures are made using Equations 1 and 2 and are displayed in Figure 3.3. Since the findings for these measures contravene expectations, I repeat this analysis using measures of parents' educational aspirations and expectations for their child contained in the NELS and ELS, which are displayed in Figure 3.4. Although the indicators are the same, they are from different datasets and measured along different scales. Therefore, I report the standardized estimates.

The findings in Figure 3.5 show the results for whether parents' perceptions of barriers and the importance of schooling have implications for youths' academic orientation. I present these findings in a series of mini-graphs in Figure 3.5. I show the youth averages on various outcomes for parents who are low, average, and high on the measures for parents' perceptions of discrimination, beliefs about barriers, and views about education. Specifically, I employ the following equation:

$$Y_{G11} = \alpha + \beta_1 \text{(black)} + \delta_1 \text{(DiscrimPar}_{G7}) + \delta_2 \text{(RaceBarrierPar}_{G7}) +$$
$$\lambda_1 \text{(DiscrimChild}_{G7}) + \lambda_2 \text{(RaceBarrierChild}_{G7}) + \xi_1 \text{(EducAsp}_{G7}) +$$
$$\xi_2 \text{(EducSuccessLife}_{G7}) + \gamma_1 \text{(DiscrimPar}_{G7} * \text{black)} +$$
$$\gamma_2 \text{(RaceBarrierPar}_{G7} * \text{black)} + \gamma_3 \text{(DiscrimChild}_{G7} * \text{black)} +$$
$$\gamma_4 \text{(RaceBarrierChild}_{G7} * \text{black)} + \gamma_5 \text{(EducAsp}_{G7} * \text{black)} +$$
$$\gamma_6 \text{(EducSuccessLife}_{G7} * \text{black)} + \beta_2 (Y_{G7}) + X\beta_3 + e \qquad (6)$$

where youth outcomes are measured when youth were in grade 11 (Y_{G11}), δ_1 and $_2$ represent the estimates for parents' belief that they have experienced discrimination (DiscrimPar) and that race has made it harder for them to get ahead in life (RaceBarrierPar), respectively. The next two estimates, λ_1 and $_2$, represent the estimates for parents' belief that their child will experience discrimination because of race (DiscrimChild) and that race will make it harder for them to get ahead in life (RaceBarrierChild), respectively. The estimates represented by ξ are for parents' educational aspirations (EducAsp) for the youth and their belief that their child will not be successful in life if they are not successful in school (EducSuccessLife). The next six estimates (γ) are intended to examine whether parents' beliefs about discrimination toward themselves and their child and their views about the importance of education have a stronger association with the youth outcomes for blacks than whites. Finally, X represents the matrix of the aforementioned SES variables and observations specified in the model, and β_3 represents its associated vector of coefficients. The findings from this equation are displayed as follows:

Figure A.3:   Example of How the Association between Parents' Beliefs about Discrimination and Youth Outcomes Are Displayed

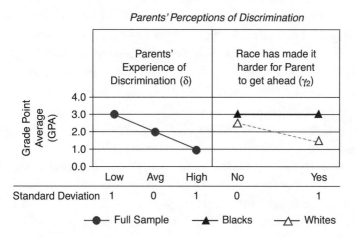

The minigraph in Figure A.3 shows the *slope* or changes in the youth outcome—listed on the y-axis—associated with increases in the indicator for parents' beliefs about discrimination—listed along the x-axis. The left panel indicates that youth whose parents report fewer experiences of discrimination have higher GPAs than those whose parents report experiencing high levels of discrimination. The right panel shows that parents' belief that race has made it difficult for them to get ahead in life is unrelated to GPA for black youth and is associated with a decline in GPA for white youth. These slopes were obtained using the following equation:

$$\mu_{outcome} +/- [(\eta) (\sigma_{predictor})] \tag{7}$$

where μ is the mean of the youth outcome, η refers to the estimate obtained from Equation 6 for the parental measure listed along the top of the x-axis, and σ represents the standard deviation for the parental measure. When the parental measure is dichotomous, such as when parents assess whether "race has made (will make) it difficult for them (for youth) to get ahead in life," the following equation was employed:

$$\mu_{outcome} +/- [\eta / 2] \tag{8}$$

Thus, minigraphs such as those displayed in Figure A.3 enable me to convey both youths' averages on the outcomes and how the outcomes are associated with the parental factors. The association between the parental and youth measures is displayed as the average score for youth at two levels of the parental indicator: one standard deviation below and one standard deviation above the mean of the parental indicator (labeled "low" and "high," respectively), passing through the mean (labeled "average") of the youth outcomes. In cases where the slope differs by race, the slope is graphed separately for blacks and whites. The youth outcomes in Figure 3.5 are 1) the value they attribute to schooling, 2) their educational aspirations, 3) their educational expectations, 4) the barriers they anticipate in the future, 5) their educational aspirations minus their educational expectations, and 6) their academic achievement.

The final two figures in Chapter 3 (3.6 and 3.7) are analogous to Figures 3.2 and 3.5 discussed above. The main differences are in the predictors; whereas Figure 3.2 considered parents' beliefs about discrimination, Figure 3.6 considers parental *messages* about the value of schooling and the barriers present within the opportunity structure, and presents indicators of both the positive and negative messages youth attain about schooling from their peers. These measures are from the eleventh-grade wave of the MADICS. The bottom panel of Figure 3.6 shows racial comparisons on a measure for youths' assessment of their peers' academic orientation obtained from the tenth-grade wave of both the NELS and ELS. Thus, the results in Figure 3.6 were obtained using Equations 1 and 2 and displayed in the manner described in Figure A.1. Similarly, Figure 3.7 repeats the analysis described for Figure 3.5 with the messages from parents and peers as the predictors. The analysis in Figure 3.7 is cross-sectional, however, with both predictors and outcomes measured in grade 11. The parental message measures were asked only in the eleventh-grade wave of the MADICS.

Chapter 4

The purpose of this chapter is to outline a conceptual distinction between different beliefs about the opportunity structure and discuss the potential implications of these beliefs for academic outcomes. Much of the analysis relies on the MADICS. I begin by assessing whether black youth perceive lower value from schooling than whites and whether they perceive greater barriers despite schooling than whites. These perceptions are intended to measure youths' beliefs about opportunities for upward mobility and were assessed when they were in grade 11. These findings are displayed in the top panel of Figure 4.2 in the manner described for Figure A.1 using Equation 1. The resistance model predicts that β_1 will be negative when belief about the *value of schooling* is the outcome, and positive when belief about *barriers despite schooling* is the outcome.

The bottom panel of Figure 4.2 graphs the racial difference in beliefs (β_1) under four conditions. The first condition is simply the unadjusted difference from Equation 1. The second condition shows β_1 from Equation 2, which shows the racial difference after accounting for SES. Since pre–high school achievement is likely to influence beliefs in high school, the third condition shows β_1 after accounting for students' achievement (Ach) prior to high school (grade 7), which can be expressed as follows:

$$\text{Beliefs}_{G11} = \alpha + \beta_1 \text{ (black)} + X\beta_2 + \beta_3 \text{ (Ach}_{G7}) + e \qquad (9)$$

Finally, since many scholars note that messages about education provided by family and friends are critical to beliefs and attitudes students develop about school (Fordham and Ogbu 1986; Mickelson 1990; Steinberg, Dornbusch, and Brown 1992), I include a vector consisting of messages about school received from family and friends (M_{G11}):

$$\text{Beliefs}_{G11} = \alpha + \beta_1 \text{(black)} + X\beta_2 + \beta_3 (\text{Ach}_{G7}) + M_{G11}\beta_4 + e \quad (10)$$

where the message vector is comprised of three measures. The first assesses parents' messages about the value of schooling (for example, "my parents tell me that a good education is very important in order to get a good job). The second measure assesses parents' messages about barriers to upward mobility (my parents say people like us are not always paid or promoted according to our education). The final measure assesses youths' perceptions of their peers' value toward schooling (how many of the friends you spend most of your time with do well in school).

In Figure 4.3, I examine how youths' beliefs are associated with academic achievement and college enrollment. I estimate the following equation for each group:

$$\text{Achv}_{G11} = \alpha + X\beta_1 + \beta_2 (\text{Ach}_{G7}) + M_{G11}\beta_3 + \delta_1 (\text{Value}_{G11}) +$$
$$\delta_2 (\text{Barriers}_{G11}) + \delta_3 (\text{Attitudes}_{G11}) + e \quad (11)$$

where achievement in grade 11 (Achv_{G11}) is a function of youths' beliefs about the value of school (δ_1), beliefs about barriers despite schooling (δ_2), and affective attitudes toward schooling (δ_3) net of background factors, prior achievement, and the messages vector. These findings are presented in the top panel of Figure 4.3 in the manner described for Figure A.3. I use logistic regression to estimate a model for *likelihood of enrolling in college* similar to Equation 11 that includes a control for eleventh grade achievement. I graph the odds ratio for δ_1 through $_3$ in the bottom panel of Figure 4.3.

In the next portion of the analysis I determine whether youth believe that their sex will make it harder for them to get ahead in life. I also determine whether they believe that race will be a barrier for getting ahead as well. These results are graphed in Figure 4.6 using the following equations:

$$Y_{G8} = \alpha + \beta_1 (\text{WhiteFem}) + \beta_2 (\text{BlackM}) + \beta_3 (\text{BlackFem}) + e \quad (12)$$

and

$$Y_{G8} = \alpha + \beta_1 (\text{WhiteFem}) + \beta_2 (\text{BlackM}) + \beta_3 (\text{BlackFem}) +$$
$$X\beta_4 + \beta_5 (\text{Ach}_{G7}) + e \quad (13)$$

where Y_{G8} represents the belief that sex (and race) will make it difficult to get ahead in life, α represents the estimated mean on the belief for white males, and β_1, β_2, and β_3 represent the estimated means for white females, black males, and black females, respectively. The findings are displayed in the manner described for Figure A.1.

The next set of analyses examine whether youths' beliefs about sex and race as a barrier to upward mobility examined in Figures 4.5 and 4.6 (measured in grade 8) have implications for their investment in schooling and academic outcomes, which are all measured in grade 11. Three types of investment are assessed: psychological, behavioral, and academic. Psychological investment is measured by students' *educational aspirations, educational expectations*, and the *importance they attribute to school* for success in the labor market. Behavioral investment is measured by the frequency with which students *seek help* to improve academically, and the amount of time they spend on *school activities/clubs* (for example, student government), *homework*, and *educational activities* outside school. Finally, analyses are conducted for two academic outcomes: achievement (grades) and college enrollment (one-year post–high school). These outcomes are first regressed on gender and race interactions to determine the extent to which group differences exist on school investment. Students' perceptions of barriers within the opportunity structure are then included in the models to examine whether they lead to a decline in school investment:

$$Y_{G11} = \alpha + \beta_1 \, (WhiteFem) + \beta_2 \, (BlackM) + \beta_3 \, (BlackFem) + X\beta_4 +$$
$$\beta_5 \, (Ach_{G7}) + \delta_1 \, (Sex/Job_{G8}) + \delta_2 \, (Sex/Edu_{G8}) + \delta_3 \, (Sex/ahead_{G8}) +$$
$$\delta_4 \, (Race/Job_{G8}) + \delta_5 \, (Race/Edu_{G8}) + \delta_6 \, (Race/ahead_{G8}) + e \qquad (14)$$

where the aforementioned youth outcomes are assessed in grade 11 (Y_{G11}), δ_1, δ_2, and δ_3 are the estimated change in the outcomes associated with increases in the belief that sex will be a barrier for youths' desired job, level of education, and getting ahead in life, respectively, and δ_4 through $_6$ estimate the same three beliefs with regard to race. In Table 4.1, I report only the δs from Equation 14 that are statistically significant for each outcome. The rest are labeled NS for not significant.

The final set of analyses in Chapter 4 is presented in the bottom panel of Figure 4.7 (the top panel displays raw percentages). Equation 12 was used for the first two outcomes, which measure the importance youth attribute to education for their future, using the MADICS (grade 11) and ELS (grade 10). I report the estimated difference relative to white males (β) for each group. The final two outcomes assess students' grades in the MADICS (grade 11) and NELS (grade 10) using Equation 13.

Chapter 5

The purpose of Chapter 5 is to provide racial comparisons across a wide range of indicators that measure academic orientation. The manner in which the results are displayed in Figures 5.2, 5.3 and 5.10 (based on the MADICS), along with the analytic strategy for the findings presented in these figures, is described above in the General Strategy section of this appendix (see description of Figure A.2). There is one exception to the modeling strategy, however; the adjusted estimates in these figures (obtained using Equation 2) also include a control for students' grade level (grade 8 and grade 11, with grade 7 omitted). The racial comparisons in these figures are based on pooled cross-sections. Because an individual can enter the sample three times (in grades 7, 8, and 11), robust standard errors are used to account for correlation across individuals. To determine whether blacks fare worse on the outcomes as they move closer to adulthood relative to whites, developmental effects were tested by interacting grade level and race. These findings are not reported because these analyses did not yield significant estimates (I discuss this further in Chapter 5).

The findings in Figures 5.4 through 5.7 are based on time diaries from the CDS (further information on the time diaries can be found in Chapter 5). The findings in Figure 5.4 represent the mean in minutes for the activities listed for both white and black youth. The findings are *not* conditional on having spent time in the activity. Also, as mentioned in Chapter 5, the weekday and weekend day were randomly selected. In order to provide a sense for how much of the racial differences observed in Figure 5.4 can be attributed to background factors, I regressed time on all educational activities displayed in Figure 5.4 during the weekend day (multiplied by two to represent a typical weekend) on several background factors. The full model can be expressed as follows:

$$\text{Minutes} = \alpha + \beta_1 \text{(black)} + X\beta_2 + \beta_3 \text{(\#books)} + \beta_4 \text{(ReadAbility)} + e \ (15)$$

where the average time on all educational activities (minutes) is a function of race (β_1), the SES vector ($X\beta_2$), number of books in the home (β_3), and students' reading ability as assessed by the Woodcock-Johnson achievement test (β_4). These findings are displayed in Figure 5.5. Specifically, after graphing the racial difference (β_1) from Equation 1, I graph β_1 from a series of models in which each factor expressed in Equation 15 is added separately, culminating with the full model. Whereas all factors in vector X were assessed in CDS-I (household income, parental education, family structure, and youths' sex), number of books and reading ability were assessed in CDS-II to ensure that youth in grades 1 through 6 (most of whom were between the ages of 0 and 5 in CDS-I) have data points for these factors. The analyses displayed in Figures 5.4 and 5.5 were repeated for a sample restricted to adolescent youth (grades 7–12) and displayed in Figures 5.6 and 5.7.

In Figure 5.8, I examine whether there is a racial difference in the social cost associated with good academic performance. The indicators in the top panel are based only on the grade 7 wave of the MADICS and were analyzed using the following equation:

$$\text{Social Standing} = \alpha + \beta_1 (\text{black}) + \beta_2 (\text{HA}) + \beta_3 (\text{LA}) + X\beta_4 + \delta_1 (\text{HA} * \text{black}) + \delta_2 (\text{LA} * \text{black}) + e \tag{16}$$

where youths' social standing is being predicted by whether s/he is a high achiever (HA), a low achiever (LA), the vector of SES, and two interaction terms. High and low academic achievers refer to students in the top and bottom quartile of the GPA distribution, respectively (average achievers or students in the middle of the achievement distribution serve as the reference group). The estimates relevant for the resistance model are indicated by δ. According to the resistance model, δ_1 should be negative, indicating that high-achieving blacks have a lower social standing than their high-achieving white counterparts. Similarly, δ_2 should be positive, indicating that low-achieving blacks have a greater social standing than low-achieving whites (the opposite is expected when the indicator of social standing is *trouble getting along with peers*). The measures of social standing in the bottom panel of Figure 5.8 are estimated using Equation 16 with one difference: the equation for these measures includes controls for grade level (grades 8 and 11). The points on the graph were plotted as shown in Table A.1.

Table A1: Graphing Strategy for Figure 5.8 Using Equation 16

Achievement Level	Whites	Blacks
Low Achievers	$\alpha + \beta_3$	$\alpha + \beta_1 + \beta_3 + \delta_2$
Average Achievers	α	$\alpha + \beta_1$
High Achievers	$\alpha + \beta_2$	$\alpha + \beta_1 + \beta_2 + \delta_1$

Finally, the analysis shown in Figure 5.9 is for the black youth in the MADICS and simply shows the percentage of youth within each achievement level (as established for Figure 5.8) that believe getting good grades is "acting white" and those who do not believe this to be the case.

The next set of analyses is contained in Figures 5.11 and 5.12. These findings are intended to test the resistance model in the United Kingdom and are based on the LSYPE. The analytic strategy differs in three ways. First, British Asians are included in the analysis. Second, as is conventional within the British context, social class is measured as parents' occupation. Third, perception of barriers (or discrimination) is included to explain potential minority disadvantages in academic orientation. Therefore, the findings in Figure 5.11 were obtained using the following equation:

$$Y = \alpha + \beta_1 \text{ (black)} + \beta_2 \text{ (Asian)} + \beta_3 \text{ (SC)} + \beta_4 \text{ (Sex)} + \beta_5 \text{ (Discrim)} + e \ (17)$$

where SC is an indicator of parental occupation, β_4 is the estimate for youths' sex, and β_5 is the estimate for youths' experiences of discrimination (that is, whether they have ever been treated unfairly by teachers because of their skin, ethnicity, race, or religion).

Three estimates are displayed for black and Asian youth in Figure 5.11 in the manner described in Figure A.2. The first estimate shows the unadjusted means for black and Asian youth on the outcomes relative to whites. The second estimate for each group was obtained from an equation that includes social class and youths' sex. Finally, the third estimate is based on the full model shown in Equation 17. The same analytic approach was applied to the measures displayed in Figure 5.12. However, since the measures in Figure 5.12 are dichotomous (yes/no), the findings were estimated using logistic regression with the same predictors shown in Equation 17. I graph the odds ratios in Figure 5.12 for each group based on the same three model variants described for Figure 5.11 above.

The final figure in Chapter 5 (Figure 5.13) shows findings for analysis that examine whether ethnic minorities experience a greater social cost for good academic performance than whites within the United Kingdom. The estimates were obtained as follows:

$$Y = \alpha + \beta_1 \text{ (black)} + \beta_2 \text{ (Asian)} + \beta_3 \text{ (SC)} + \beta_4 \text{ (Sex)} + \beta_5 \text{ (Discrim)} +$$
$$\delta_1 \text{ (Value)} + \delta_2 \text{ (English)} + \delta_3 \text{ (Math)} + R^*V\xi_1 + R^*E\xi_2 + R^*M\xi_3 + e \ (18)$$

where Y is the outcome for youth's social standing, δ_1 is the estimate for the value youths attribute to schooling, δ_2 and $_3$ are the estimates for youths'

English and math ability, respectively, R*V, R*E, and R*M represent vectors that contain a product of race and value of schooling, race and English scores, and race and math scores, respectively, for each racial group in the model (blacks and Asians), and the ξs represent the associated vectors of coefficients. The slopes were graphed through the mean on the outcomes for each group using the strategy described for Figure A.3. Since the findings were the same for the academic measures, for the sake of brevity, I graphed only the findings for *value of schooling*, where δ_1 represents the slope for white youth and the slopes for blacks and Asians is represented by the sum of δ_1 and each group's respective ξ_1.

Chapter 6

In Chapter 6, I examine whether a raceless identity is an effective strategy for academic success among black youth. The data are from the high school wave of the MADICS (grade 11). The first two figures in Chapter 6 describe the profiles that are examined and show the percentage of students from each profile that affirms each racial attitude measure. These figures do not warrant discussion beyond that provided in Chapter 6. In Figure 6.3 I show findings for how each race profile compares on various measures of academic orientation (represented by Y) using the following equation:

$$Y = \alpha + \beta_1 \text{(Dissimilar)} + \beta_2 \text{(MildAmbiv)} + \beta_3 \text{(Ambiv)} +$$
$$\beta_4 \text{(Similar)} + e \qquad (19)$$

where the estimate for each race profile should be interpreted relative to the black youth in the "race neutral" profile represented by α. Thus, Figure 6.3 simply graphs each β, and α is fixed to zero for the purpose of presentation. The actual value for each α is listed in the notes for Figure 6.3. Finally, the findings in Table 6.1 are basic mean comparisons obtained using a series of bivariate regressions as expressed in Equation 1 in which the academic outcome represented by Y (achievement, educational aspirations, value of school, and detachment from school) is regressed on each racial attitude, β_1 always represents the "affirm" group, and α represents the "do not affirm" group.

Chapter 7

In Chapter 7, I examine whether academic skills prior to high school are more important for academic success than an oppositional academic orientation during high school. The data are from the first three waves of the NELS and from the CDS. The first two figures in Chapter 7 display the unadjusted means for whites, Asians, and blacks on various measures of academic behavior during high school (Figure 7.2) and on achievement prior to high school and for grade 12 (Figure 7.3). Since these figures simply graph basic means, they do not warrant discussion beyond that provided in Chapter 7.

Figure 7.4 displays the key findings for Chapter 7. Specifically, this figure shows the change (both actual and percentage) in the Asian-white and black-white achievement gaps that result from controlling for schooling behaviors during high school and academic skills prior to high school. For this analysis, the baseline model is expressed as follows:

$$Ach_{G12} = \alpha + \beta_1 \text{ (Asians)} + \beta_2 \text{ (black)} + X\beta_3 + e \qquad (20)$$

where achievement in grade 12 (Ach_{G12}) is a function of race and the vector for SES. The first bar in each panel of Figure 7.4 graphs β_1 and β_2 for Asians and blacks, respectively, with α fixed to zero for the purpose of presentation. Thus, the estimate for each group can be interpreted relative to the achievement of white youth. Since Asian Americans do not differ from whites in reading achievement, the top panel does not display the bars for the Asian estimates.

The second bar for each panel in Figure 7.4 shows the racial achievement gaps after accounting for schooling behaviors during high school. The estimates were obtained from the following equation:

$$Ach_{G12} = \alpha + \beta_1 \text{ (Asians)} + \beta_2 \text{ (black)} + X\beta_3 + BEH_{G10}\delta_1 + e \qquad (21)$$

where BEH_{G10} represents a vector of schooling behaviors consisting of the schooling behaviors during grade 10 examined in Figure 7.2 and δ represents the associated vector of coefficients. The third bar is based on a model that replaces schooling behaviors with a vector for academic skills prior to high school consisting of both reading and math scores from the standardized tests administered by the NELS in grade 8 and displayed in Figure 7.3. The fourth bar replaces the vector for schooling behaviors in Equation 21 with grades prior to high school (in grade 8), which are also displayed in Figure 7.3. Finally, the last bar in each panel in Figure 7.4 shows the estimated achievement for Asians and blacks relative to whites in a full model that accounts for all the aforementioned factors as follows:

$$Ach_{G12} = \alpha + \beta_1 \text{ (Asians)} + \beta_2 \text{ (black)} + X\beta_3 + BEH_{G10}\delta_1 + $$
$$PS_{G8}\delta_2 + \delta_3 \text{ (PG}_{G8}) + e \qquad (22)$$

where PS_{G8} and PG_{G8} represent prior skills and prior grades in grade 8, respectively.

Next, I determine the extent to which the estimated behavioral effects are overestimated resulting from the omission of prior academic skills. In Figure 7.5, I show the percent change in the estimated effect for each schooling behavior that occurs when the behavioral estimates from Equation 21 are compared to those in Equation 22. Thus, whereas the open circles in the graph show the behavioral estimates obtained from Equation 21, the full circles show the behavioral estimates obtained using Equation 22.

Figures 7.6 and 7.7 show the findings for analysis similar to those employed to obtain the findings displayed in Figures 7.3 and 7.4, respectively, for youth prior to entering high school using the CDS. Specifically, in the top panel of Figure 7.6 I graph the racial differences in schooling behaviors, measured as the daily average of minutes spent on academic activities, for youth in middle school. In the bottom panel, I graph youths' achievement during and prior to middle school (grades 1 through 3). In Figure 7.7, I graph the change (both actual and percentage) in the black-white achievement gaps that results from controlling for schooling behaviors during middle school and for academic skills prior to middle school. The following equation served as the basis for this analysis:

$$Ach_{MS} = \alpha + \beta_1 (black) + X\beta_2 + BEH_{MS}\delta_1 + PS_{G1-3}\delta_2 + e \qquad (23)$$

where Ach_{MS} represents achievement during middles school, BEH_{MS} represents the schooling behaviors during middle school displayed in the top panel of Figure 7.6, and PS_{G1-3} represents academic skills (reading and math) assessed in grades 1 through 3 and displayed in the bottom panel of Figure 7.6. The first bar for both panels in Figure 7.7 shows β_1 from a model that includes only the SES vector (X). The second bar shows β_1 from a model that includes the vectors for both SES and middle school behaviors. This model is reestimated replacing the vector for middle school behaviors with a vector for academic skills prior to middle school (PS_{G1-3}) and displayed in the third bar of both panels. Finally, the fourth bar in Figure 7.7 shows the β_1 obtained from Equation 23.

Chapter 8

The purpose of Chapter 8 is to provide a test of the marginalization hypotheses—that youth from marginalized groups resist schooling. I selected the United Kingdom because 1) it was one of the six countries highlighted by

Ogbu (1978) for which good data exists, 2) the British education system is more stratified than the U.S. system, and 3) it is an industrially advanced society that is rapidly diversifying. Thus, the United Kingdom is similar enough to the United States but provides a sufficiently different context that might yield patterns hidden within the United States. In developing my research strategy, I had to create comparison groups that were appropriate to the British context. That meant stratifying the sample by social class rather than race. Although I test the primary underlying assumption of the resistance model, that marginalization is associated with academic disinvestment, since race is not the central focus of this chapter, these analyses are not a test of the resistance model. I also replicate this analysis for the United States.

Despite stratifying the samples from both countries by social class, the measures for social class differed for each country. It is important to identify measures of social class that are meaningful to how youth construct the purpose of education and therefore guide their orientation toward schooling. Furthermore, for the purposes of this study, a single-indicator approach to social class facilitates greater ease and more meaningful interpretation of findings than would be the case for composite indices of social class comprised of numerous factors. The use of single indicators is consistent with a move among some inequality scholars who advocate using independent rather than composite measures of social class. In a critique of the widely embraced Duncan SEI measure, Hauser and Warren (1997) argue that a social class composite divided into single measures allows researchers to select the measure(s) most suitable for their research question. They also caution that composite measures may produce erroneous conclusions. I avoid this pitfall by using the measure for each country that I view as most relevant to youths' academic orientation.

For the U.S. sample, I stratify social class according to parents' level of education. Parental education offers a stronger measure of social class because it is more closely related to parental expectations for children's academic performance and parents' effectiveness in communicating their expectations to their children. While financial/material capital is generally good for overall child well-being, it does not necessarily follow that parents with greater financial/material capital will attribute more importance to education.

In contrast to the United States, social class within the British context is conceived of as culture; having to do with habitus, life experiences, and social practices. The single factor that best captures social class within the British context is occupation. There has been some apprehension among

British scholars toward using income as a measure of social class because there are some people in culturally working-class occupations who earn high incomes and others in culturally middle-class occupations who earn less. Thus, children whose parents are in the former group are likely to have working-class views toward education despite their parents' high earnings, whereas children whose parents are in the latter group are likely to have middle-class views toward education despite their parents' lower earnings. Likewise, although in Britain education can be used as a marker of social class, it is not a pure one. Until very recently, only a small percentage of people in Britain attended university compared to the United States. However, there are many middle-class professions within the United States for which a college degree is a prerequisite (for example, middle management), which historically has not been the case within the United Kingdom. To the extent that social class can be mapped within the United Kingdom, it is often mapped into one's occupation. Furthermore, since the United Kingdom and the United States have different education systems, years of schooling do not correspond to the same educational level across the two countries. Therefore, social class is stratified in a manner that is recognizable to readers from each country.

In the top panel of Figure 8.1, I graph the unadjusted differences in achievement between the social class groups within the United Kingdom using the standardized betas that result from the following equation:

$$Ach_{UK} = \alpha + \beta_1 \, (\text{UpMid}) + \beta_2 \, (\text{LoMid}) + \beta_3 \, (\text{Low}) + e \qquad (24)$$

where achievement within the United Kingdom (Ach_{UK}) is a function of social class expressed in the form of three dummy variables: upper middle class, lower middle class, and lower class (see Appendix D for a description of these categories). The estimates for each of these categories should be interpreted relative to youth in the upper-class group, which is represented by α and fixed to zero for the purpose of presentation in Figure 8.1. The findings in the second panel of Figure 8.1 are based on the same modeling strategy, where the outcome is achievement within the United States and β_1 through $_3$ represent the estimates for *some college, high school graduate,* and *less than high school graduate,* respectively. These estimates should be interpreted relative to youth whose parents are college graduates. In the bottom panel of Figure 8.1, I show the racial achievement gap in both the United Kingdom and the United States as a basis on which to compare the size of the achievement gaps by social class observed in the top two panels of Figure 8.1. The estimates are the unadjusted standardized betas from an equation that includes an estimate for each racial group listed in the figure. Whereas the estimates for the British sample can be interpreted relative to non-lower-class whites, those displayed in the right panel for the analysis based on the NELS and CDS can be interpreted relative to whites within the United States.

In Figure 8.2, I show findings for analysis that compare the social class groups within the United Kingdom on various measures of academic orientation using the BCS70. Two estimates are displayed for each group in the manner described above for Figure A.2 based on the following equation:

$$Y = \alpha + \beta_1 \text{(UpMid)} + \beta_2 \text{(LoMid)} + \beta_3 \text{(Low)} + \beta_4 \text{(Sex)} + \beta_5 \text{(Discrim)} + e \tag{25}$$

where Y is the measure for academic orientation and *Discrim* is a measure for whether youth report that they have been treated unfairly/unjustly in the last twelve months due to sex, skin color, dress, family background, speech, religion, or other reason. The unadjusted estimates represented by the open circle were obtained from an abridged version of Equation 25 in which the measures for sex and discrimination were excluded. The estimates represented by the full circle were obtained using Equation 25. The findings in Figure 8.3 were obtained using the same two models (the abridged and full versions of Equation 25). Although the outcome is a dichotomous measure (yes/no to having had an unexcused absence), I employ OLS rather than logistic regression so that the estimates can be interpreted as proportions rather than log odds.

In Table 8.1, I display findings for the analysis of academic orientation by social class within the United States using the MADICS. The findings are based on two versions of the following equation:

$$Y = \alpha + \beta_1 \text{(SC)} + \beta_2 \text{(HS)} + \beta_3 \text{(LessHS)} + X\beta_4 + \beta_5 \text{(Race)} + \beta_6 \text{(Sex)} + \beta_7 \text{(Grade)} + e \tag{26}$$

where (Y) represents the academic orientation outcome, β_1 through $_3$ are the estimates for youth whose parents have some college education (SC), are high school graduates (HS), and have less than a high school degree (LessHS), respectively, β_4 is a vector of coefficients associated with the SES vector that includes parental income and family structure, and β_5, β_6, and β_7 are estimates that correspond to youths' race, sex, and grade level, respectively. The unadjusted estimates were obtained from an abridged version of

Equation 26 in which the measures for parental income, family structure, race, sex, and grade level were excluded. The adjusted estimates were obtained using equation 26. The analysis was based on pooled cross-sections (and robust standard errors) that included youth from all grades for which data were available.

The final figure in Chapter 8 (8.4), shows findings that examine whether negative sanctioning for high academic orientation is associated with social class. The findings are presented in minigraphs such as those described in Figure A.3. Thus, the association between academic orientation and social standing for youth in each category of social class is displayed as the average score for youth who are one standard deviation below and one standard deviation above the mean of the measure for academic orientation, passing through the mean of the indicator for social standing. The following equation was employed for each graph in the top panel of Figure 8.4:

$$
\begin{aligned}
Y = \alpha &+ \beta_1 \, (\text{UpMid}) + \beta_2 \, (\text{LoMid}) + \beta_3 \, (\text{Low}) + \beta_4 \, (\text{Sex}) + \beta_5 \, (\text{Discrim}) + \\
&\delta_1 \, (\text{Value}) + \delta_2 \, (\text{Vocab}) + \delta_3 \, (\text{TeachAs}) + \lambda_1 \, (\text{Value} * \text{UpMid}) + \\
&\lambda_2 \, (\text{Value} * \text{LoMid}) + \lambda_3 \, (\text{Value} * \text{Low}) + \xi_1 \, (\text{Vocab} * \text{UpMid}) + \\
&\xi_2 \, (\text{Vocab} * \text{LoMid}) + \xi_3 \, (\text{Vocab} * \text{Low}) + \gamma_1 \, (\text{TeachAs} * \text{UpMid}) + \\
&\gamma_2 \, (\text{TeachAs} * \text{LoMid}) + \gamma_3 \, (\text{TeachAs} * \text{Low}) + e \qquad (27)
\end{aligned}
$$

where Y represents the indicator for social standing, δ_1, δ_2, and δ_3 represent the estimates for the value youth attribute to schooling, their vocabulary scores, and teacher assessments, respectively, and the λs, ξs, and γs represent the interaction terms between each social class category and the value youth attribute to school, vocabulary scores, and teacher assessments, respectively. The slopes are displayed for youth in each of the social class categories. Thus, δ_1 is graphed for youth in the upper-class group. The estimates for the other groups were obtained by adding δ_1 to their corresponding λ. (Since the findings were the same for each predictor, I chose to graph only the interaction terms for social class and value of schooling for the sake of brevity.)

The bottom panel of Figure 8.4 shows findings for the same analysis conducted using the MADICS. The estimates graphed were obtained from an extended version of Equation 26, as follows:

$$
\begin{aligned}
Y = \alpha &+ \beta_1 \, (\text{SC}) + \beta_2 \, (\text{HS}) + \beta_3 \, (\text{LessHS}) + X\beta_4 + \beta_5 \, (\text{Race}) + \\
&\beta_6 \, (\text{Sex}) + \delta_1 \, (\text{GPA}) + \lambda_1 \, (\text{GPA} * \text{SC}) + \lambda_2 \, (\text{GPA} * \text{HS}) + \\
&\lambda_3 \, (\text{GPA} * \text{LessHS}) + e \qquad (28)
\end{aligned}
$$

where GPA represents grade point average (grade level is dropped because the analysis is conduct only among youth in grade 7). Similar to the findings displayed in the top panel of Figure 8.4, δ_1 is graphed for youth whose parents hold a college degree or greater, and the estimates for the other groups were obtained by adding δ_1 to their corresponding λ.

APPENDIX D: DESCRIPTION OF MEASURES

Table A2: Means, Standard Deviations, and Descriptions for Variables Used in Chapter 3

Variable Name	Description	Metric	Means (SD)		N	Alpha	Data
			Whites	Blacks			
Figure 3.2[a]							
Parents' Perceptions of Barriers for Self							
Parent Discrim.	Over your lifetime, in general, how often have you felt discriminated against because you are (Race)?	1 = Never 5 = Very often	1.95 (1.08)	3.10 (1.29)	923	—	MADICS
Parent get Ahead	Do you think it has been harder for you to get ahead in life because you are (Race)?	0 = No 1 = Yes	.03	.40	923	—	MADICS
Parents' Perceptions of Barriers for Child							
Child Discrim.	How much do you think people will discriminate against (child) because s/he is (Race)?	1 = Not at all 4 = A lot	1.52 (.67)	2.45 (.80)	924	—	MADICS
Child get Ahead	Do you think it will be harder for (child) to get ahead because s/he is (Race)?	0 = No 1 = Yes	.10	.41	923	—	MADICS
Figure 3.3[a]							
Parents' Perceptions of importance of schooling							
Educational Aspirations	If finances were not a problem and everything else went right, how far would you like to see (child) go in school?	1 = < HS diploma 9 = J.D./Ph.D./M.D.	8.15 (1.14)	8.35 (1.20)	948	—	MADICS

Construct	Description	Scale			N		Source
School = life	My 7th grader will not be successful in life if s/he isn't successful in school.	1 = SD b 5 = SA	3.66 (1.01)	3.89 (.98)	937	—	MADICS

Figure 3.4c

Parents' Aspirations for Youth

Construct	Description	Scale			N		Source
Educational Aspirations	Youths' response to the Following: How far in school do you think your mother wants you to get?	1 = < than HS 6 = > 4yr Col. Degree	4.86 (1.04)	4.93 (1.20)	7,727	—	NELS
Educational Aspirations	Parents' response to the following: How far in in school do you want your tenth grader to go?	1 = < than HS 6 = J.D./Ph.D./M.D.	4.38 (.98)	4.72 (1.10)	9,331	—	ELS

Parents' Expectations for Youth

Construct	Description	Scale			N		Source
Educational Expectations	Things often don't go right, so how far do you think (CHILD) will actually go in school?	1 = < HS diploma 8 = J.D./Ph.D./M.D.	6.78 (1.61)	6.71 (1.80)	1,400	—	MADICS
Educational Expectations	Parents' response to the following: How far in school do you expect your eighth grader to go?	1 = < than HS 6 = > 4yr Col. Degree	4.48 (1.24)	4.52 (1.32)	8,232	—	NELS

Table A2   (continued)

Figure 3.5[a]

Youth Outcomes (Parental predictors are described earlier under Figure 3.2 and 3.3)

Variable Name	Description	Metric	Means (SD)		N	Alpha	Data
			Whites	Blacks			
Perceived Value of Education	(a) I have to do well in school if I want to be a success in life. (b) Getting a good education is the best way to get ahead in life for the kids in my neighborhood, (c) achievement and effort in school lead to job success later on, (d) education really pays off in the future for people like me.	1 = SD 5 = SA	4.06 (.75)	4.16 (.72)	860	.812	MADICS
Educational Aspirations	If you could do exactly what you wanted, how far would you like to go in school?	1 = < HS diploma 8 = J.D., Ph.D., M.D.	7.51 (1.51)	7.75 (1.48)	846	—	MADICS
Educational Expectations	We can't always do what we most want to do. How far do you think you actually will go in school?	1 = < HS diploma 8 = J.D., Ph.D., M.D.	6.86 (1.58)	6.93 (1.63)	844	—	MADICS
Perceived Barriers	People like me aren't treated fairly at work no matter how much education they have.	1 = SD 5 = SA	2.39 (.90)	2.91 (.94)	869	—	MADICS
Limited Educ. Opportunities	Discrepancy between educational aspirations and educational expectations.		.66 (.94)	.82 (1.20)	844	—	MADICS
Achievement	Student GPA in grade 11	0–4.0	3.04 (.79)	2.82 (.72)	789	—	MADICS

Figure 3.6

Parental Messages about Education and Barriers

Message about Value of school	My parents tell me that a good education is very important in order to get a good job.	1 = SD 5 = SA	4.20 (.78)	4.29 (.87)	871	—	MADICS
Message about Barriers	My parents say people like us are not always paid or promoted according to our education.	1 = SD 5 = SA	2.82 (.88)	3.20 (.97)	867	—	MADICS

Peer Schooling Messages

Positive Academic Orientation	How many of the friends you spend most of your time with (a) do well in school? (b) plan to go to college? (c) like to discuss schoolwork or other intellectual things with you? (d) think it is important to work hard on school-work?	1 = None of them 5 = All of them	3.41 (.80)	3.39 (.78)	860	.792	MADICS
Negative Academic Orientation	How many of the friends you spend most of your time with (a) think working hard to get good grades is a waste of time? (b) cheat on school tests? (c) don't like having to come to school? (d) think being popular with friends is more important than getting A's in school? (e) think it's okay not to do their homework if their friends want to do something else instead?	1 = None of them 5 = All of them	2.31 (.68)	2.17 (.66)	850	.680	MADICS

Table A2   (continued)

Variable Name	Description	Metric	Means (SD)		N	Alpha	Data
			Whites	Blacks			
Peer Schooling Messages (National)							
Academic Orientation	Youths' assessment of the importance their friends place on the following: (a) 1) regular class attendance, (b) getting good grades, (c) studying, (d) completing high school, and (e) continuing education beyond high school.	1 = Not important 5 = Very important	2.48 (.45)	2.59 (.45)	7,706	.845	NELS
			2.47 (.46)	2.54 (.44)	7,340	.838	ELS

Figure 3.7

Youth outcomes are described in this table under Figure 3.5.

Parental and peer predictors are described in this table under Figure 3.6.

Notes:

a. The sample is restricted to youth present in grade 11; the measures in Figure 3.2 and 3.3 were predictors assessed when youth were in grade 7, and the measures described under Figure 3.5 were youth outcomes assessed in grade 11.

b. SD refers to strongly disagree and SA refers to strongly agree.

c. Measures are from the first wave of each dataset. Also, while all analyses based on national data are weighted, the Ns reported are for the unweighted sample.

Table A3: Means, Standard Deviations, and Descriptions for Variables Used in Chapter 4

Variable Name	Description	Metric	Means (SD)		N	Alpha	Data
			Whites	Blacks			
Figure 4.2							
Youth Outcomes							
Value of School	Details for this measure are contained under subheading *Figure 3.5* in Table A2.						
Perceived Barriers	See Table A2, Figure 3.5.						
Bottom Panel Controls							
Grades	Student grade point average in grade 7	0–4.0	3.37 (.48)	3.11 (.51)	770	—	MADICS
Message about Value of School	See Table A2, Figure 3.6.						
Message about Barriers	See Table A2, Figure 3.6.						
Peer Academic Orientation	See Table A2, Figure 3.6, peers' *positive academic orientation.*						

Table A3 (continued)

Variable Name	Description	Metric	Means (SD)		N	Alpha	Data
			Whites	Blacks			
Figure 4.3							
Youth Outcomes							
Grades	See Table A2, Figure 3.5, *achievement*.						
College Enrollment	Enrolled in college one year post-high school.	0 = No 1 = Yes	.74	.65	666	—	MADICS
Youth Predictors							
Value of School	See Table A2, Figure 3.5.						
Perceived Barriers	See Table A2, Figure 3.5.						
Affect Toward Schooling	(a) most of my classes or subjects are boring.* (b) homework is a waste of time.* (c) In general, you like school a lot. (d) Grades are very important to you.	1 = SD 5 = SA	3.45 (.74)	3.61 (.65)	827	.624	MADICS

Figure 4.4

No analysis is presented in this figure.

Figure 4.5

Anticipated Discrimination Based on Sex and Race

Sex/Job	How much do you think discrimination because of your sex might keep you from getting the job you want?	0 = Not at all 1 = Little to a lot	.30	.47	792	—	MADICS
Sex/Education	How much do you think discrimination because of your sex might keep you from getting the amount of education you want?	0 = Not at all 1 = Little to a lot	.18	.39	791	—	MADICS
Race/Job	How much do you think discrimination because of your race might keep you from getting the job you want?	0 = Not at all 1 = Little to a lot	.24	.66	793	—	MADICS
Race/Education	How much do you think discrimination because of your race might keep you from getting the amount of education you want?	0 = Not at all 1 = Little to a lot	.17	.56	791	—	MADICS

Figure 4.6

Youths' Perceptions of Sex and Race as Barriers

Sex as Barrier	Do you think it will be harder or easier for you to get ahead in life because you are a (boy/girl)?	1 = A lot Easier 5 = A lot Harder	2.97 (.67)	2.98 (.86)	794	—	MADICS

Table A3 (continued)

Variable Name	Description	Metric	Means (SD)		N	Alpha	Data
			Whites	Blacks			
Race as Barriers	(a) Because of your race, no matter how hard you work, you will always have to work harder than others to prove yourself; (b) because of your race, it is important that you do better than other kids at school in order to get ahead.	1 = SD 4 = SA	1.56 (.63)	2.50 (.93)	777	.843	MADICS

Table 4.1

Psychological Investment

Variable Name	Description	Metric	Whites	Blacks	N	Alpha	Data
Educational Aspirations	See Table A2, Figure 3.5.						
Educational Expectations	See Table A2, Figure 3.5.						
Educational Importance	Achievement and effort in school lead to job success later on.	1 = SD 5 = SA	4.02 (.90)	4.13 (.85)	870	—	MADICS

Behavioral Investment

Variable Name	Description	Metric	Whites	Blacks	N	Alpha	Data
Seek Help	When you're having trouble on schoolwork, how often do you go to (a) your teachers for help? (b) other adults in the school, like a tutor, for help? (c) other students for help? (d) your parent(s) for help? (e) your friends for help?	1 = Almost Never 5 = Almost Always	2.69 (.75)	2.82 (.74)	830	.609	MADICS

School Activities/Clubs	During the last year how often did you spend time on any other school activities (such as clubs or student government)?	1 = < once a month 7 = Usually every day	3.30 (2.12)	3.00 (2.23)	948	—	MADICS
Homework	Think about the last two weeks, about how often did you do homework?	1 = Never 6 = Daily, > an hour	4.37 (1.67)	4.22 (1.59)	924	—	MADICS
Educational Activities	Think about the last two weeks, about how often did you: (a) watch news, educational or cultural shows on TV? (b) read books or magazines for pleasure? (c) read newspapers?	1 = Never 6 = Daily, > an hour	3.30 (1.12)	3.28 (1.21)	934	.618	MADICS

Academic Outcomes

Grades	See Table A2, Figure 3.5, achievement.						
College Enrollment	See this table, Figure 4.3.						

Figure 4.7

Top Panel

Importance of School for Job	Achievement and effort in school lead to job success later on.	0 = ~SA 1 = SA	.33	.37	870	—	MADICS
Importance of School for Job	I go to school because education is important for getting a job later on.	0 = ~SA 1 = SA	.59	.72	10,210	—	ELS

Table A3 (continued)

| Variable Name | Description | Metric | Means (SD) | | N | Alpha | Data |
			Whites	Blacks			
Importance of Grades	Grades are very important to you.	0 = ~SA 1 = SA	.42	.46	946	—	MADICS
Importance of Grades	How important are good grades to you.	0 = ~Very important 1 = Very important	.48	.63	10,585	—	ELS
Bottom Panel							
Importance of School	I have to do well in school if I want to be a success in life.	1 = SD 5 = SA	4.21 (.96)	4.35 (.91)	867	—	MADICS
Importance of School	I study to ensure that my future will be financially secure.	1 = Almost Never 4 = Almost Always	2.68 (.97)	2.72 (.98)	7,855	—	ELS
Grades	See Table A2, Figure 3.5, *achievement.*	MADICS					
Grades	Youths' grades in math, English, history, and Science.	0 – 4.0	2.93 (.74)	2.72 (.68)	6,328	—	NELS

Note: * Item is reverse coded. Also, SD refers to strongly disagree and SA refers to strongly agree. While all analyses based on national data are weighted, the Ns reported are for the unweighted sample.

Table A4: Means, Standard Deviations, and Descriptions for Variables Used in Chapter 5 [a]

Variable Name	Description	Metric	Means (SD) Whites	Means (SD) Blacks	N	Alpha	Data
Figure 5.2							
Perceived Value of Schooling							
Perceived Returns to Education	(a) I have to do well in school if I want to be a success in life. (b) Schooling is not so important for kids like me.* (c) Getting a good education Is the best way to get ahead in life for the kids in my neighborhood.	1 = SD 5 = SA	4.13 (.69)	4.22 (.70)	3,227	.608	MADICS
Educational Aspirations	If you could do exactly what you wanted, how far would you like to go in school?	1 = 8th grade or less 9 = J.D., Ph.D., M.D.	7.62 (1.43)	7.74 (1.51)	3,239	—	MADICS
Educational Expectations	We can't always do what we most want to do. How far do you think you *actually will* go in school?	1 = 8th grade or less 9 = J.D., Ph.D., M.D.	6.95 (1.50)	6.88 (1.70)	3,231	—	MADICS
Limited Educ. Opportunities	Discrepancy between educational aspirations and educational expectations.	Min. = -6 Max. = 7	.66 (1.07)	.86 (1.36)	3,230	—	MADICS
Affect toward Schooling							
Affect Toward Schooling[b]	(a) most of my classes or subjects are boring.* (b) homework is a waste of time.* (c) In general, you like school a lot. (d) Grades are very important to you.	1 = SD 5 = SA	3.60 (.69)	3.70 (.64)	2,216	.648	MADICS

Table A4 (continued)

Variable Name	Description	Metric	Means (SD) Whites	Means (SD) Blacks	N	Alpha	Data
Go to School Because Enjoy	Importance of the following reason for attending school: I go to school because I enjoy my classes.	1 = Not imp. reason 7 = Very important	4.16 (1.70)	4.46 (1.77)	3,223	—	MADICS
Go to School Because have to	Importance of the following reason for attending school: I go to school because I have to.	1 = Not imp. reason 7 = Very important	5.02 (2.06)	4.99 (2.13)	3,208	—	MADICS
Figure 5.3							
Academic Investment							
Seek Help	When you're having trouble on schoolwork, how often do you go to (a) your teachers for help? (b) other adults in the school, like a tutor, for help? (c) other students for help? (d) your parent(s) for help? (e) your friends for help?	1 = Almost Never 5 = Almost Always	2.87 (.76)	2.99 (.74)	3,197	.600	MADICS
Time on School Activities/Clubs	During the last year how often did you spend time on any other school activities (such as clubs or student government)?	1 = < once a month 6 = Usually every day	1.81 (2.00)	1.64 (2.09)	3,344	—	MADICS
Time on Homework[b]	Think about the last two weeks, about how often did you do homework?	1 = Never 6 = Daily, > an hour	4.70 (1.42)	4.64 (1.42)	2,316	—	MADICS

Variable	Description	Scale			N	Reliability	Source
Time on Educational Activities[b]	Think about the last two weeks, about how often did you: (a) watch news, educational or cultural shows on TV? (b) read books or magazines for pleasure? (c) read newspapers?	1 = Never 6 = Daily, > an hour	3.03 (1.05)	3.04 (1.13)	2,326	.581	MADICS
Importance of Academics	Compared to other things you do, how important are each of the following activities to you?: (a) Math (b) Other school subjects.	1 = Much less 7 = Much more	4.95 (1.34)	5.37 (1.31)	3,241	.810	MADICS

Resistance to Schooling

Variable	Description	Scale			N	Reliability	Source
Skip School/ Cut Classes	How often, if ever, have you skipped school or cut classes?	1 = Never 4 = Often	1.52 (.87)	1.54 (.92)	3,303	—	MADICS
Suspensions[c]	Number of times youth has been suspended from middle school and high school (asked in grades 8 and 11, respectively).	1 to 10 or more	.33 (1.19)	.70 (1.62)	1,845	—	MADICS
Importance Non-Academics	Compared to other things you do, how important are sports to you?	1 = Much less 7 = Much more	4.26 (1.93)	4.43 (1.88)	3,325	—	MADICS

Figure 5.4

Weekday (based on time diaries)

Variable	Description	Scale			N	Reliability	Source
Homework	General homework activities.	Minutes	35:28 (55:13)	40:02 (48:27)	2,016	—	CDS
Educational Activities	Includes being tutored, non-school professional classes or lectures, studying/ research/reading library activities, reviewing homework with parents/caregiver, and other educational activities.	Minutes	4:29 (20:43)	5:51 (23:34)	2.016	—	CDS

Table A4 (continued)

| Variable Name | Description | Metric | Means (SD) | | N | Alpha | Data |
			Whites	Blacks			
Leisure Reading	Includes looking at or reading books, magazines, reviews, pamphlets, newspapers, other non-school related reading, and being read to/listening to a story.	Minutes	11:18 (24:54)	4:32 (15:32)	2,016	—	CDS
Weekend Day (based on time diaries)							
Homework	Same as weekday measure.		15:20 (48:19)	5:32 (22:26)	1,994	—	CDS
Educational Activities	Same as weekday measure.		4:52 (30:58)	3:10 (24:24)	1,994	—	CDS
Leisure Reading	Same as weekday measure.		14:06 (34:59)	8:20 (33:26)	1,994	—	CDS
Figure 5.5							
Controls for Outcomes in Figure 5.4							
Sex (1 = Female)	Proportion of youth that are female.	0 = No / 1 = Yes	.51	.45	2,155	—	CDS
Grade Level	Youths' grade level in school.	1 to 12	6.46	6.80	2,155	—	CDS
Parents' Income (USD / 1000)	Total Household income in 1996 USD.	USD	60.71 (48.10)	26.93 (23.93)	2,128	—	CDS

Variable	Description	Coding	Mean (SD)	Mean (SD)	N		Source
Parents' Education	Total years of schooling for household head.	1–16, Actual years 17 = Post-grad work	13.74 (2.31)	12.19 (2.39)	2,059	—	CDS
Family Structure	Whether youth lives in a two-parent home.	0 = No / 1 = Yes	.87	.49	2,155	—	CDS
Number of Books	Parents' response to the following: About how many books does child have?	1 = None 5 = 20 or more	4.76 (.66)	4.28 (.92)	2,150	—	CDS
Reading Ability	Scores on the Woodcock-Johnson reading achievement standardized test, which is a summation of the letter-word and passage comprehension scores.	Min. = 30 Max. = 194	110.12 (16.55)	96.42 (16.26)	2,134	—	CDS

Figure 5.6

Description of measures is the same as Figure 5.4. The unadjusted means are displayed in Figure 5.6 in Chapter 5.

Figure 5.7

See information in this table under Figure 5.5.

Figure 5.8

Social Standing

Variable	Description	Coding	Mean (SD)	Mean (SD)	N		Source
Make Friends[d]	Compared to other kids your age, how well do you do in making friends?	1 = Much worse 7 = Much better	5.09 (1.49)	5.53 (1.42)	1,133	—	MADICS
Trouble Getting Along with Peers[d]	How often do you have trouble getting along with other kids?	1 = Almost Never 5 = Almost Always	1.95 (1.01)	1.96 (1.10)	1,144	—	MADICS

Table A4 (continued)

Variable Name	Description	Metric	Means (SD) Whites	Means (SD) Blacks	N	Alpha	Data
Popularity	Compared to other kids your age, how popular are you?	1 = Much less 7 = Much more	4.43 (1.40)	4.91 (1.49)	2,862	—	MADICS
Number of Friends[c]	Youths' assessment of how satisfied with s/he is with the number of friends s/he has	0 = Wish I had more 1 = Have plenty	.72	.78	1,716	—	MADICS
Figure 5.9							
Direct Measure for "Acting White" Hypothesis							
Act White	Is getting good grades part of "acting White"?	0 = No / 1 = Yes	—	.17	527	—	MADICS
Figure 5.10							
Peer Schooling Messages							
Positive Academic Orientation	How many of the friends you spend most of your time with (a) do well in school? (b) plan to go to college? (c) like to discuss schoolwork or other intellectual things with you? (d) think it is important to work hard on school-work?	1 = None of them 5 = All of them	3.40 (.73)	3.44 (.75)	3,194	.714	MADICS

Measure	Item	Response scale			N	α	Data
Negative Peers Behaviors	How many of the friends you spend most of your time with (a) are in youth or street gangs? (b) have stolen something worth more than $50? (c) put pressure on you to use drugs?	1 = None of Them 5 = All of them	1.23 (.45)	1.26 (.52)	3,171	.695	MADICS
Negative Peer Values[c]	Would your friends think it was cool or uncool if you (a) drank beer, wine, or liquor? (b) used pot, marijuana or other illegal drugs? (c) had a baby or fathered a baby while in high school? (d) talked back to teachers (e) did what you wanted to do even if it meant breaking a school rule? (f) did risky and dangerous things?	1 = Very Uncool 5 = Very Cool	2.52 (.82)	2.50 (.81)	1,899	.810	MADICS
Negative Academic Orientation[c]	How many of the friends you spend most of your time with (a) think working hard to get good grades is a waste of time? (b) cheat on school tests? (c) don't like having to come to school? (d) think being popular with friends is more important than getting A's in school? (e) think it's okay not to do their homework if their friends want to do something else instead?	1 = None of them 5 = All of them	2.29 (.69)	2.16 (.68)	1,826	.686	MADICS

Note: * Item is reverse coded. Also, SD refers to strongly disagree and SA refers to strongly agree. While all analyses based on national data (CDS and LSYPE) are weighted, the Ns reported are for the unweighted sample.

a. Although many of the measures in this chapter are similar to those used in previous chapters, the descriptive statistics are different due to different sample restrictions.

b. These measures were not collected in the eighth grade and consist of 94 percent or greater of the total seventh and eleventh grade sample.

c. These measures were not collected in the seventh grade and consist of 94 percent or greater of the total eighth and eleventh grade sample.

d. These measures were used only for analysis among seventh graders and consist of 98 percent or greater of the total seventh grade sample.

e. Analysis was conducted only among black youth in grade 7.

Table A4: Means, Standard Deviations, and Descriptions for Variables Used in Chapter 5 [a]

Variable Name	Description	Metric	Means (SD)			N	Alpha	Data
			Whites	Asian	Blacks			
Figure 5.11								
Academic Orientation among British Youth								
Read for Pleasure	Frequency with which youth reads for pleasure.	1 = Never 6 = Most days	4.32 (1.60)	4.38 (1.60)	4.60 (1.50)	13,221	—	LSYPE
Happy at School	I am happy when I am at school.	1 = SD 4 = SA	3.01 (.71)	3.26 (.60)	3.07 (.69)	12,699	—	LSYPE
Value of School	(a) School is a waste of time for me,* (b) school work is worth doing, (c) the work I do in lessons is a waste of time.*	1 = SD 4 = SA	3.30 (.54)	3.41 (.50)	3.36 (.49)	12,272	.601	LSYPE
Academic Disengagement	(a) Most of the time I do not want to go to school, (b) On the whole, I like being at School,* (c) I work as hard as I can in school,* (d) In an lesson, I often count the minutes until it ends, (e) I am bored in (all or most) of my lessons.	1 = SD 4 = SA	2.28 (.56)	2.02 (.48)	2.19 (.53)	11,249	.764	LSYPE
Figure 5.12								
Resistance to Schooling								
No Post-Comp. School Desired	Youth does not want to continue schooling beyond age 16.	0 = Stay on 1 = Do not stay	.16	.03	.03	12,561	—	LSYPE

	Description	Coding				N		Source
Behavior	Whether youth's parents have ever been contacted by school(s) about youth's behavior.	0 = No 1 = Yes	.24	.14	.33	12,758	—	LSYPE
Suspended	Whether youth has ever been temporarily suspended or excluded from school.	0 = No 1 = Yes	.08	.05	.14	12,807	—	LSYPE

Figure 5.13

Peer Sanctioning Measures

	Description	Coding				N		Source
Friends over to Home	The number of times the youth has had friends visit their home in the last 7 days.	1 = None 4 = 6 or more	1.99 (.96)	1.64 (.80)	1.79 (.88)	13,208	—	LSYPE
Go out with Friends	The number of times the youth has gone out with friends in the last 7 days.	1 = None 4 = 6 or more	2.61 (1.03)	1.97 (.95)	2.30 (.94)	13,213	—	LSYPE

Controls for all Analyses Based on LSYPE

	Description	Coding				N		Source
Discrimination	Do you think you have ever been treated unfairly by teachers at your school because of your skin, ethnicity, race, or religion?	0 = No 1 = Yes	.09	.29	.45	12,401	—	LSYPE

Table A4 (continued)

Variable Name	Description	Metric	Means (SD)			N	Alpha	Data
			Whites	Asian	Blacks			
Social Class	Highest level of education by either parent coded as follows: (4) higher managerial and professional occupation; (3) lower managerial and professional and intermediate occupation; (2) small employers, low supervisors, and technical semi-routine and routine labor; (1) never worked or long term unemployment.	1 to 4	2.65 (.73)	2.16 (.81)	2.45 (.86)	12,479	—	LSYPE

Note: * Item is reverse coded. Also, SD refers to strongly disagree and SA refers to strongly agree. While all analyses based on national data (CDS and LSYPE) are weighted, the Ns reported are for the unweighted sample.

a. Although many of the measures in this chapter are similar to those used in previous chapters, the descriptive statistics are different due to different sample restrictions.

b. These measures were not collected in the eighth grade and consist of 94 percent or greater of the total seventh and eleventh grade sample.

c. These measures were not collected in the seventh grade and consist of 94 percent or greater of the total eighth and eleventh grade sample.

d. These measures were used only for analysis among seventh graders and consist of 98 percent or greater of the total seventh grade sample.

e. Analysis was conducted only among black youth in grade 7.

Table A5: Means, Standard Deviations, and Descriptions for Variables Used in Chapter 6

Variable Name	Description	Metric	Means (SD)	N	Alpha	Data
Figure 6.1						
No analysis is presented in this figure.						
Figure 6.2						
Youth Racial Attitudes						
Happy	I am happy that I am blacks.	0 = ~ SA 1 = SA	.68	596	—	MADICS
Regret	I often regret that I am black.	0 = SD 1 = ~SD	.24	596	—	MADICS
Success Helps Other Blacks	It will help other Blacks if I am successful.	0 = SD/D/Neither 1 = Agree/SA	.64	596	—	MADICS
Benefits for Blacks' Success	It helps me when other Black people are successful.	0 = SD/D/Neither 1 = Agree/SA	.67	596	—	MADICS
Figure 6.3						
Youth Academic Orientation						
Achievement	See Table A2, Figure 3.5, *achievement.*	0 – 4.0	2.81 (.72)	484	—	MADICS
Educational Aspirations	See Table A2, Figure 3.5.	1 = 8th grade or less 9 = J.D., Ph.D., M.D.	7.75 (1.48)	513	—	MADICS

Table A5 (continued)

Variable Name	Description	Metric	Means (SD)	N	Alpha	Data
Value of School	See Table A2, Figure 3.5.	1 = SD 5 = SA	4.15 (.72)	525	.793	MADICS
Detachment From School	(a) Schooling is a waste of time. (b) I don't really care care about schooling. (c) Schooling is not so important for kids like me.	1 = SD 5 = SA	1.89 (.83)	529	.758	MADICS

Note: SD refers to strongly disagree, D refers to disagree, and SA refers to strongly agree.

Table A6: Means, Standard Deviations, and Descriptions for Variables Used in Chapter 7

Variable Name	Description	Metric	Means (SD) Whites	Asian	Blacks	N	Alpha	Data
Figure 7.2								
Negative Schooling Behaviors								
Disruptive	Teachers' responses to: How often is this student disruptive in class?	1 = Never 5 = All the time	1.60 (.82)	1.52 (.80)	1.91 (.99)	6,322	—	NELS
In trouble	How many times did the following happen to you in the first half of the current school year?: I got in trouble for not following school rules.	0 = Never 4 = 10 or >	.62 (.91)	.45 (.72)	.60 (.82)	7,035	—	NELS
Troublemaker	Do you think other students see you as a troublemaker?	0 = Not at all 2 = Very much	.31 (.53)	.24 (.49)	.21 (.49)	6,734	—	NELS
Positive Schooling Behaviors								
Homework	Overall about how much time do you spend on homework each week out of school?	0 = None 7 = > 15 hours	2.56 (1.72)	3.17 (1.91)	2.39 (1.48)	6,940	—	NELS
Effort	Teachers' responses to: Does this student usually work hard for good grades?	0 = No 1 = Yes	.68 (.47)	.75 (.43)	.56 (.50)	4,790	—	NELS
Attentive	Teachers' responses to: How often is this student attentive in class?	1 = Never 5 = All the time	3.98 (.83)	4.09 (.74)	3.77 (.83)	4,903	—	NELS

Table A6 (continued)

Variable Name	Description	Metric	Means (SD)			N	Alpha	Data
			Whites	Asian	Blacks			
Figure 7.3								
Prior skills (Grade 8)								
Reading	Item Response Theta (IRT) estimated number right.	10.61 = Min. 43.83 = Max.	28.95 (8.45)	28.40 (9.04)	23.57 (7.60)	7,070	—	NELS
Math	IRT estimated number right.	16.03 = Min. 66.81 = Max.	38.87 (11.71)	40.72 (12.22)	29.89 (9.92)	7,069	—	NELS
GPA	Cumulative grade point average.	0 to 4.0	3.01 (.75)	3.20 (.70)	2.72 (.71)	7,263	—	NELS
Educational Outcomes (Grade 12)								
Reading	IRT estimated number right.	10.41 = Min. 51.16 = Max.	34.76 (9.69)	35.41 (10.21)	28.24 (9.58)	7,311	—	NELS
Mathematics	IRT estimated number right.	16.97 = Min. 78.10 = Max.	50.74 (13.92)	54.37 (14.12)	39.32 (12.30)	7,311	—	NELS
Grades	Combined grades in reading, math, science, and social studies.	0 to 4.0	2.14 (.82)	2.35 (.72)	1.58 (.66)	6,600	—	NELS

Figure 7.4

See measures described under Figures 7.2 and 7.3.

Figure 7.5

See measures described under Figures 7.2 and 7.3.

Note: All analyses are weighted. The Ns reported are for the unweighted sample.

Table A6: Means, Standard Deviations, and Descriptions for Variables Used in Chapter 7

Variable Name	Description	Metric	Means (SD)		N	Alpha	Data
			Whites	Blacks			
Figure 7.6							
Schooling Behaviors (based on time diaries)							
Homework	Daily average, calculated as ([weekday x 5] + [weekend day x 2]) /7, on general homework activities.	Minutes	37:22 (51:14)	34:22 (27:30)	293	—	CDS
Educational Activities	Daily average on the following: being tutored, non-school professional classes or lectures, studying/research/reading, library activities, reviewing homework with parents/ caregiver, and other educational activities	Minutes	4:02 (13:35)	2:26 (7:46)	293	—	CDS
Leisure Reading	Daily average on the following: looking at or reading books, magazines, reviews, pamphlets, newspapers, other non-school related reading, and being read to/listening to a story.	Minutes	11:29 (22:55)	4:50 (17:35)	293	—	CDS
Middle School Achievement							
Reading	Scores on the Woodcock-Johnson reading achievement standardized test, which is a summation of the letter-word and passage comprehension scores.	Min. = 30 Max. = 193	110.02 (18.87)	90.72 (18.31)	312	—	CDS

Math	Scores on the Woodcock-Johnson math achievement standardized test, which is a based on a summation of the calculation and applied problems tests.	Min. = 55 Max. = 146	111.04 (15.74)	95.27 (12.16)	310 —	CDS

Prior Skills: Achievement during grade school

Reading	Scores on similar Woodcock-Johnson reading achievement test described for middle school.	Min. = 44 Max. = 153	111.65 (16.54)	101.83 (16.23)	286 —	CDS
Math	Scores on similar Woodcock-Johnson math achievement test described for middle school.	Min. = 33 Max. = 149	111.46 (16.73)	102.99 (14.56)	285 —	CDS

Figure 7.7

See measures described under Figure 7.6.

Note: All analyses are weighted. The Ns reported are for the unweighted sample.

Table A7: Means, Standard Deviations, and Descriptions for Variables Used in Chapter 8

Variable Name	Description	Metric	Means
Measures of social class for all data used in this chapter (Highest for either parent):			
BCS (N = 16,801)			
High Class	Professional or managerial.	0 = No / 1 = Yes	.21
Upper-Middle	Skilled non-manual.	0 = No / 1 = Yes	.29
Lower-Middle	Skilled manual or semi-skilled.	0 = No / 1 = Yes	.47
Lower Class	Unskilled labor.	0 = No / 1 = Yes	.03
LSYPE (N = 12,752)			
High Class	Higher managerial and professional occupation.	0 = No / 1 = Yes	.14
Upper-Middle	Lower managerial and professional and intermediate.	0 = No / 1 = Yes	.33
Lower-Middle	Small employers, low supervisors, and technical semi-routine and routine labor.	0 = No / 1 = Yes	.48
Lower Class	Never worked or long term unemployment.	0 = No / 1 = Yes	.05
NELS (N = 10,737)			
Omitted group	Four-year college degree or greater.	0 = No / 1 = Yes	.20
Some Col.	Some college education.	0 = No / 1 = Yes	.41

HS Grad.	High school diploma.	0 = No / 1 = Yes	.22
< HS Grad.	Less than a high school diploma.	0 = No / 1 = Yes	.17
CDS (N = 1,196)			
Omitted group	Four-year college degree or greater.	0 = No / 1 = Yes	.29
Some Col.	Some college education.	0 = No / 1 = Yes	.22
HS Grad.	High school diploma.	0 = No / 1 = Yes	.29
< HS Grad.	Less than a high school diploma.	0 = No / 1 = Yes	.20
MADICS (N = 3,352)			
Omitted group	Four-year college degree or greater.	0 = No / 1 = Yes	.33
Some Col.	Some college education.	0 = No / 1 = Yes	.32
HS Grad.	High school diploma.	0 = No / 1 = Yes	.29
< HS Grad.	Less than a high school diploma.	0 = No / 1 = Yes	.06

Note: * Item is reverse coded. Also, SD refers to strongly disagree and SA refers to strongly agree. Analyses based on the LSYPE, NELS, and CDS are weighted. The Ns reported are for the unweighted sample. See notes from Table A4 for further information on the items from the MADICS used in this chapter.

Table A7: Means, Standard Deviations, and Descriptions for Variables Used in Chapter 8

Variable Name	Description	Metric	Means (SD)	N	Alpha	Data
Figure 8.1						
Achievement among British Youth						
Vocabulary Score	Standardized scores from the Assessment Performance Unit test administered by teachers for the BCS70.	Min. = -3.80 Max. = 2.12	.00 (1.00)	4,439	—	BCS
Teacher Evaluations	Teacher's rating of youth's academic performance and underlying ability compared to other students of similar age.	1 = Bottom 5% 7 = Top 5%	4.37 (1.26)	3,705	—	BCS
English	Scores on the National Key Stage Tests taken at age 14.	Min. = 21 Max. = 45	33.80 (6.56)	13,897	—	LSYPE
Math	Scores on the National Key Stage Tests taken at age 14.	Min. = 15 Max. = 51	36.15 (8.24)	14,043	—	LSYPE
Achievement for the U.S. Sample						
Reading	IRT estimated number right.	Min. = 10.55 Max. = 51.16	33.19 (10.03)	9,142	—	NELS
Math	IRT estimated number right.	Min. = 16.97 Max. = 78.10	48.15 (14.43)	9,145	—	NELS
Reading	Scores on the Woodcock-Johnson reading achievement standardized test (same measure used in Figure 7.6).	Min. = 30 Max. = 193	104.96 (19.54)	1,075	—	CDS

Variable	Description	Coding	Mean (SD)	N	α	Data
Math	Scores on the Woodcock-Johnson math achievement standardized test (same measure used in Figure 7.6).	Min. = 49 Max. = 171	105.08 (16.60)	1,072	—	CDS

Figure 8.2

Academic Orientation among British Youth

Variable	Description	Coding	Mean (SD)	N	α	Data
Number of School Activities	The number of school-based activities in which the youth participated.	0 = Min. 7 = Max.	1.86 (1.53)	6,417	—	BCS
Value of School	(a) Continuing in full-time education only puts off the time when you become unemployed;* (b) It is best to leave school as soon as possible to get job experience;* (c) Job experience is more important than getting qualifications.*	1 = Agree fully 3 = Disagree	2.44 (.47)	5,467	.576	BCS
Academic Disengagement	(a) I feel school is largely a waste of time; (b) I think homework is a bore; (c) I find it difficult to keep my mind on my work; (d) I never take school work seriously; (e) I do not like school; (f) there is no point in planning for the future, you should take things as they come.	1 = Not true at all 3 = Very true	1.68 (.43)	6,076	.754	BCS

Figure 8.3

Academic Orientation among British Youth

Variable	Description	Coding	Mean (SD)	N	α	Data
Unexcused Absence	Whether youth has had an unexcused absence (e.g., non-health related).	0 = No 1 = Yes	.43	6,298	—	BCS

Table A7 (continued)

Variable Name	Description	Metric	Means (SD)	N	Alpha	Data
Figure 8.4						
Social Standing Measures						
Number of Friends	Compared with an average teenager of my same age and sex, the number of good friends I have is:	1 = Far less 5 = Far more	3.32 (.87)	4,181	—	BCS
Lonely	Do you often feel lonely as school?	0 = No / 1 = Yes	.08	6,003	—	BCS
Make Friends	Compared to other kids your age, how well do you do in making friends?	1 = Much worse 7 = Much better	5.38 (1.46)	1,133	—	MADICS
Trouble Getting Along with Peers	How often do you have trouble getting along with other kids?	1 = Almost Never 5 = Almost Always	1.95 (1.07)	1,144	—	MADICS
Table 8.1						
Perceptions and Attitudes						
Perceived Returns to Education	(a) I have to do well in school if I want to be a success in life. (b) Schooling is not so important for kids like me, * (c) Getting a good education Is the best way to get ahead in life for the kids in my neighborhood.	1 = SD 5 = SA	4.19 (.70)	3,227	.608	MADICS
Educational Aspirations	If you could do exactly what you wanted, how far would you like to go in school?	1 = 8th grade or less 9 = J.D., Ph.D, M.D.	7.70 (1.48)	3,239	—	MADICS

Measure	Item/Question	Response Scale	Mean (SD)	N	Reliability	Source
Educational Expectations	We can't always do what we most want to do. How far do you think you *actually will* go in school?	1 = 8th grade or less 9 = J.D., Ph.D., M.D.	6.91 (1.63)	3,231	—	MADICS
Affect Toward Schooling	(a) most of my classes or subjects are boring.* (b) homework is a waste of time.* (c) In general, you like school a lot. (d) Grades are very important to you.	1 = SD 5 = SA	3.66 (.66)	2,216	.648	MADICS
Go to School Because Enjoy	Importance of the following reason for attending school: I go to school because I enjoy my classes.	1 = Not imp. reason 7 = Very important	4.36 (1.75)	3,223	—	MADICS
Limited Educ. Opportunities	Discrepancy between educational aspirations and educational expectations.	Min. = -6 Max. = 7	.79 (1.27)	3,230	—	MADICS
Go to School Because have to	Importance of the following reason for attending school: I go to school because I have to.	1 = Not imp. reason 7 = Very important	5.00 (2.11)	3,208	—	MADICS

Schooling Behaviors

Measure	Item/Question	Response Scale	Mean (SD)	N	Reliability	Source
Seek Help	When you're having trouble on schoolwork, how often do you go to (a) your teachers for help? (b) other adults in the school, like a tutor, for help? (c) other students for help? (d) your parent(s) for help? (e) your friends for help?	1 = Almost Never 5 = Almost Always	2.95 (.75)	3,197	.600	MADICS
Time on School Activities/Clubs	During the last year how often did you spend time on any other school activities (such as clubs or student government)?	1 = < once a month 6 = Usually every day	1.70 (2.05)	3,344	—	MADICS

Table A7 (continued)

Variable Name	Description	Metric	Means (SD)	N	Alpha	Data
Time on Homework	Think about the last two weeks, about how often did you do homework?	1 = Never 6 = Daily, > an hour	4.66 (1.42)	2,316	—	MADICS
Time on Educational Activities	Think about the last two weeks, about how often did you: (a) watch news, educational or cultural shows on TV? (b) read books or magazines for pleasure? (c) read newspapers?	1 = Never 6 = Daily, > an hour	3.04 (1.10)	2,326	.581	MADICS
Importance of Academics	Compared to other things you do, how important are each of the following activities to you?: (a) Math (b) Other school subjects.	1 = Much less 7 = Much more	5.22 (1.33)	3,241	.810	MADICS
Skip School / Cut Classes	How often, if ever, have you skipped school or cut classes?	1 = Never 4 = Often	1.53 (.90)	3,303	—	MADICS
Suspensions	Number of times youth has been suspended from middle school and high school (asked in grades 8 and 11, respectively).	1 to 10 or more	.57 (1.49)	1,845	—	MADICS
Importance Non-Academics	Compared to other things you do, how important are sports to you?	1 = Much less 7 = Much more	4.37 (1.90)	3,325	—	MADICS

Peer Orientation

Positive Academic Orientation	How many of the friends you spend most of your time with (a) do well in school? (b) plan to go to college? (c) like to discuss schoolwork or other intellectual things with you? (d) think it is important to work hard on school-work?	1 = None of them 5 = All of them	3.42 (.75)	3,194	.714	MADICS
Negative Academic Orientation	How many of the friends you spend most of your time with (a) think working hard to get good grades is a waste of time? (b) cheat on school tests? (c) don't like having to come to school? (d) think being popular with friends is more important than getting A's in school? (e) think it's okay not to do their homework if their friends want to do something else instead?	1 = None of them 5 = All of them	2.21 (.69)	1,826	.686	MADICS

Note: * Item is reverse coded. Also, SD refers to strongly disagree and SA refers to strongly agree. Analyses based on the LSYPE, NELS, and CDS are weighted. The Ns reported are for the unweighted sample. See notes from Table A4 for further information on the items from the MADICS used in this chapter.

NOTES

1. Introduction to Oppositional Culture

1. I use the term "black" to refer to people of African Diaspora residing within the United States.

2. The test score gap is not synonymous with the achievement gap. Standardized tests are simply one measure of achievement. I elaborate on this point later in this chapter.

3. In fact, an edited volume by Ogbu—*Minority Status, Oppositional Culture, and Schooling*—was published posthumously in 2008, five years after his death.

4. I provide a brief discussion on the limitations of standardized testing in Appendix A.

5. Many private-sector employers also use standardized tests for hiring, placing, and promoting employees. Hedges and Nowell (1998:167) write: "If very high scores are needed to excel in a field, or if gatekeepers believe that this is so, the fact that whites are ten to twenty times more likely to have high scores makes it almost impossible for blacks to be well represented in high-ranking positions. This under-representation seems to hold for all types of tests: the consequences are not limited to scientific or technical fields." Jencks and Phillips (1998) echo this sentiment in predicting that if selective colleges and professional schools based their admissions decisions entirely on test performance, accepting only students scoring in the top percentiles, their enrollment would currently be 96 or 97 percent white and Asian. This would exclude almost all the nation's future black leaders.

6. Although not directly related to achievement, Conley (1999) shows that blacks' higher levels of unemployment and high school dropout rates is not due to race (or genetics); he also finds that blacks are actually less likely to engage in socially deviant behaviors than whites once social class (that is, family wealth and assets) is taken into account.

7. Ainsworth (2002) highlights the benefits of spatial concentration of advantage; he finds that as the percentage of adults with a college education and a professional or managerial occupation within a community increases, so do youths' educational aspirations and achievement. Furthermore, Ainsworth shows that the ben-

efits of having high-status residents in a neighborhood seems to overshadow the effects of negative neighborhood characteristics and that more than half of the detrimental effect of living in economically deprived neighborhoods is attributable to a lack of high-status residents in such neighborhoods.

8. Lucas (1999) shows that children from working-class origins are more likely to attend vocational tracks while their middle-class counterparts attend academic tracks, that upward track mobility is rather difficult, and that track location has an effect on achievement and educational attainment. Another manner in which inequality is perpetuated is through the valorization of particular forms of cultural expressions (Bourdieu and Passeron 1977). Schools embody the culture and ideology of the dominant group, whose value system and behavioral norms are regarded as superior; those who effectively enact these arbitrary cultural tools are said to have the "cultural capital" critical to obtaining (or maintaining) high-class status. Thus, social inequalities are reproduced because working-class youth have the added burden of acquiring the class-specific cultural knowledge that schools and teachers promote. There is a line of research that lends support to the notion that schools have limited effectiveness in diminishing the link between class origin and destination (Hanushek 1989, 1997, 2007; Coleman et al. 1966). The general conclusion from Hanushek's work is that the "common surrogates for teacher and school quality (class size, teachers' education, and teachers' experience, among the most important) are not systematically related to performance" (1989:49). Hanushek's research echoes the conclusion of the classic *Coleman Report* (Coleman et al. 1966:325), which determined that "schools bring little influence to bear on a child's achievement that is independent of his background and general social context; and that this very lack of an independent effect means that the inequalities imposed on children by their home, neighborhood, and peer environment are carried along to become the inequalities with which they confront adult life at the end of school." It is important to note that Hanushek's work has been heavily contested (Hedges, Laine, and Greenwald 1994a, 1994b; also see Alan Krueger in Heckman and Krueger 2004:33–39).

9. Structural explanations refer to theories that provide compelling narratives that persistent patterns of behavior stem from responses to external contingencies.

10. Because the purpose of this book is to examine whether black youth have a culture oppositional toward education relative to whites, I do not distinguish between native and non-native blacks. Unlike some groups whose minority group classification is unambiguous (for example Hawaiians, Native Americans, and African Americans as involuntary minorities and Asian Americans as voluntary minorities), as discussed earlier, it is difficult to distinguish whether black immigration is voluntary or involuntary. Despite the classification scheme's usefulness within the framework when applied to race, the reasons behind what makes a "push" factor

for immigration voluntary or involuntary are underdeveloped. Thus, in addition to the fact that group classification can vary within racial groups, some "push" factors can be classified as both voluntary and involuntary. Although datasets rich in educational measures (including those used in this study) contain immigration status, they do not have clean measures for whether the immigration was voluntary or involuntary; the motivation for the immigration and whether the immigrant would regard their migration to be voluntary or involuntary is not assessed. This is perhaps why race has been the primary characteristic used by researchers; nearly all studies of the resistance model use whites, blacks, and Asian Americans to represent dominant, involuntary, and voluntary groups, respectively. In a more general sense within the education arena, the immigrant-domestic born distinction among blacks is made primarily by colleges and universities for admissions data. This distinction is not made regarding achievement; achievement and testing data track the black-white achievement gap and not the domestic-born black-white gap. Therefore, given the ambiguity associated with the application of the minority classification scheme, in this study I use the black-white distinction to be consistent with previous research. Supplemental analyses in which I exclude immigrant blacks reveal that the findings remain nearly identical to those reported in this book; all primary conclusions remain unchanged. The results of these analyses, which will be featured in a future article, are available upon request.

2. Discrimination and Barriers

1. The studies by both Elliott and Smith (2004) and Smith (2005) omit the Detroit site from their analyses because of a lack of information on key labor market variables (for example, level of workplace power).

2. On a related note, Elliott and Smith (2004) find that all groups benefit equally from in-group favoritism in the promotion process (selection of people with similar race/sex to fill positions immediately beneath one), but that the opportunity to take advantage of in-group favoritism is greater for white males relative to blacks by a ratio of eight to one.

3. That is, skin shade is genetic, but intelligence within the black community does not vary by skin shade (Hill 2002).

4. The findings from numerous studies suggest that racial inequality in wages is greater at the highest levels of education and occupations (Grodsky and Pager 2001; Tomaskovic-Devey, Thomas, and Johnson 2005) and that racial inequality in promotion increases at higher levels of power (Baldi and McBrier 1997; Elliott and Smith 2004; Smith 2001; Wilson, Sakura-Lemessy, and West 1999). These findings are consistent with the theory of the functionality of market-based discrimination, which was proposed by prominent economist William Darity Jr. (2001). The theory posits that as subaltern groups—in this case, blacks—improve their human

capital characteristics, the exclusionary or discriminatory practices of the dominant group will intensify. Given this evidence, Ogbu's claim that black Americans
are skeptical toward education appears quite reasonable.

5. The colorblind narrative is a variation of modern laissez-faire liberalism, which
emphasizes free individual expression and freedom of competition. Blau (2003:26)
notes that belief in free competition legitimizes unequal outcomes so that "the
distributional processes that yield inequalities of wealth, income, and status can
therefore be construed by many people as fair and just." She contends that whereas
whites often consider these processes to be impartial, disadvantage has a black
face. She argues: "Because social life became increasingly easy to analogize in
competitive market terms, whites could legitimize superior occupational and
earnings outcomes as being the consequences of many good personal choices . . .
Whites justify racial inequalities as therefore being fair while considering themselves to be blind to color" (2003:26).

3. Origins of Youth Perceptions

1. See Appendix B for a complete description of the sources of data used in this study.
2. See Appendix C for a detailed description of the analytic plan for all analyses conducted in this study and Appendix D for a description of the measures employed
in each chapter.
3. Although rather small, the racial differences are statistically significant at the .05
level.
4. To obtain unbiased population estimates, analyses are based on weighted data using the appropriate NELS and ELS panel weights to adjust for sampling design
(stratification, disproportionate sampling of certain strata, and clustered, multistage
probability sampling), sample attrition, and nonresponse (Ingles et al. 1994).
5. Since findings are being displayed for the same indicator across different datasets,
it is not possible to make comparisons based on the actual values from parents'
responses. Each dataset uses a different scale for the question, and the responses
were obtained from different samples. Therefore, in order to make the estimates
comparable, they have been standardized.
6. Value of schooling is measured as the average of youths' responses to the following
questions on a 5-point scale (5 = strongly agree): 1) I have to do well in school if I
want to be a success in life, 2) getting a good education is the best way to get ahead
in life for the kids in my neighborhood, 3) achievement and effort in school lead
to job success later on, and 4) education really pays off in the future for people like
me. Perceived barriers are measured as youths' average along the same scale on the
following question: People like me aren't treated fairly at work no matter how
much education they have. Educational aspirations and expectations range from 1
(less than a high school diploma) to 8 (J.D., M.D., Ph.D.). Youths' GPAs serve as
the measure of academic achievement.

5. Racial Differences in Academic Orientation of Youth

1. See Appendix D for a description of measures used throughout this study.
2. See Appendix C for the analytic plan for all analyses conducted in this study.
3. The standard error is useful in illustrating the size of uncertainty in the estimate. Since the statistics are based on a sample of students drawn from a population, they are estimates of the "true" value that would be observed if the entire population were to be surveyed. Therefore, estimates have a margin of error, which in statistics is referred to as the standard error because it represents the average discrepancy of the means that would be obtained among all possible samples (of a given size) drawn from the population and the real population mean. Given the assumption of normality (that the values in the population are distributed in a manner that can be described by a bell-shaped curve), an estimate is significant only if it is twice the size of the standard error. This means that in the case of a positive estimate (say, 0.3), the standard error (say, 0.1) could be subtracted from the estimate twice and the estimate would still remain above zero, which would suggest that we could be 95 percent confident that the true value in the population is greater than zero—or simply significant. However, since subtracting a standard error of 0.2 from an estimate of 0.3 twice would equal -0.1, we could not be 95 percent certain that the population value we are estimating is greater than zero. In this case, the estimate would be described as not significant (NS).
4. Recall that grade 11 is the last time data were collected in the MADICS prior to the completion of compulsory schooling.
5. This work stems from collaboration with Jeremy Staff and Ricardo Sabates on a larger project on youth ambitions in the United States and the United Kingdom.

6. Should Blacks Become Raceless to Improve Achievement?

1. Although the "acting white" hypothesis stems from the study published by Fordham and Ogbu (1986), the concept is often attributed to Ogbu. However, the concept was developed by Fordham (see Fordham 2008).
2. Racial identity models do not assume that a particular racial identity is optimal. For example, while the Multidimensional Model of Racial Identity by Sellers et al. (1998) posits that the relative importance of one's racial identity varies across both individuals (centrality to one's self-definition) and social settings (salience from cues within the social context that determine the importance of given identities), Cross, Parham, and Helms (1991) note that the effects of both rejecting or embracing a black racial identity vary across social contexts. Sellers et al. (1998) suggest that high-achieving black students' identity as good students may be more important than race, thereby negating the need to distance themselves from or embrace race.
3. Arroyo and Zigler (1995) assess race and achievement group differences in responses to a racelessness scale. Their scale is comprised of four components:

achievement attitudes, impression management, alienation, and stereotypical beliefs. However, with the exception of the stereotype component—which assesses
the extent to which students agree with societal stereotypes about blacks—the
items for the other components are race neutral; they inquire about general attitudes toward the importance of school (achievement attitudes), whether students
are concerned about how they are perceived by other students (impression management), and the extent to which they feel alienated from other people in the
same age group (alienation). As such, the racelessness scale used by Arroyo and
Zigler does not assess the extent to which blacks feel a sense of connection to their
race. In addition to examining whether race/ethnic connection among blacks in
high school is associated with school achievement, in this chapter I examine
whether a race/ethnic connection relates to educational aspirations, value attributed to schooling, and detachment from schooling.

4. A student who affirms that they are *happy to be black* does not necessarily mean
s/he will not *regret being black*. Similarly, nor does a *regret of being black* mean that
one will not be *happy to be black*. Students may not be high or low on either concept, particularly those for whom race is not central to their self-definition (Sellers
et al. 1998).

7. Shifting the Focus Away from Culture

1. To illustrate how the omission of a variable can lead to biased findings, consider
the following general example in which the "true" model for school achievement
(Y) for the *ith* child *at time t* is determined by schooling behaviors (X_1), prior skill
level (Z_{it-1}), and an error term (ε) such that:

$$Y_{it} = \beta_0 + \beta_1 X_{1i} + \beta_2 Z_{it-1} + \varepsilon \tag{1}$$
$$Z_{it-1} = \alpha_0 + \alpha_x X_{1i} + u_2 \tag{2}$$

Where Z_{it-1} (prior skills) is a function of a set of factors (for example, parental academic involvement during childhood or the quality of a child's educational experience) occurring at an earlier time. Substituting (2) into (1) leads to (3) whereby:

$$Y_{it} = \beta_0 + \beta_1 X_{1i} + \beta_2 [\alpha_0 + \alpha_x X_{1i} + u_2] + \varepsilon \tag{3}$$

Rearranging the factors in (4) gives:

$$Y_{it} = [\beta_0 + \beta_2 \alpha_0] + [\beta_1 + \beta_2 \alpha_x] X_{1i} + [\beta_2 u + \varepsilon] \tag{4}$$

Thus, by omitting skill level (Z_{it-1}) from Equation (1), the estimated coefficient for
the vector of *behaviors* (X_1) would be $[\beta_1 + \beta_2 \alpha_x]$ (for the purpose of clarity, a coefficient for socioeconomic background factors that may affect achievement is not
shown). The analysis I present in this chapter shows the extent to which the effects
that students' schooling behaviors during high school have on their academic
achievement toward the end of their high school careers are overestimated.

2. The analyses are restricted to include only those students present in the sample from grades 8 through 12, and who completed standardized math and reading tests developed by the Educational Testing Service (78 percent of both whites and Asian Americans and 73 percent of blacks within the NELS). Supplemental analysis showed minimal sample exclusion bias.

3. Disruptive in class is measured along a 5-point scale (1 = never to 5 = all of the time). The number of times in trouble is also measured along a 5-point scale (0 = never to 4 = ten times or more). Troublemaker is measured along a 3-point scale (0 = Not at all to 2 = Very much).

4. Time spent on homework is measured on an 8-point scale (0 = none to 7 = over 15 hours). Teachers' view on whether the students put forward effort for good grades is dichotomous (0 = no, 1 = yes). Finally, teachers' estimate of how often the student is attentive in class ranges from 1 (never) to 5 (all the time).

5. To the extent a bias exists by not accounting for social class, it only has implications for mean differences across the groups; it is reasonable to expect results for behavioral "effects" on achievement—and their level of decline once prior skills are taken into account—to remain unaffected once social class is controlled.

6. Achievement is measured as students' test scores (reading and math) and grades for several reasons. First, these are common outcomes used for evaluating students' academic performance. Second, using separate measures of achievement allows for the determination of whether the patterns observed are robust. Third, test scores and grades might not be uniform in what they measure. For example, prior grades may capture more aspects of previous behavioral issues than test scores. Finally, using multiple measures of previous academic aptitude will help identify the source of the bias resulting from the omission of prior skills.

7. In order to obtain an estimate for the amount of time students typically spend on academic activities daily, the activities are the sum of the weekday multiplied by five and the weekend day multiplied by two.

8. Does Marginalization Equal Resistance to Schooling?

1. Formal schooling in the United Kingdom consists of three stages: primary (ages 4–10), secondary (ages 11–15), and higher education (ages 16 and beyond)—generally completed in three years. The university attended is contingent upon the type of secondary school attended. Specifically, students who attend grammar or technical secondary schools have a greater opportunity to gain admission into the more prestigious universities, whereas those who complete comprehensive and modern secondary schools typically attain unskilled or semiskilled employment. Students' scores on the 11-plus exam taken at the conclusion of primary school largely determine which type of secondary school they attend.

2. Several points regarding my social class stratification strategy are worthy of note. First, I chose to not use a composite index of social class because the use of single

indicators is consistent with a move among some inequality scholars who advocate for independent rather than composite measures of social class. Second, since the United Kingdom and the United States have different education systems, parents' years of schooling do not correspond to the same educational level across the two countries. Therefore, social class is stratified in a manner that is recognizable to readers from each country. I elaborate on each of these points in Appendix C.

9. Refocusing Understanding of Racial Differences

1. It bears repeating that while a strong racial identity appears to enhance schooling outcomes, a black nationalistic ideology, which stresses that the black experience is unique and that blacks should control their own destiny with minimal input or contact with other groups, can be maladaptive. Studies by Sellers, Chavous, and Cooke (1998) and Oyserman et al. (2003) find that a more multicultural or minority identity—an ideology that emphasizes similarities among oppressed groups and recognizes that their in-group must overcome obstacles and barriers yet still have a positive connection to other in-groups and the larger society—is more adaptive for academic success.

2. Standard deviation is calculated in the following manner: (1) each test taker's score is subtracted from the mean for the entire sample; (2) each of these mean deviations is squared; (3) the squared mean deviations are added; then (4) divided by the total number of units in the sample, which produces the average squared deviation for every unit in the sample; and (5) the square root of the result from step 4 is the standard deviation. Typically, 68 percent of the sample is between -1 and 1 standard deviation from the mean for the entire sample and 95 percent of the sample is between -2 and 2 standard deviations from the sample mean. The standard deviation can be calculated separately for blacks relative to the mean for blacks in the sample (say an average of 70) and for whites relative to the white distribution (say an average of 80). Rather than expressing the average difference between these two subsamples in the raw unit specific to the exam (which in this case would be a 10-point gap), the difference in means can be expressed in standard deviation units. (If the full sample that includes both whites and blacks has a standard deviation of 20, then a 10-point gap is a standardized gap of 0.5). Therefore, a black-white achievement gap of one standard deviation is rather large and means that 76 percent of whites in the sample will score above blacks while only 24 percent of blacks will score higher than whites.

3. The extent to which this process is as deterministic as Heckman argues is debatable. The factors discussed by Heckman are not the only reasons for the gap, as the gap in skills widens *after* youth enter the school system, which I discuss in the next section. Furthermore, it is unclear how much these factors explain racial differences in early academic skills.

4. In addition to documenting the growth of the achievement gap over time, Fryer and Levitt (2004, 2006) provide an assessment of several hypotheses regarding the black-white gap. They also include Hispanics and control for "other" racial groups in their analysis of gap changes over time. However, I limit my summary of their work to portions of their analysis relevant to my discussion in this chapter.

5. Examples of this might include wearing shorts in the winter, listening to heavy metal music, using extremely clear diction that sounds rehearsed; having a stiff walk, and exhibiting a lack of general "coolness" or swagger—awkward style or body mechanics (particularly when set to music).

Appendix A

1. This reference applies to basketball. In the National Basketball Association (NBA) a team must shoot the ball at the basket within twenty-four seconds of gaining possession (thirty-five seconds in college).

2. Whereas the first question comes from the ACT, the second was drawn from the SAT. The answers to these questions are $6x^6 + x^3$ and ½, respectively.

BIBLIOGRAPHY

Ainsworth, James W. 2002. "Why Does It Take a Village? The Mediation of Neighborhood Effects on Educational Achievement." *Social Forces* 81:117–152.

Ainsworth-Darnell, James W., and Douglas B. Downey. 1998. "Assessing the Oppositional Culture Explanation for Racial/Ethnic Differences in School Performance." *American Sociological Review* 63:536–553.

Akom, A. A. 2003. "Reexamining Resistance as Oppositional Behavior: The Nation of Islam and the Creation of a Black Achievement Ideology." *Sociology of Education* 76:305–325.

Anderson, Deborah, and David Shapiro. 1996. "Racial Differences in Access to High-Paying Jobs and the Wage Gap between Black and White Women." *Industrial and Labor Relations Review* 49:273–286.

Anderson, James D. 1988. *The Education of Blacks in the South, 1860–1935.* Chapel Hill: University of North Carolina Press.

Archer, Louise, and Merryn Hutchings. 2000. "'Bettering Yourself?': Discourses of Risk, Cost and Benefit in Ethnically Diverse, Young Working-Class Non-Participants' Constructions of Higher Education." *British Journal of Sociology of Education* 21:555–574.

Arroyo, Carmen G., and Edward Zigler. 1995. "Racial Identity, Academic Achievement, and the Psychological Well-Being of Economically Disadvantaged Adolescents." *Journal of Personality and Social Psychology* 69:903–914.

Ashcroft, Kate, Stephen Bigger, and David Coates. 1996. *Researching into Equal Opportunities in College and Universities.* London: Kogan Page.

Bae, Yupin, Susan Choy, Claire Geddes, Jennifer Sable, and Thomas Snyder. 2000. *Trends in Educational Equity of Girls and Women.* U.S. Department of Education, National Center for Education Statistics. Washington, DC: U.S. Government Printing Office.

Baldi, Stephane, and Debra Branch McBrier. 1997. "Do the Determinants of Promotion Differ for Blacks and Whites?" *Work and Occupations* 24:478–497.

Ball, Stephen J., Jackie Davies, Miriam David, and Diane Reay. 2002. "'Classification' and 'Judgement': Social Class and the 'Cognitive Structures' of Choice of Higher Education." *British Journal of Sociology of Education* 23:51–72.

Banfield, Edward C. 1970. *The Unheavenly City*. Boston: Little, Brown.

Banks, Olive. 1968. *The Sociology of Education*. London: Batsford.

Bell, Wendell, and Robert V. Robinson. 1980. Cognitive Maps of Class and Racial Inequalities in England and the United States." *American Journal of Sociology* 86:320–349.

Berry, John W., Ype H. Poortinga, Marshall H. Segall, and Pierre R. Dasen. 2002. *Cross-Cultural Psychology*. Cambridge: Cambridge University Press.

Bertrand, Marianne, and Sendhil Mullainathan. 2004. Are Emily and Brendan More Employable Than Lakisha and Jamal? A Field Experiment on Labor Market Discrimination. *American Economic Review* 94:991–1013.

Bird, John, A. Shebani, and Dianne Francombe. 1992. *Ethnic Monitoring and Admissions to Higher Education*. Bristol University: Employment Department.

Blau, Judith R. 2003. *Race in the Schools: Perpetuating White Dominance?* Boulder, CO: Lynne Rienner.

Bol, Linda, and Robert Q. Berry III. 2005. "Secondary Mathematics Teachers' Perceptions of the Achievement Gap." *High School Journal* 88:32–45.

Bonilla-Silva, Eduardo. 2006. *Racism without Racists: Color-Blind Racism and the Persistence of Racial Inequality in the United States*. Lanham, MD: Rowman and Littlefield.

Bourdieu, Pierre, and Jean Claude Passeron. 1977. *Reproduction in Education, Society, and Culture*. London: Sage.

Bowen, William G., and Derek Bok. 1998. *The Shape of the River: Long-Term Consequences of Considering Race in College and University Admissions*. Princeton, NJ: Princeton University Press.

Bowles, Samuel, and Herbert Gintis. 1976. *Schooling in Capitalist America: Educational Reform and the Contradictions of Economic Life*. New York: Basic Books.

Bowman, Philip, and Cleopatra Howard. 1985. "Race-Related Socialization, Motivation, and Academic Achievement: A Study of Black Youths in Three-Generation Families." *Journal of the American Academy of Child Psychiatry* 24:134–141.

Braddock, Jomills Henry. 1990. "Improving the Education and Achievement of African American Males." *Hearing on the Office of Educational Research and Improvement*. Hearing before the Subcommittee on Select Education of the Committee on Education and Labor, House of Representatives. Washington, DC: U.S. Government Printing Office.

Breen, Richard, and John H. Goldthorpe. 2001. "Class, Mobility and Merit: The Experience of Two British Birth Cohorts." *European Sociological Review* 17:81–101.

———. 1999. "Class Inequality and Meritocracy: A Critique of Saunders and an Alternative Analysis." *British Journal of Sociology* 50:1–27.

British National Statistics. 2001. *Census 2001: Key Statistics for Local Authorities in England and Wales*. Newport, U.K.: Office of National Statistics.

Brooks-Gunn, Jeanne, Pamela K. Klebanov, and Greg J. Duncan. 1996. "Ethnic Differences in Children's Intelligence Test Scores: Role of Economic Deprivation, Home Environment, and Maternal Characteristics." *Child Development* 67:396–408.

Brooks-Gunn, Jeanne, Pamela K. Klebanov, Judith Smith, Greg J. Duncan, and Kyunghee Lee. 2003. "The Black-White Test Score Gap in Young Children: Contributions of Test and Family." *Applied Developmental Science* 7:239–252.

Brown, Susan K., and Charles Hirschman. 2006. "The End of Affirmative Action in Washington State and Its Impact on the Transition from High School to College." *Sociology of Education* 79:106–130.

Browne, Irene, and Joya Misra. 2003. "The Intersection of Gender and Race in the Labor Market." *Annual Review of Sociology* 29:487–513.

Bruce, Philip A. 1889. *The Plantation Negro as a Freeman: Observations on His Character, Condition, and Prospects in Virginia*. Whitefish, MT: Kessinger.

Buchmann, Claudia, and Thomas A. DiPrete. 2006. "The Growing Female Advantage in College Completion: The Role of Family Background and Academic Achievement." *American Sociological Review* 71:515–541.

Burke, Peter. 1991. "Identity Processes and Social Stress." *American Sociological Review* 56:836–849.

Bynner, John, Elsa Ferri, and Peter Shepherd. 1997. *Twenty-Something in the 1990s: Getting on, Getting by, Getting Nowhere*. Aldershot, UK: Ashgate.

Bynner, John, and Samantha Parsons. 2002. "Social Exclusion and the Transition from School to Work: The Case of Young People Not in Employment, Education, or Training (NEET)." *Journal of Vocational Behaviour* 60:289–309.

Carneiro, Pedro, James J. Heckman, and Dimitriy V. Masterov. 2005. "Labor Market Discrimination and Racial Differences in Premarket Factors." *Journal of Law and Economics* 48:1–39.

Carter, Prudence. 2005. *Keepin' It Real*. New York: Oxford University Press.

Center on Education Policy. 2009. "State High School Exit Exams: Trends in Test Programs, Alternate Pathways, and Pass Rates." Washington, DC: Center on Education Policy.

Chafetz, Janet Saltzman. 1997. "Feminist Theory and Sociology: Underutilized Contributions for Mainstream Threoy." *Annual Review of Sociology* 23:97–120.

Chavous, Tabbye M., Debra Hilkene Bernat, Karen Schmeelk-Cone, Cleopatra H. Caldwell, Laura Kohn-Wood, and Marc A. Zimmerman. 2003. "Racial Identity and Academic Attainment among African American Adolescents." *Child Development* 74:1076–1090.

Coard, Bernard. 1971. *How the West Indian Child Is Made Educationally Subnormal in the British School System: The Scandal of the Black Child in Schools in Britain*. London: New Beacon Books.

Coard, Stephanie, Scyatta Wallace, Howard Stevenson, and Lori Brotman, 2004. "Towards Culturally Relevant Preventive Interventions: The Consideration of

Racial Socialization in Parent Training with African-American Families." *Journal of Child and Family Studies* 13:277–293.

Cohen, Philip. 1988. "The Perversions of Inheritance: Studies in the Making of Multiracist Britain." Pp. 9–118 in *Multi-Racist Britain*, edited by P. Cohen and H. S. Bains. London: Macmillan.

Coleman, James S. 1961. *The Adolescent Society.* New York: Free Press.

———. 1966. "Equal Schools or Equal Students." *Public Interest* 4:70–75.

Coleman, James S., Ernest Q. Campbell, Carol J. Hobson, James McPartland, Alexander M. Mood, Frederic D. Weinfeld, and Robert L. York. 1966. *Equality of Educational Opportunity.* Washington, D.C.: U.S. Government Printing Office.

Coleman, Major G. 2003. "Job Skill and Black Male Wage Discrimination." *Social Science Quarterly* 84:892–905.

Coleman, Major G., William A. Darity, and Rhonda V. Sharpe. 2008. "Are Reports of Discrimination Valid? Considering the Moral Hazard Effect." *American Journal of Economics and Sociology* 67:149–175.

Conley, Dalton. 1999. *Being Black, Living in the Red: Race, Wealth, and Social Policy in America.* Berkeley: University of California Press.

Constantine, Madonna, and Sha'kema Blackmon. 2002. "Black Adolescents' Racial Socialization Experiences: Their Relations to Home, School, and Peer Self-Esteem." *Journal of Black Studies* 32:322–335.

Cook, Philip J., and Jens Ludwig. 1997. "Weighing the 'Burden of Acting White': Are There Race Differences in Attitudes toward Education?" *Journal of Policy Analysis and Management* 16:256–278.

———. 1998. "The Burden of 'Acting White': Do Black Adolescents Disparage Academic Achievement?" Pp. 375–400 in *The Black-White Test Score Gap*, edited by C. Jencks and M. Phillips. Washington, DC: Brookings Institution.

Cosby, Bill, and Alvin E. Poussaint. 2007. "Come On, People: On the Path from Victims to Victors. Nashville, TN: Thomas Nelson.

Cose, Ellis. 1993. *The Rage of a Privileged Class.* New York: Harper Collins.

Cotter, David A., Joan M. Hermsen, and Reeve Vanneman. 2004. *Gender Inequality at Work.* New York: Russell Sage.

Crocker, Jennifer, and Brenda Major. 1989. "Social Stigma and Self Esteem: The Self-Protective Properties of Stigma." *Psychological Review* 96:608–630.

Cross, William E., Thomas A. Parham, and Janet E. Helms. 1991. "The Stages of Black Identity Development: Nigrescence Models." Pp. 319–338 in *Black Psychology*, edited by R. Jones. Berkeley: Cobb and Henry.

Currie, Janet. 2005. "Health Disparities and Gaps in School Readiness." *The Future of Children* 15:117–138.

D'Agostino, Jerome V., and Sonya L. Powers. 2009. "Predicting Teacher Performance with Test Scores and Grade Point Average: A Meta-Analysis. *American Education Research Journal* 46:146–182.

Darity, William Jr. 2001. "The Functionality of Market-Based Discrimination." *International Journal of Social Economics* 28:980–986.

Datnow, Amanda, and Robert Cooper. 1997. "Peer Networks of African American Students in Independent Schools: Affirming Academic Success and Racial Identity." *Journal of Negro Education* 66:56–72.

Davis-Kean, Pamela E., and Jacquelynne S. Eccles. 2005. "Influences and Challenges to Better Parent-School Collaborations." Pp. 57–73 in *School-Family Partnerships for Children's Success*, edited by E. N. Patrikakou, R. P. Weissberg, S. Redding, and H. J. Walberg. New York: Teachers College Press.

Delpit, Lisa. 1995. *Other People's Children: Cultural Conflict in the Classroom.* New York: New Press.

Demo, David, and Michael Hughes. 1990. "Socialization and Racial Identity among Black Americans." *Social Psychology Quarterly* 53:364–374.

Diamond, John B., Antonia Randolph, and James P. Spillane. 2004. "Teachers' Expectations and Sense of Responsibility for Student Learning: The Importance of Race, Class, and Organizational Habitus." *Anthropology & Education Quarterly* 35:75–98.

Dickens, William T. 2005. "Genetic Differences in School Readiness." *Future of Children* 15:55–69.

Dickens, William T., and James R. Flynn. 2006. "Black Americans Reduce the Racial IQ Gap: Evidence from Standardization Samples." *Psychological Science* 17:913–920.

DiPrete, Thomas, and Claudia Buchmann. 2006. "Gender-Specific Trends in the Value of Education and the Emerging Gender Gap in College Completion." *Demography* 43:1–24.

Downey, Douglas B., and James W. Ainsworth-Darnell. 2002. "The Search for Oppositional Culture among Black Students." *American Sociological Review* 67:156–164.

Downey, Douglas B., and Shana Pribesh. 2004. "When Race Matters: Teachers' Evaluations of Students' Classroom Behavior." *Sociology of Education* 77:267–282.

Duncan, Greg J., and Jeanne Brooks-Gunn. 1997. *Consequences of Growing Up Poor.* New York: Russell Sage.

Duncan, Greg J., and Katherine A. Magnuson. 2005. "Can Family Socioeconomic Resources Account for Racial and Ethnic Test Score Gaps?" *Future of Children* 15:35–54.

Edwards, Audrey, and Craig K. Polite. 1992. *Children of the Dream.* New York: Doubleday.

Elliott, James R., and Ryan A. Smith. 2004. "Race, Gender, and Workplace Power." *American Sociological Review* 69:365–386.

Entwisle, Doris R., and Karl L. Alexander. 1992. "Summer Setback: Race, Poverty, School Composition, and Mathematics Achievement in the First Two Years of School." *American Sociological Review* 57:72–84.

Espenshade, Thomas J., and Alexandria Walton Radford. 2009. *No Longer Separate, Not Yet Equal*. Princeton, NJ: Princeton University Press.

Farkas, George. 1993. "Structured Tutoring for At Risk Children in the Early Years." *Applied Behavioral Science Review* 1:69–92.

———. 1996. *Human Capital or Cultural Capital? Ethnicity and Poverty Groups in an Urban School District*. NewYork: Aldine de Gruyter.

Farkas, George, Robert Grobe, Daniel Sheehan, and Yuan Shuan. 1990. "Cultural Resources and School Success: Gender, Ethnicity, and Poverty Groups within an Urban School District." *American Sociological Review* 27:807–827.

Farkas, George, Christy Lleras and Steve Maczuga. 2002. "Does Oppositional Culture Exist in Minority and Poverty Peer Groups?" *American Sociological Review* 67:148–155.

Farkas, George, and Keven Vicknair. 1996. "Appropriate Tests of Racial Wage Discrimination Require Controls for Cognitive Skills." *American Sociological Review* 61:557–660.

Feagin, Joe R., and Melvin P. Sikes. 1994. *Living with Racism: The Black Middle-Class*. Boston: Beacon Press.

Ferguson, Ann Arnett. 2000. *Bad Boys: Public Schools in the Making of Black Masculinity*. Ann Arbor: University of Michigan Press.

Ferguson, Ronald F. 2001. "A Diagnostic Analysis of Black-White GPA Disparities in Shaker Heights, Ohio." Pp. 347–414 in *Brookings Papers on Education Policy 2001*, edited by Diane Ravitch. Washington, DC: Brookings Institution.

———. 2003. "Teachers' Perceptions and Expectations and the Black-White Test Score Gap." *Urban Education* 38:460–507.

Fischer, Claude S., Michael Hout, Martin Sanchez Jankowski, Samuel R. Lucas, Ann Swidler, and Kim Voss. 1996. *Inequality by Design: Cracking the Bell Curve Myth*. Princeton, NJ: Princeton University Press.

Ford, Donna Y. 1996. *Reversing Underachievement among Gifted Black Students: Promising Practices and Programs*. New York: Teachers College Press.

Ford, Donna Y., and J. John Harris III. 1996. "Perceptions and Attitudes of Black Students Toward School, Achievement, and Other Educational Variables." *Child Development* 67:1141–1152.

Fordham, Signithia. 1988. "Racelessness as a Factor in Black Students' School Success: Pragmatic Strategy or Pyrrhic Victory?" *Harvard Educational Review* 58:54–84.

———. 1996. *Blacked Out: Dilemmas of Race, Identity, and Success at Capital High*. Chicago: University of Chicago Press.

———. 2008. "Beyond Capital High: On Dual Citizenship and the Strange Career of 'Acting White.'" *Anthropology & Education Quarterly* 39:227–246.

Fordham, Signithia, and John U. Ogbu. 1986. "Black Students' School Success: Coping with the Burden of 'Acting White.'" *Urban Review* 18:176–206.

Freeman, Catherine, Benjamin Scafidi, and David L. Sjoquist. 2005. "Racial Segregation in Georgia Public Schools, 1994–2001: Trends, Causes, and Impact on Teacher Quality." Pp. 148–163 in *School Segregation: Must the South Turn Back?*, edited by John Charles Boger and Gary Orfield. Chapel Hill: University of North Carolina Press.

Fryer, Ronald G., and Steven D. Levitt. 2004. "Understanding the Black-White Test Score Gap in the First Two Years of School." *Review of Economics and Statistics* 86:447–464.

———. 2006. "The Black-White Test Score Gap through Third Grade." *American Law and Economics Review* 8:249–281.

Fryer, Roland, and Paul Torelli. 2010. "An Empirical Analysis of 'Acting White.'" *Journal of Public Economics* 94:380–396.

Gans, Herbert J. 1968. "Culture and Class in the Study of Poverty: An Approach to Antipoverty Research." Pp. 201–228 in *On Understanding Poverty: Perspectives from the Social Sciences*, edited by Daniel P. Moynihan. New York: Basic Books.

Gecas, Viktor, and Peter Burke. 1995. "Self and Identity." Pp. 41–67 in *Sociological Perspectives in Social Psychology*, edited by Karen Cook, Gary Alan Fine, and James House. Boston: Allyn and Bacon.

Goldsmith, Arthur H., Darrick Hamilton, and William Darity Jr. 2006. "Shades of Discrimination: Skin Tone and Wages." *American Economic Review* 96:242–245.

Goldthorpe, John H. 1987. *Social Mobility and Class Structure in Modern Britain.* Oxford: Clarendon Press.

Grissmer, David, Ann Flanagan, and Stephanie Williamson. 1998. "Why Did the Black-White Test Score Gap Converge in the 1970s and 1980s?" Pp. 182–226 in *The Black-White Test Score Gap*, edited by C. Jencks and M. Phillips. Washington, DC: Brookings Institution.

Grodsky, Eric, and Devah Pager. 2001. "The Structure of Disadvantage: Individual and Occupational Determinants of the Black-White Wage Gap." *American Sociological Review* 66:542–567.

Hanson, Sandra L. 1994. "Lost Talent: Unrealizing Educational Aspirations and Expectations among U.S. Youths. *Sociology of Education* 67:159–183.

Hanushek, Eric A. 1989. "The Impact of Differential Expenditures on School Performance." *Educational Researcher* 18:45–52.

———. 1997. "Assessing the Effects of School Resources on Student Performance: An Update." *Educational Evaluation and Policy Analysis* 19:141–164.

———. 2007. "Throwing Money at Schools." *Journal of Policy Analysis and Management* 1:19–41.

Hanushek, Eric A., John F. Kain, and Steven G. Rivkin. 2004. "Why Public Schools Lose Teachers." *Journal of Human Resources* 39:326–354.

Harris, Angel L. 2006. "I (Don't) Hate School: Revisiting 'Oppositional Culture' Theory of Blacks' Resistance to Schooling." *Social Forces* 85:797–834.

———. 2008. "Optimism in the Face of Despair: Black-White Differences in Beliefs about School as a Means for Upward Social Mobility." *Social Science Quarterly* 89:629–651.

Harris, Angel L., and Kris Marsh. 2010. "Is a Raceless Identity an Effective Strategy for Academic Success Among Blacks." *Social Science Quarterly* 91:1242–1263.

Harris, Angel L., and Keith Robinson. 2007. "Schooling Behaviors or Prior Skills?: A Cautionary Tale of Omitted Variable Bias within the Oppositional Culture Theory." *Sociology of Education* 80:139–157.

Harris, Angel L., and Marta Tienda. 2010. "Minority Higher Education Pipeline: Consequences of Changes in College Admissions Policy in Texas." *Annals of the American Academy of Political and Social Science* 627:60–81.

Hatcher, Richard. 1998. "Class Differentiation in Education: Rational Choices? *British Journal of Sociology of Education* 19:5–22.

Hauser, Robert, and John Warren. 1997. "Socioeconomic Indexes for Occupations: A Review, Update, and Critique. *Sociological Methodology* 27:177–298.

Heckman, James J. 1998. "Detecting Discrimination." Journal of Economic Perspectives 12:101–116.

———. 2006. "Skill Formation and the Economics of Investing in Disadvantaged Children." *Science* 312: 1900–1002.

Heckman, James J., and Alan B. Krueger. 2004. *Inequality in America: What Role for Human Capital Policies.* Cambridge, MA: MIT Press.

Heckman, James J. and Peter Siegelman. 1993. "The Urban Institute Audit Studies: Their Methods and Findings." Pp. 187–258 in *Clear and Convincing Evidence: Measurement of Discrimination in America*, edited by Michael Fix and Raymond J. Struyk. Lanham, MD: Urban Institute.

Hedges, Larry V., and Amy Nowell. 1998. "Black-White Test Score Convergence since 1965." Pp. 149–181 in *The Black-White Test Score Gap*, edited by C. Jencks and M. Phillips. Washington, DC: Brookings Institution.

———. 1999. "Changes in the Black-White Gap in Achievement Test Scores." *Sociology of Education* 72:111–135.

Hedges, Larry V., Richard D. Laine, and Rob Greenwald. 1994a. "Does Money Matter? A Meta-Analysis of Studies of the Effects of Differential School Inputs on Student Outcomes." *Educational Researcher* 23:5–14.

———. 1994b. "Money Does Matter Somewhere: A Reply to Hanushek." *Educational Researcher* 23:9–10.

Hemmings, Annette. 1998. "The Self Transformations of African-American Achievers." *Youth & Society* 29(2):330–368.

Herbert, Bob. 1995. "A Nation of Nitwits." *The New York Times.* March 1, p. A15.

Herrnstein, Richard, and Charles Murray. 1994. *The Bell Curve: Intelligence and Class Structure in American Life.* New York: Free Press.

Hill, Mark E. 2002. "Skin Color and Intelligence in African Americans: A Reanalysis of Lynn's Data." *Population and Environment* 24:209–214.

Hochschild, Jennifer L. 1995. *Facing Up to the American Dream: Race, Class, and the Soul of the Nation*. Princeton, NJ: Princeton University Press.

Hofferth, Sandra L., and John F. Sandberg. 2001. "How American Children Spend Their Time." *Journal of Marriage and Family* 63:295–308.

hooks, bell. 1994. *Teaching in Transgress: Education as the Practice of Freedom*. London: Routledge.

Horvat, Erin McNamara, and Kristine S. Lewis. 2003. "Reassessing the Burden of 'Acting White': The Importance of Peer Groups in Managing Academic Success." *Sociology of Education* 76:265–280.

Hughes, Diane. 2003. "Correlates of African American and Latino Parents' Messages to Children about Ethnicity and Race: A Comparative Study of Racial Socialization." *American Journal of Community Psychology*. 31:15–32.

Hughes, Diane, and Lisa Chen. 1997. "When and What Parents Tell Children about Race: An Examination of Race-Related Socialization among African American Families." *Applied Developmental Science* 1:200–214.

Hughes, Diane, and Deborah Johnson, 2001. "Correlates in Children's Experiences of Parents' Racial Socialization Behaviors." *Journal of Marriage and Family* 63:981–995.

Ingels, Steven J., Kathryn L. Dowd, James L. Stipe, John D. Baldridge, Virginia H. Bartot, and Martin R. Frankel. 1994. *National Education Longitudinal Study of 1988, Second Follow-Up: Dropout Component Data File User's Manual*. Washington, DC: U.S. Department of Education.

Jackson, C. Kirabo. 2009. "Student Demographics, Teacher Sorting, and Teacher Quality: Evidence from the End of School Desegregation." *Journal of Labor Economics* 27:213–256.

Jacobs, Jerry. 1996. "Gender Inequality and Higher Education." *Annual Review of Sociology* 22:153–185.

Jaffe, A. J., Ruth M. Cullen, and Thomas D. Boswell. 1980. *The Changing Demography of Spanish Americans*. New York: Academic Press.

Jensen, Arthur. 1969. "How Much Can We Boost IQ and Scholastic Achievement?" *Harvard Educational Review* 39:1–123.

Jencks, Christopher, and Meredith Phillips. 1998. "The Black-White Test Score Gap: An Introduction." Pp. 1–51 in *The Black-White Test Score Gap*, edited by C. Jencks and M. Phillips. Washington, DC: Brookings Institution.

Johnson, William R., and Derek Neal. 1998. "Basic Skills and the Black-White Earnings Gap." Pp. 480–497 in *The Black-White Test Score Gap*, edited by C. Jencks and M. Phillips. Washington, DC: Brookings Institution.

Joy, Lois. 2003. "Salaries of Recent Male and Female College Graduates: Educational and Labor Market Effects." *Industrial and Labor Relations Review* 56:606–621.

Juster, F. T., and Frank Stafford. 1991. "The Allocation of Time: Empirical Findings, Behavioral Models, and Problems of Measurement." *Journal of Economic Literature* 29:471–522.

Kao, Grace. 1995. "Asian-Americans as Model Minorities? A look at Their Academic Performance." *American Journal of Education* 103:121–159.

Kane, Thomas J. 1998. "Racial and Ethnic Preferences in College Admissions." Pp. 431–456 in *The Black-White Test Score Gap*, edited by C. Jencks and M. Phillips. Washington, DC: Brookings Institution.

Kent, Mary Mederios. 2007. "Immigration and America's Black Population." *Population Bulletin* 62:1-16.

Kerckhoff, Alan C. 2000. "Transition from School to Work in Comparative Perspective" Pp. 453–474 in *Handbook of the Sociology of Education*, edited by M. T. Hallinan. New York: Kluwer Academic/Plenum.

———. 2003. "From Student to Worker." Pp. 251–267 in *Handbook of the Life Course*, edited by J. T. Mortimer and M. Shanahan. New York: Kluwer Academic/ Plenum.

Knudsen, Eric I., James J. Heckman, Judy L. Cameron, and Jack P. Shonkoff. 2006. "Economic, Neurobiological, and Behavioral Perspectives on Building America's Future Workforce." *Proceedings of the National Academy of Sciences* 103:10,155–10,162.

Kohn, Melvin, and Carmi Schooler. 1983. *Work and Personality*. Norwood, NJ: Ablex.

Krysan, Maria. 2008. "Data Update to *Racial Attitudes in America*." An update and website to complement *Racial Attitudes in America: Trends and Interpretations, Revised Edition*, Howard Schuman, Charlotte Steeh, Lawrence Bobo, and Maria Krysan, 1997, Harvard University Press. Retrieved on June 1, 2010 from (http:// www.igpa.uillinois.edu/programs/racial-attitudes/).

Kuncel, Nathan R., Sarah A. Hezlett, and Deniz S. Ones. 2001. "A Comprehensive Meta-Analysis of the Predictive Validity of the Graduate Record Examinations: Implications for Graduate Student Selection and Performance." *Psychological Bulletin* 127:162–181.

Lareau, Annette. 2003. *Unequal Childhoods: Class, Race, and Family Life*. Berkeley: University of California Press.

Lareau, Annette, and Erin McNamara Horvat. 1999. "Moments of Social Inclusion and Exclusion: Race, Class, and Cultural Capital in Family-School Relationships." *Sociology of Education* 72:37–53.

Lesane-Brown, Chase, Tony Brown, Cleopatra Caldwell, and Robert Sellers. 2005. "The Comprehensive Race Socialization Inventory." *Journal of Black Studies* 36:163–190.

Lewis, Amanda E. 2003. *Race in the Schoolyard: Reproducing the Color Line in School*. New Brunswick, NJ: Rutgers University Press.

Lewis, Oscar. 1961. *The Children of Sanchez*. New York: Random House.

———. 1968. "The Culture of Poverty." Pp. 187–220 in *On Understanding Poverty: Perspectives from the Social Sciences*, edited by Daniel P. Moynihan. New York: Basic Books.

Lipset, Seymour Martin. 1963. "The Value Patterns of Democracy: A Case Study in Comparative Analysis." *American Sociological Review* 28:515–531.

Litwack, Leon F. 1998. *Trouble in the Mind: Black Southerners in the Age of Jim Crow.* New York: Vintage Books.

Livingston, Andrea, and John Wirt. 2004. *The Condition of Education 2004 in Brief* (NCES 2004–076). U.S. Department of Education, National Center for Education Statistics. Washington, DC: U.S. Government Printing Office.

Lopez, Nancy. 2003. *Hopeful Girls, Troubled Boys.* New York: Routledge.

Lucas, Samuel Roundfield. 1999. *Tracking Inequality: Stratification and Mobility in American High Schools.* New York: Teachers College Press.

———. 2008. *Theorizing Discrimination in an Era of Contested Prejudice.* Philadelphia: Temple University Press.

MacLeod, Jay. 2009. *Ain't No Making It: Aspirations and Attainment in a Low-Income Neighborhood.* Philadelphia: Westview Press.

Marini, Margaret Mooney, and Pi-Ling Fan. 1997. "The Gender Gap in Earnings at Career Entry." *American Sociological Review* 62:588–604.

Marryshow, Derrick, Eric A. Hurley, Brenda A. Allen, Kenneth M. Tyler, and A. Wade Boykin. 2005. "Impact of Learning Orientation on Black Children's Attitudes toward High-Achieving Peers." *American Journal of Psychology* 118:603–618.

Marshall, Gordon, Adam Swift, and Stephen Robert. 1997. *Against the Odds? Social Class and Social Justice in Industrial Societies.* Oxford: Clarendon Press.

Martin, Joyce A., Brady E. Hamilton, Paul D. Sutton, Stephanie J. Ventura, Fay Menacker, and Sharon Kirmeyer. 2006. "Births: Final Data for 2004." *National Vital Statistics Reports* 55:1–102. Hyattsville, MD: National Center for Health Statistics.

Massey, Douglas, and Nancy Denton. 1993. *American Apartheid.* Cambridge, MA: Harvard University Press.

Mason, Patrick L. 1997. "Race, Culture and Skills: Interracial Wage Differentials among African Americans, Latinos and Whites." *Review of Black Political Economy* 25:5–39.

———. 2000. "Persistent Discrimination: Racial Disparity in the United States, 1968–1988." *American Economic Review* 90:312–316.

———. 2007. "Intergenerational Mobility and Interracial Inequality: The Return to Family Values." *Industrial Relations* 46:51–80.

Mattern, Krista D., Brian F. Patterson, Emily J. Shaw, Jennifer L. Kobrin, and Sandra M. Barbuti. 2008. *Differential Validity and Prediction of the SAT* (College Board Research Report No. 2008-5). New York: The College Board.

McCall, George. 2003. "The Me and the Not-Me: Positive and Negative Pole of Identity." Pp. 11–25 in *Advances in Identity Theory and Research,* edited by Peter J. Burke, Timothy J. Owens, Richard T. Serpe, and Peggy A. Thoits. New York: Plenum.

McCall, Leslie. 2000. Explaining Levels of Within-Group Wage Inequality in U.S. Labor Markets. *Demography* 37:415–430.

McCloyd, Vonnie C. 1990. "The Impact of Economic Hardship on Black Families and Children: Psychological Distress, Parenting, and Socioemotional Development." *Child Development* 61:311–346.

McCreary, Micah L., Lesley A. Slavin, and Eloise J. Berry. 1996. "Predicting Problem Behavior and Self-Esteem among African American Adolescents." *Journal of Adolescent Research* 11:216–234.

McKown, Clark, and Rhona S. Weinstein. 2008. "Teacher Expectations, Classroom Context, and the Achievement Gap." *Journal of School Psychology* 46:235–261.

McNeil, Linda M. 2000. *Contradictions of School Reform: Educational Costs of Standardized Testing.* New York: Routledge.

McWhorter, John. 2000. *Losing the Race.* New York: Free Press.

Meier, Deborah. 2000. *Will Standards Save Public Education?* Boston: Beacon Press.

Metcalf, Hilary. 1997. *Class and Higher Education: The Participation of Young People from Lower Social Classes.* London: Council for Industry and Higher Education.

Mickelson, Roslyn Arlin. 1989. "Why Does Jane Read and Write So Well?: The Anomaly of Women's Achievement." *Sociology of Education* 62:47–63.

——. 1990. "The Attitude-Achievement Paradox among Black Adolescents." *Sociology of Education* 63:44–61.

——. 2001. "Subverting Swann: First- and Second-Generation Segregation in the Charlotte-Mecklenburg Schools." *American Educational Research Journal* 38: 215–252.

Miller, David B. 1999. "Racial Socialization and Racial Identity: Can They Promote Resiliency for African American Adolescents?" *Adolescence* 34:493–501.

Modood, Tariq. 1993. "The Number of Ethnic Minority Students in British Higher Education: Some Grounds for Optimism. *Oxford Review of Education* 19:167–182.

Morris, Edward W. 2005. " 'Tuck in that Shirt!': Race, Class, Gender, and Discipline in an Urban School." *Sociological Perspectives* 48:25–48.

——. 2007. "Ladies" or "Loudies"?: Perceptions and Experiences of Black Girls in Classrooms." *Youth & Society* 38:490–515.

Mortimore, Peter, Pam Sammons, Louise Stoll, David Lewis, and Russell J. Ecob. 1988. *School Matters: The Junior Years.* London: Open Books.

Moser, Claus A., and Graham Kalton. 1972. *Survey Methods in Social Investigation.* 2nd ed. New York: Basic Books.

Moynihan, Daniel Patrick. 1965. *The Negro Family: The Case for National Action.* Washington, DC: Office of Planning and Research, U.S. Department of Labor.

Muller, Patricia A., Frances K. Stage, and Jillian Kinzie. 2001. "Science Achievement Growth Trajectories: Understanding Factors Related to Gender and Racial-Ethnic

Differences in Precollege Science Achievement." *American Educational Research Journal* 38:981–1012.

Neal, Derek A., and William R. Johnson. 1996. "The Role of Premarket Factors in Black-White Wage Differences." *Journal of Political Economy* 104:869–895.

Neal, La Vonne I., Audrey Davis McCray, Gwendolyn Webb-Johnson, and Scott T. Bridgest. 2003. "The Effects of African American Movement Styles on Teachers' Perceptions and Reactions." *The Journal of Special Education* 37:49–57.

Newham Council. 1989. *Boosting Educational Achievement*. London: Newham Council.

Nisbett, Richard E. 1998. "Race, Genetics, and IQ." Pp. 86–102 in *The Black-White Test Score Gap*, edited by C. Jencks and M. Phillips. Washington, D.C.: Brookings Institution.

Noble, Kimberly G., Nim Tottenham, and B. J. Casey 2005. "Neuroscience Perspectives on Disparities in School Readiness and Cognitive Achievement." *The Future of Children* 15:71–89.

Noguera, Pedro A. 2003. *City Schools and the American Dream*. New York: Teachers College Press.

O'Connor, Carla. 1997. "Dispositions toward (Collective) Struggle and Educational Resilience in the Inner City." *American Educational Research Journal* 34:593–629.

———. 1999. "Race, Class, and Gender in America: Narratives of Opportunity among Low-Income African American Youth." *Sociology of Education* 72:137–157.

Oettinger, Gerald S. 1996. "Statistical Discrimination and the Early Career Evolution of the Black-White Wage Gap." *Journal of Labor Economics* 14:52–78.

Ogbu, John U. 1978. *Minority Education and Caste: The American System in Cross-Cultural Perspective*. New York: Academic Press.

———. 1990. "Minority Education in Comparative Perspective." *Journal of Negro Education* 59:45–57.

———. 1991. "Minority Responses and School Experiences." *Journal of Psychohistory* 18:433–456.

———. 1994. "Racial Stratification in the United States." *Teachers College Record* 96:264–298.

———. 2003. *Black American Students in an Affluent Suburb: A Study of Academic Disengagement*. Mahway, NJ: Lawrence Erlbaum.

———. 2008. *Minority Status, Oppositional Culture, and Schooling*. New York: Routledge.

Ogbu, John U., and Herbert D. Simons. 1998. "Voluntary and Involuntary Minorities: A Cultural-Ecological Theory of School Performance with Some Implications for Education." *Anthropology and Education Quarterly* 29:155–188.

O'Neill, June. 1990. "The Role of Human Capital in Earnings Differences Between Black and White Men." *Journal of Economic Perspectives* 4:25–45.

Organization for Economic Cooperation and Development. 2000. *Education at a Glance, OECD Indicators 2000*. Paris: OECD.

Organizing for America. (2004, July 27). *Keynote Address at the 2004 Democratic National Convention*. Retrieved on June 1, 2010 from (http://www.barackobama .com/2004/07/27/keynote_address_at_the_2004_de.php).

Oyserman, Daphna, Larry Gant, and Joel Ager. 1995. "A Socially Contextualized Model of African American Identity: Possible Selves and School Persistence." *Journal of Personality and Social Psychology* 69:1216–1232.

Oyserman, Daphna, Markus Kemmelmeier, Stephanie Fryberg, Hezi Brosh, and Tamera Hart-Johnson. 2003. "Racial-Ethnic Self-Schemas." *Social Psychology Quarterly* 66:333–347.

Padilla, Yolanda C., Jason D. Boardman, Robert A. Hummer, and Marilyn Espitia. 2002. "Is the Mexican American 'Epidemiologic Paradox' Advantage at Birth Maintained through Early Childhood?" *Social Forces* 80:1101–1123.

Pager, Devah. 2007. *MARKED: Race, Crime, and Finding Work in an Era of Mass Incarceration*. Chicago: University of Chicago Press.

Pager, Devah, and Diana Karafin. 2009. "Bayesian Bigot? Statistical Discrimination, Stereotypes, and Employer Decision Making." *ANNALS of the American Academy of Political and Social Science* 621:70–93.

Parliamentary Select Committee. 1973. *Parliamentary Select Committee on Immigration and Race Relations*. Session 1972–73, Education, Volume 1. London: H.M.S.O.

Patterson, Orlando. 1997. *The Ordeal of Integration: Progress and Resentment in America's "Racial" Crisis*. New York: Civitas/Counterpoint.

Peter, Katharin and Laura Horn. 2005. *Gender Differences in Participation and Completion of Undergraduate Education and How They Have Changed Over Time* (NCES 2005-169). U.S. Department of Education, National Center for Education Statistics. Washington, DC: U.S. Government Printing Office.

Phillips, Meredith, James Crouse, and John Ralph. 1998. "Does the Black-White Test Score Gap Widen After Children Enter School?" Pp. 229–264 in *The Black-White Test Score Gap*, edited by C. Jencks and M. Phillips. Washington, DC: Brookings Institution.

Public Agenda. 2000. *Great Expectations: How the Public and Parents—White, African American and Hispanic—View Higher Education* (Report #00–2). Washington, DC: The National Center for Public Policy and Higher Education.

Pyke, Karen, and Denise L. Johnson. 2003. "Asian American and Racialized Femininities: 'Doing' Gender across Cultural Worlds." *Gender & Society* 17:33–53.

Reay, Diane. 1996. "Dealing with Difficult Differences: Reflexivity and Social Class in Feminist Research." *Feminism and Psychology* 6:443–456.

Reichman, Nancy E. 2005. "Low Birth Weight and School Readiness." *Future of Children* 15:91–116.

Rodgers, William M. III, and William E. Spriggs. 1996. "What Does the AFQT Really Measure: Race, Wages, Schooling and the AFQT Score." *Review of Black Political Economy* 24:13–46.

———. 2002. "Accounting for the Racial Gap in AFQT Scores: Comment on Nan L. Maxwell, 'The Effect on Black-White Wage Differences in the Quantity and Quality of Education.'" *Industrial and Labor Relations Review* 55:533–541.

Roscigno, Vincent J., and James W. Ainsworth-Darnell. 1999. "Race, Cultural Capital, and Educational Resources: Persistent Inequalities and Achievement Returns." *Sociology of Education* 72:158–178.

Rosner, Jay. 2003. "On White Preferences." *Nation* 276:24.

Sackett, Paul R., Matthew J. Borneman, and Brian S. Connelly. 2008. "High-Stakes Testing in Higher Education and Employment: Appraising the Evidence for Validity and Fairness." *American Psychologist* 63:215–227.

Sacks, Peter. 1999. *Standardized Minds: The High Price of America's Testing Culture and What We Can Do About It.* Cambridge, MA: Perseus Books.

Sampson, Robert J., Jeffrey D. Morenoff, and Felton Earis. 1999. "Beyond Social Capital: Spatial Dynamics of Collective Efficacy for Children." *American Sociological Review* 64:633–660.

Sandefur, Gary D., Molly Martin, Jennifer Eggerling-Boeck, Susan E. Mannon, and Ann M. Meier. 2001. "An Overview of Racial and Ethnic Demographic Trends." Pp. 40–102 in *America Becoming: Racial Trends and Their Consequences*, Vol. 1, edited by N. J. Smelser, W. J. Wilson, and F. Mitchell. Washington, DC: National Academy Press.

Sanders, Mavis G. 1997. "Overcoming Obstacles: Academic Achievement as a Response to Racism and Discrimination." *Journal of Negro Education* 66:83–93.

Sankofa, Biko M., Eric A. Hurley, Brenda A. Allen, and A. Wade Boykin. 2005. "Cultural Expression and Black Students' Attitudes toward High Achievers." *Journal of Psychology* 139:247-259.

Schoendorf, Kenneth C., Carol J. Hogue, Joel C. Kleinman, and Diane L. Rowley. 1992. "Mortality among Infants of Black as Compared with White College-Educated Parents." *New England Journal of Medicine* 326:1522–1526.

Schuman, Howard, Charlotte Steeh, Lawrence Bobo, and Maria Krysan, 1997. *Racial Attitudes in America: Trends and Interpretations.* Rev. ed. Cambridge, MA: Harvard University Press.

Sellers, Robert M., Tabbye M. Chavous, and Deanna Y. Cooke. 1998. "Racial Ideology and Racial Centrality as Predictors of African American College Students' Academic Performance." *Journal of Black Psychology* 24:8–27.

Sellers, Robert M., Mia Smith, J. Nicole Shelton, Stephanie J. Rowley, and Tabbye M. Chavous. 1998. "Multidimensional Model of Racial Identity: A Reconceptualization of African American Racial Identity." *Personality and Social Psychology Review* 2:18–39.

Smith, Andrea, and Richard N. Lalonde. 2003. "'Racelessness' in a Canadian Context? Exploring the Link between Black Students' Identity, Achievement, and Mental Health." *Journal of Black Psychology* 29:142–164.

Smith, David. 1981. *Unemployment and Racial Minorities*. London: Policy Studies Institute.

Smith, Elsie M. J. 1989. Black Racial Identity Development. *Counseling Psychologist* 17:277–288.

Smith, Marshall S. 2000. "Assessment Trends in a Contemporary Policy Context." Pp. 264–272 in *Analytic Essays in the Assessment of Student Achievement* (NCES 2000–050), edited by D. W. Grissmer and J. M. Ross. Washington, DC: U.S. Department of Education, National Center for Education Statistics.

Smith, Ryan A. 1997. "Race, Income, and Authority at Work: A Cross-Temporal Analysis of Black and White Men (1972–1994). *Social Problems* 44:19–37.

———. 2001. "Particularism in Control over Monetary Resources at Work: An Analysis of Racial Ethnic Differences in the Authority Outcomes of Black, White, and Latino Men." *Work and Occupations* 28:447–468.

———. 2005. "Do the Determinants of Promotion Differ for White Men Versus Women and Minorities?: An Exploration of Intersectionalism Through Sponsored and Contest Mobility Processes." *American Behavioral Scientist* 48:1157–1181.

Sowell, Thomas. 1994. "Knowledge Is not 'White', Ignorance: A Good Formula for Self Destruction." *Atlanta Journal-Constitution*, June 28, A8.

Spencer, S. J., and Claude M. Steele. 1992. "The Effect of Stereotype Vulnerability on Women's Math Performance." Paper presented at the 100th Annual Convention of the American Psychological Association, Washington, DC.

Staples, Brent. 1996. "Editorial Notebook: Hostility Toward the Gifted; The Life and Times of P.S. 308." *New York Times*, April 22, A12.

Steele, Claude. 1988. "The Psychology of Self-Affirmation." *Advances in Experimental Social Psychology* 21:261–302.

———. 1997. "A Threat in the Air: How Stereotypes Shape Intellectual Identity and Performance. *American Psychologist* 52:613–629.

Steele, Claude M., and Joshua Aronson. 1995. "Stereotype Threat and the Intellectual Test Performance of African Americans. *Journal of Personality and Social Psychology* 69:797–811.

Steele, Shelby. 1990. *The Content of Our Character*. New York: Harper Perennial.

Steinberg, Laurence. 1996. *Beyond the Classroom*. New York: Simon and Schuster.

Steinberg, Laurence, Sanford Dornbusch, and Bradford Brown. 1992. "Ethnic Differences in Adolescent Achievement: An Ecological Perspective." *American Psychologist* 47:723–729.

Stevenson, Howard C. Jr., Rick Cameron, Teri Herrero-Taylor, and Gwendolyn Y. Davis. 2002. "Development of the Teenager Experience of Racial Socialization

Scale: Correlates of Race-Related Socialization Frequency from the Perspective of Black Youth." *Journal of Black Psychology* 28:84–106.

Swain, Carol M. 2001. "Affirmative Action: Legislative History, Judicial Interpretations, Public Consensus." Pp. 318–347 in *America Becoming: Racial Trends and Their Consequences*, Vol. 1, edited by N. J. Smelser, W. J. Wilson, and F. Mitchell. Washington, DC: National Academy Press.

Tatum, Beverly Daniel. 1992. "African-American Identity Development, Academic Achievement, and Missing History." *Social Education* 56:331–333.

Taylor, Robert, Linda M. Chatters, M. Belinda Tucker, and Edith Lewis. 1990. Developments in Research on Black Families: A Decade Review. *Journal of Marriage and the Family* 52:993–1014.

Thernstrom, Stephen, and Abigail Thernstrom. 1997. *America in Black and White: One Nation Indivisible*. New York: Simon and Schuster.

Thernstrom, Abigail, and Stephan Thernstrom. 2003. *No Excuses: Closing the Racial Gap in Learning*. New York: Simon and Schuster.

Thomas, Anita, and Suzette Speight. 1999. "Racial Identity and Racial Socialization Attitudes of African American Parents." *Journal of Black Psychology* 25:152–170.

Tienda, Marta. 2005. "Growing Up Ethnic in the United Kingdom and the United States: Comparative Contexts for Youth Development." Pp. 21–49 in *Ethnicity and Causal Mechanisms*, edited by M. Rutter and M. Tienda. Cambridge: Cambridge University Press.

Tomaskovic-Devey, Donald, Melvin Thomas, and Kecia Johnson. 2005. "Race and the Accumulation of Human Capital across the Career: A Theoretical Model and Fixed-Effects Application." *American Journal of Sociology* 111:58–89.

Tomlinson, Sally. 1991. "Ethnicity and Educational Attainment in England: An Overview." *Anthropology and Education Quarterly* 22:121–139.

Tyler, Kenneth M., A. Wade Boykin, and Tia R. Walton. 2006. "Cultural Considerations in Teachers' Perceptions of Student Classroom Behavior and Achievement." *Teaching and Teacher Education* 22:998–1005.

Tyson, Karolyn. 2002. "Weighing In: Elementary-Age Students and the Debate on Attitudes toward School among Black Students." *Social Forces* 80:1157–1189.

———. 2003. "Notes from the Back of the Room: Problems and Paradoxes in the Schooling of Young Black Students." *Sociology of Education* 76:326–343.

Tyson, Karolyn, William Darity Jr., and Domini Castellino. 2005. "Black Adolescents and the Dilemmas of High Achievement." *American Sociological Review* 70:582–605.

U.S. Census Bureau. 2000. *The Hispanic Population in the United States: Population Characteristics, March 2000*. Current Population Report. Pp. 20–535. Washington, DC: U.S. Department of Commerce, Figure 1.

U.S. Census Bureau. 2009. *Educational Attainment—People 25 Years Old and Over, by Total Money Earnings in 2008, Work Experience in 2008, Age, Race, Hispanic Origin, and Sex.* Washington, DC: US Department of Commerce Table PINC-03.

U.S. Department of Education. 1992. *A Profile of Parents of Eighth Graders.* Washington, DC: National Center for Education Statistics.

———. 2002. *National Education Longitudinal Study of 1988 Base Year to Fourth Follow-Up Student Component Data File User's Manual.* Washington, DC: National Center for Education Statistics.

Van De Werfhorst, Herman G., Alice Sullivan, and Sin Yi Cheung. 2003. "Social Class, Ability and Choice of Subject in Secondary and Tertiary Education in Britain." *British Educational Research Journal* 29:41–62.

Vars, Fredrick E., and William G. Bowen. 1998. "Scholastic Aptitude Test Scores, Race, and Academic Performance in Selective Colleges and Universities." Pp. 457–479 in *The Black-White Test Score Gap,* edited by C. Jencks and M. Phillips. Washington, DC: Brookings Institution.

Voelkl, Kristin. 1993. "Academic Achievement and Expectations among African-American Students." *Journal of Research and Development in Education* 27:42–55.

Wax, Amy. 2009. *Race, Wrongs, and Remedies: Group Justice in the 21st Century.* Lanham, MD: Rowman and Littlefield/Hoover Institution Press.

Weinberg, Meyer. 1977. *A Chance to Learn: A History of Race and Education in the United States.* Cambridge: Cambridge University Press.

Williams, Heather. 2005. *Self-Taught: African American Education in Slavery and Freedom.* Chapel Hill: University of North Carolina Press.

Williams, Jenny. 1997. *Negotiating Access to Higher Education: The Discourse of Selectivity and Equity.* Buckingham, UK: Open University Press.

Willis, Paul. 1977. *Learning to Labor: How Working Class Kids Get Working Class Jobs.* Farnborough, UK: Saxon House.

Wilson, George, and Debra Branch McBrier. 2005. "Race and Loss of Privilege: African American/White Differences in the Determinants of Job Layoffs from Upper-Tier Occupations." *Sociological Forum* 20:301–321.

Wilson, George, and Vincent J. Roscigno. 2010. "Race and Downward Mobility from Privileged Occupations: African American/White Dynamics across the Early Work-Career." *Social Science Research* 39:67–77.

Wilson, George, Ian Sakura-Lemessy, and Jonathan P. West. 1999. "Reaching the Top: Racial Differences in Mobility Paths to Upper-Tier Occupations." *Work and Occupations* 26:165–186.

Wilson, William Julius. 1987. *The Truly Disadvantaged: The Inner City, the Underclass, and Public Policy.* Chicago: University of Chicago Press.

———. 1996. *When Work Disappears: The World of the New Urban Poor.* New York: Knopf.

Wong, Carol A., Jacquelynne S. Eccles, and Arnold Sameroff. 2003. "The Influence of

Ethnic Discrimination and Ethnic Identification on African American Adolescents' School and Socioemotional Adjustment." *Journal of Personality* 71:1197–1232.

Young, Alford. 1999. "Navigating Race: Getting Ahead in the Lives of 'Rags to Riches' Young Men." Pp. 30–82 in *Cultural Territories of Race,* edited by Michele Lamont. Chicago: University of Chicago Press.

Zhao, Bo, Jan Ondrich, and John Yinger. 2006. "Why Do Real Estate Brokers Continue to Discriminate? Evidence from the 2000 Housing Discrimination Study." *Journal of Urban Economics* 59:394–419.

ACKNOWLEDGMENTS

Many factors have contributed to the completion of this book. First, I had the privilege of relying on several excellent scholars for helpful comments. In particular, I benefited greatly from the encouraging and constructive feedback I received from Mustafa Emirbayer, Thomas Espenshade, Douglas Massey, Carolyn Rouse, Matthew Salganik, Nicole Shelton, and Marta Tienda. These scholars read earlier drafts of various portions of this (and in some cases the entire) manuscript. I am also grateful to Paul DiMaggio, who saw promise in an early draft of this manuscript, which I found reassuring. Second, I must thank Kris Marsh, Keith Robinson, Ricardo Sabates, and Jeremy Staff for being such great collaborators throughout the period that I was completing this manuscript. They will recognize much of the work in this book, as my collaboration with them served as the impetus for several chapters. I also wish to thank Andrea Henderson, who provided some research assistance on portions of this work. Third, I am in debt to Douglas Downey who, unbeknownst to him, has served as a model for me to think about youth, culture, and schooling. I must thank George Farkas and Roslyn Mickelson. Although I sit on the opposite side of the debate on the oppositional culture theory, they have *always* been kind to me, given me career advice, and made me feel welcomed within the educational sociology community. Fourth, I owe a very special thank you to Devah Pager and Lauren Lee-Houghton, who both read *numerous* drafts of this manuscript and provided useful comments with blazing turn-around time. However, any faults or ideological positions found in this work should be attributed to me alone.

I would not have been able to complete this project without the generosity of various funding agencies. The Maryland Adolescent Development in Context Study (MADICS)— the dataset that served as the basis for a substantial portion of this manuscript—was supported in part by NICHD Grant R01 HD33437 to Jacquelynne S. Eccles and Arnold J. Sameroff, by the Spencer Foundation Grant MG #200000275 to Tabbye Chavous and Jacquelynne S. Eccles, and by the MacArthur Network on Successful Adolescent Development in High Risk Settings (Chair: R. Jessor). I thank the Jacobs Foundation for the Young Scholars Grant, which funded a portion of this project. I also thank the Institute for Advanced Study (IAS), where I spent the 2009–2010 academic year on leave, which gave me the time and space to complete this project. At IAS I was surrounded by an amazing interdisciplinary group of senior scholars from whom I learned much. I owe a special thanks to Danielle Allen from IAS for giving me the title to this book.

I must also acknowledge the individuals that contributed to my growth as a scholar. First, I thank my professors at Grambling State University. From them I learned of my academic potential, which gave me the confidence to apply to graduate school. Second, I thank the members of my master's thesis committee, Scott Frey, Sue Williams, the late Donald Adamchak, and the late Leonard Bloomquist. From them I learned how to be a scholar. I owe a special thanks to Leonard Bloomquist. As the chair of my M.A. thesis committee, he had perhaps the largest impact on my academic development. It was under Leonard's guidance that something "clicked" for me, and from whom I received many of the skills necessary to complete a rigorous doctoral program at the University of Michigan. I was a very demanding student, frequently knocking on his door for unscheduled meetings. Leonard always made time for me and was tolerant of my unconventional work habits. Sadly, Leonard will not get to see the full effect that his mentorship had for me, as he passed away two months following my dissertation defense. However, I still carry many of his lessons forward. Third, I thank David Williams (co-chair), Mary Corcoran (co-chair), Tabbye Chavous, Bob Schoeni, and Yu Xie for their guidance at Michigan, which served as the initial platform for this manuscript. Fourth, I thank Oksana Malanchuk and Jacquelynne Eccles for their generosity in allowing me to use the MADICS dataset, which shortened the time it took me to complete my Ph.D. program.

Although all of the aforementioned scholars were instrumental in the completion of this project or in my scholarly development in general, my acknowledgements would feel incomplete if I did not thank the people who were important in my journey leading up to this book. I owe the most credit to my grandparents Victoria and Pedro Barreto. When my mother passed away at the age of twenty-one, they took on the unenviable responsibility of raising my sister Jackie and me in Gowanus Housing Projects in Brooklyn, New York. Although Victoria and Pedro were not well educated (ninth and third grade, respectively), they always preached about the value of a good education. Despite the fact that a large proportion of the household income came from welfare assistance, they sacrificed so that they could pay the tuition necessary for me to attend Catholic school through grade 8. However, my grandmother was most proud of the fact that I avoided drugs, alcohol, and trouble. A major component of her parenting consisted of cautioning me about the dangers of drugs. She was *extremely* overprotective and did not allow me to "hang out" as much as my friends. Although I could not appreciate my upbringing, it allowed me to accomplish things that once seemed improbable. I surpassed my grandparents' expectations by simply attending college. Pedro and Victoria will not see how I benefited from the many years that they sacrificed to raise me when they should have been enjoying each other (Pedro passed on in 1996 and Victoria 2001,). Nevertheless, they continue to serve as a moral compass. They deserve to be acknowledged. To them I owe my deepest gratitude.

I wish to acknowledge Danette and Darlene Molina. When I was seventeen, they encouraged me to attend college, which at the time did not seem like a viable option. I applied to several schools and was accepted by one: Grambling State University (GSU), a historically black college in rural northern Louisiana. Excluding my grandparents' homeland of Puerto

Rico, I had never ventured beyond New York City. I had neither the resources nor plans to attend GSU. To my surprise, on an evening three days prior to the registration period at GSU, Danette informed me that she would get me to Grambling. She arrived at Gowanus in a rented 1993 Crown Victoria with Darlene and two of their classmates from law school. I packed my bags and said goodbye to my shocked grandparents. Danette, Darlene, and their two classmates drove twenty-four consecutive hours to Monroe, Louisiana (thirty miles from Grambling), where we spent the night. After arriving at Grambling on the following day, they spent about two hours with me to make sure that I had a dorm room and that I knew what I had to do to enroll. I told them that I would repay them, to which they replied, "Repay us by doing well, and God will take care of the rest." They gave me thirty dollars and left for the long drive back. I have never taken their gesture for granted and will always strive to do well so that their effort does not go in vain. I thank Danette, Darlene, and their two classmates, who knew that I would attend Grambling before I did. They gave me more than I had any right to expect. They put my life on its current trajectory. To them I owe more than I could ever repay.

I wish to thank Vernetta Spaulding, the mother of my college roommate Tyrone, the first student I met at Grambling. Since the first month that I arrived at Grambling, she has treated me like a son. She saw something in me that she thought was worthy of her time and resources. My success became her top priority, regardless of how much inconvenience this caused her. There were many instances in which she sacrificed more for me than anyone else. She has played a significant part in the transformation that I have made since I was seventeen, and she filled a void that I needed filled. She made sure that I stayed on my current trajectory. For that I thank her.

Finally, I thank Chinyere Harris, who has been a wonderful source of support for me during this process. She has shown patience with my work habits, and tolerance for my idiosyncrasies. She has contributed to my productivity in countless ways. She keeps things running smoothly at home, which enabled me to focus on the completion of this book. This project would not have been possible without that type of support. She deserves my deepest gratitude.

INDEX

Abstract attitudes vs. concrete attitudes, 77–80, 103–104

Academic achievement: vs. academic culture, 144; as "acting white," 112–115; and beliefs in schooling and barriers, 76–77; black fictive kinship system and, 130–131; black perception of, 22–23, 132; black valuation of school and, 184; cross-cultural, 121–126; and difficulty early in schooling process, 161–162; emphasis on value of education and, 77; gender discrimination and, 90; implication of racelessness for, 134–140; by nonneutral students, 138; parents' perceptions about opportunity structure and, 63–66; perceptions of opportunity and, 54, 74–97; popularity and, 113–114; positive orientation, failure, and, 99; positive racial identity for, 133; racelessness and, 129–143; racial disparity by entry into academic cycle, 191–192; schooling behaviors as determinant of, 154–157; student belief and academic success, 76; trends in, 5; by women, 87. *See also* Academic performance; Opportunity structure

Academic culture vs. academic achievement, 144

Academic disinvestment, from racial barriers, 78–80. *See also* Academic investment

Academic improvement, black commitment to, 105

Academic investment: racial differences in, 106; social cost and, 183; social mobility and, 92–97. *See also* Academic disinvestment

Academic orientation: attitudes toward being black and, 138–139; of British ethnic groups, 122–126; as culture, 145; decline in, through school, 117; implication of racial attitudes for, 140; more favorable among blacks than whites, 183–184; racial differences and, 98–127; social class variation in UK and, 170–171; UK class-based marginalization and, 167–170; of UK youth by class, 170–173; by U.S. social class, 174–175

Academic outcomes: "acting white" and, 21–22, 23–24, 25; for involuntary minorities, 20; racial achievement gap in, 4; upward mobility and, 16, 93; youths' perceptions of opportunity and, 82–84

Academic performance: as adaptation to barriers, 20; barriers to socioeconomic mobility and, 30; as choice, 22; lower-class youth experience of social class for, 176–178; popularity and,

"Brainiac," use of term, 22, 23
Britain. *See* United Kingdom
British Cohort Study (BCS70), 168–170, 171, 207–209
"Brotherhood," 129
Bruce, Philip, 52

Callback rates, race and, 38
Caste-like minorities, 17, 19–20
Child Development Supplement (CDS), to Panel Study for Income Dynamics (PSID), 107, 157, 193, 206–207
Class. *See* Social class
Classification, group, 17–19; schooling responses and, 19–20
Coard, Bernard, 121–122
Cognitive distance, from fictive kinship system, 131–132
Cognitive skills, health and, 190. *See also* Prior skills; Skills
Cognitive trajectories, establishing of, 147, 160–161
Coleman, James, 52
Collective ethos, of black community, 13
College enrollment, implication of beliefs and attitudes toward, 83–84. *See also* Schooling
Colorblind ideology: blacks and, 46–47; whites and, 45–47
Community forces, in oppositional culture theory, 15, 17
Concrete attitudes vs. abstract attitudes, 77–80, 103–104
Confidence, MADICS indicators of, 112
Conservative-liberal perspectives, 14
Content of our Character, The (Steele), 180
Coping skills, racial identity and, 141–142
Cosby, Bill, 127, 128
Countereducational attitudes, 148

Counterproductive schooling behavior, reasons for resistance, 150–151
Credentials, audit studies of, 38–39
Cross-cultural achievement, 121–126
Cross-cultural research, 164–165
Cuba, refugees from, 19
Cultural deficiency, 2, 30, 51
Cultural-ecological theory, 15. *See also* Oppositional culture theory
Cultural explanations, for racial inequality, 13–14
Cultural forces, in cultural-ecological framework, 15, 17
Cultural inversion, 16, 20
Cultural pathology, Moynihan on, 51
Culture: academic orientation as, 145; behavioral components of, 97. *See also* Black culture
Culture of opposition, purposeful vs. unintentional, 99–100
Culture of poverty, 13, 51
Curriculum, achievement gap and, 2

Data sources, 203–210
De jure racial segregation, 30
Democracy in America (Tocqueville), 165
Disadvantaged groups, 13. See also *specific* groups
Discrimination: belief that racial inequality due to, 41; in British education, 122, 123–126; constructive responses to, 133; direct evidence of, 38–39; government-sanctioned, 30; as obstacle for U.S. blacks, 40; parental experiences with, 55, 70–73; parents' perceptions toward self and child, 58; perceptions for academic investment, 91; premarket skills and, 36; vs. skills, 35–37; in UK, 170; wage, 59; against

women, 84–87. *See also* Racial
discrimination
Disengagement from academics, 53
Disinvestment from school, 164
Disruptive behavior, racial comparisons
of, 149–150, 155
Dress, of black males, 107

Early Childhood Longitudinal Study-
Kindergarten (ECLS-K), 8
Early skill development. *See* Prior skills;
Skills
Earnings: annual vs. hourly, 35; by
gender, 86, 94; schooling related to, 34
ECLS-K, 10–11, 191, 193
Ecological forces, in cultural-ecological
framework, 15, 17
Economic tools, 16
Education: adolescent views on, 77–78;
attainment by gender, 86; barriers
based on gender and race, 87–88, 89;
belief in value of, by sex and race, 92;
black parents' aspirations for, 60–63;
in Britain, 122–126; disadvantaged
community resources and, 9; early skill
development focus and, 187–191; equal
opportunity through, 55; expected
gains from, 101; importance to girls vs.
boys, 90; for involuntary minorities,
19–20; under Jim Crow, 49–50;
parents' experiences of discrimination
and, 59; quality based on teacher
response to minority students, 186–187;
resistance to, 99–100; returns to
women, 94; for slaves, 48–49; teachers'
perceptions of black youth and,
186–187; time spent on, 107–111; in
UK, 164–167; unequal reward of, 77;
upward mobility through, 16, 21;
valuation by black parents, 61–63; for

voluntary minorities, 19; women's
returns from, 86, 94. *See also* School
resistance
Educational achievement, black vs.
white students, 1
Educational aspirations, 101; vs. expecta-
tions, 66
Educational engagement, and marginal-
ization, 120–121
Educational returns, youth perceptions
of, 102
Educational Testing Service (ETS), 201
Education Longitudinal Study (ELS,
2002), 61–62, 68, 90
Effort, racial comparisons of, 150
ELS. *See* Education Longitudinal Study
Emancipation Proclamation, 48
Employers, perceptions of blacks by, 41
Employment, and education in UK, 166
England. *See* United Kingdom
Environment, skill development and,
191
Equal Opportunity Employers, black
résumés and, 38
Ethnic identity, 134. *See also* Racial
identity
Ethnic minorities, in United Kingdom,
121–126
Ethnic pride, 133
Ethnographic studies: and blacks'
perception of returns to education in
labor market, 21; from elementary
schools, 11–12, 28; of English youth,
167; from high schools, 21; of Houston
Independent School District, 199;
of Latin American poverty, 13;
from middle schools, 12; in Shaker
Heights, 23
ETS. *See* Educational Testing Service
Evidence of oppositional culture theory,
163